Hostage in Peking

In the late 1960s, journalist Anthony Grey was held hostage for two years in Peking, during China's Cultural Revolution. Since then, the list of innocent men and women taken as political hostages in all parts of the world has grown ever longer ... in Latin America, the Far East, North America, the Middle East, in particular in Iran and Beirut.

Grey's account of his twenty-six-month imprisonment in a tiny room plastered with Maoist slogans has become a classic of its kind. The lonely fight against despair and isolation that he describes brings vividly to life the harrowing plight that every hostage must face up to...

During the 1979–81 Iran hostage crisis, when American diplomats were held prisoner in Tehran, their families circulated *Hostage in Peking* among themselves. It helped them understand the horrors their relatives were facing – and helped them prepare for the difficulties all hostages experience on regaining their freedom. Over the years many others, directly affected or not, have found understanding – and encouragement – in its pages.

Anthony Grey is now the bestselling author of the novels *Saigon* and *Peking*. This book is republished to mark his first return visit to China since that nightmare ordeal, and coincides with the showing on BBC Television of his account of that experience, *Return to Peking*.

HOSTAGE IN PEKING

Books by Anthony Grey

AUTOBIOGRAPHY
Hostage in Peking (1970)

SHORT STORIES
A Man Alone (1972)

NON-FICTION
The Prime Minister Was a Spy (1983)

NOVELS
Some Put Their Trust in Chariots (1973)
The Bulgarian Exclusive (1976)
The Chinese Assassin (1979)
Saigon (1982)
Peking (1988)

HOSTAGE IN
PEKING

ANTHONY GREY

Weidenfeld and Nicolson

London

First published in Great Britain in 1970 by
Michael Joseph Ltd

Published in paperback in 1988 by
George Weidenfeld & Nicolson Limited
91 Clapham High Street, London SW4 7TA

Copyright © Anthony Grey 1970

British Library Cataloguing in Publication Data

Grey, Anthony
    Hostage in Peking.
    1. China. Political prisoners. Grey,
    Anthony
    I. Title
    365′.45′0924

    ISBN 0–297–79503–1

Printed and bound in Great Britain by
Butler & Tanner Ltd, Frome and London

ILLUSTRATIONS

Map of my house   12–13

Between pages 128 and 129

The gate to my courtyard in June 1967, from which hung a straw effigy of a paper tiger with a top hat

Children gleefully joined in rocking the car of a Canadian correspondent when it was surrounded, with him inside it, during a demonstration

Crowds waving red books of Mao's quotations, his portrait and anti-British slogans at the gates of the British Mission in Peking during the Hong Kong crisis of May 1967

The gutted shell of the main hall of the British Mission after the Red Guard sacking

The ill-fated Ming Ming helping me with my chess game

The courtyard of my house photographed in October 1969

The eight-foot square room

My bed in the twelve-foot square room

The staircase

Slogans and paint on the furniture of my lounge

ACKNOWLEDGEMENTS

My thanks are due to those China-watching friends, they know who they are, who helped me with some parts of the manuscript for this book. They were able to go on Watching when my own view was restricted.

My thanks are also due to the following for permission to quote from works in which they hold the copyright: *The China Quarterly*, for permission to quote from an article, 'The Foreign Ministry and Foreign Affairs during the Cultural Revolution' by Melvin Gurtov, Issue No. 40, October-December 1969; *Penguin Books Ltd.*, for the poem 'Snow' by Mao Tse-tung, from MAO TSE-TUNG by Stuart Schram; and *A. Thomas & Co. (Preston) Ltd.*, for extracts from TRUE YOGA by William Zorn.

Similarly my thanks are due to *Syndication International* for permission to use three photographs in which they hold the copyright, all reproduced on the final page of illustrations. I should also like to thank Visnews Ltd. for kindly providing still pictures from cine film which I took in Peking.

dedicated
to my angel

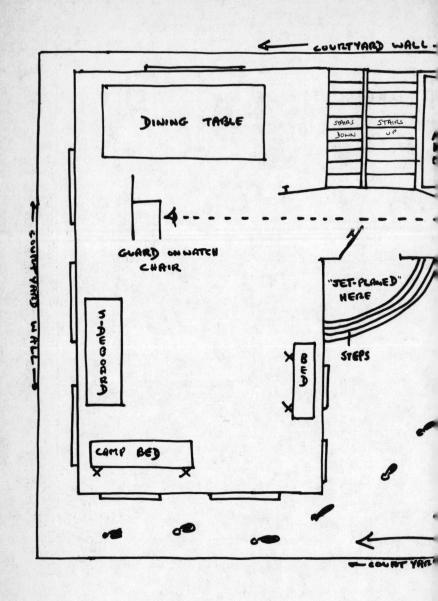

COURTYARD WALL ←

DINING TABLE

STAIRS DOWN

STAIRS UP

GUARD ON WATCH CHAIR

"JET-PLANED" HERE

STEPS

SIDEBOARD

BED

CAMP BED

COURTYARD WALL →

COURTYARD

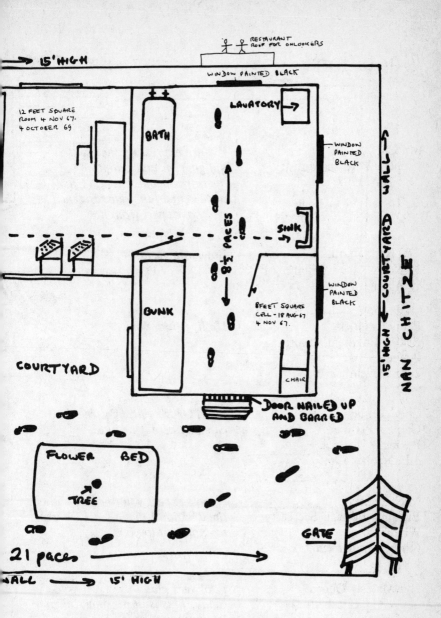

RESTAURANT
ROOF FOR ONLOOKERS

WINDOW PAINTED BLACK

15' HIGH

12 FEET SQUARE
ROOM 4 NOV 67.
4 OCTOBER 69

BATH

LAVATORY

WINDOW
PAINTED
BLACK

8½ PACES

SINK

BUNK

8 FEET SQUARE
CELL - 18 AUG 67
4 NOV 67.

WINDOW
PAINTED
BLACK

COURTYARD

CHAIR

DOOR NAILED UP
AND BARRED

FLOWER BED

TREE

GATE

21 paces

WALL → 15' HIGH

15' HIGH COURTYARD WALL

NAN CHITZE

Quotations

Mr Chi
Chinese Foreign Ministry
21st July 1967

We are expressing the greatest indignation and adopting measures against you . . . you must remain in your residence and not depart from it.

200 Red Guards
15 Nan Chihtze, Peking
18th August 1967

Bow your head!

Percy Cradock
British Chargé d'Affaires
Peking
26th November 1968

He lives in a void.

Chou En-lai
China's Premier
Peking
4th October 1969

Well, Grey's out, he's free. He can stay here if he likes.

Michael Stewart
Britain's Foreign Secretary
Whitehall
6th November 1969

I don't expect you to agree with the decision I made but I wanted to explain it to you.

Her Majesty Queen
        Elizabeth II
Buckingham Palace
11th November 1969

I am very glad to see you here today. This is just a small token for what you have been through.

Introduction

On August 18th, 1966 a million Red Guards marched across the Square of Heavenly Peace in the centre of Peking and on to the front pages of newspapers all over the world. In the days that followed, these young Communist zealots began to build a reputation for intimidation and terrorisation as they lashed out openly in the streets of China's capital at anything they considered bourgeois or anti-party. Fostered and encouraged by Mao Tse-tung himself they rampaged through the streets shearing off the long hair of women, slashing open tightly tapered Western-style trousers, forbidding the wearing of pointed shoes and making many peremptory and bizarre demands upon the capital's population. Many adults accused of bourgeois tendencies were paraded in humiliating fashion through the streets wearing tall dunce's caps and confessions of guilt on placards around their necks. There were reports of deaths and suicides. The backstage political infighting among China's ageing Communist leaders had burst out into the streets. The words 'Cultural Revolution' took their place in the ever-expanding vocabulary of the news columns and people in the West – as well as those in Communist countries too – wondered what was the meaning of this strange new Chinese phenomenon.

I was one of those who wondered. In late August 1966 I was taking a holiday in Portugal. For the past eighteen months or so I had been based in East Berlin as Reuters correspondent and had frequently travelled in the Communist states of Eastern Europe on news assignments. So the doings of Communist parties and governments were not strange to me. But as I sat at a café table in the sunlit square of Sesimbra sipping my wine and reading Peking reports in the Paris edition of the *New York Herald Tribune*, I could only shake my head in puzzlement at the developments in China. 'Odd goings-on,' I thought.

15

Exactly one year later on 18th August, 1967 I was sitting in my house in Peking as 200 Red Guards smashed their way into the courtyard. Yelling and breaking things as they came, the Red Guards mounted the stairs to the office where I waited helplessly.

This book is largely a personal account of what happened to me in China. Although an innocent bystander, I became caught fast in a struggle between two governments. But I shall also try to set out the historical, political and emotional background to the long, isolated imprisonment in my own house and the vindictive and intentionally humiliating treatment meted out to me. That it was directly due to the Cultural Revolution there is no doubt. This ironically misnamed mass movement, the greatest and most cataclysmic of a series of mass campaigns that have been inflicted on China by Mao Tse-tung's leadership, brought the whole population of 700 million under pressure to show their allegiance and loyalty to the decreed Communist principles of Mao.

It is perhaps an impertinence to try to speak with any authority of such a complex and confused movement in such a vast country, having lived freely in the foreign community in Peking for only four months. But the fact of having been there does give an added insight into the strange convulsions which gripped China and spilled over her borders into Burma, Indonesia, Nepal, India, Cambodia, Ceylon, Macao and Hong Kong, as well as countries farther away. Much remains obscure and even totally unknown about the origins and roots of the Cultural Revolution but already a perspective of a sort is discernible and I shall try to analyse and sketch in briefly some factors, especially those which affected Britain in general and myself in particular.

I feel compelled to apologise in advance for the number of I's in this book. Some cynics might believe that a book-length description of more than two years' solitary confinement by an almost-certainly egotistical journalist would be his heart's delight. But since this is the story and I was unfortunate enough, through no fault or merit of my own, to become the teller there seems no way round it.

Part 1

CHAPTER ONE

Getting Sent There

In January and February 1967 the eyes of the world's newspaper readers were riveted daily on Peking. In the dry, icy, dust-laden streets the Chinese were doing strange things to the Russians. Millions surged around the beleaguered Russian embassy shouting slogans and screaming abuse through loud-speakers in a massive three-week long, day and night, non-stop demonstration. Truck-loads of troops with fixed bayonets joined the demonstrators in shouting 'Hang Kosygin, Soviet Revisionists go home!' Many humiliations were visited on the one-time closest Communist friends of China. Restaurants put up signs saying 'No dogs or Russians here' – an ironic turn-round of a sign allegedly put up by the British in a park in their Shanghai concession years before – 'No dogs or Chinese allowed.' These five words have been burned into the modern Chinese soul by the Communist propagandists to inculcate a continuing hatred of imperialism – and now they were turned on the Russians! A final humiliation which shocked the outside world occurred at Peking airport. The wives and families of Russia's diplomats were being sent home to Moscow because of the constant pressure and threat of the mind-numbing demonstrations round the embassy. Huge crowds of Red Guards surrounded the Russians at the airport and the departing women and children were forced to crawl on their hands and knees under portraits of Mao – a reminder to Westerners of how subjects were made to kowtow to Chinese emperors of old.

The anti-Russian hysteria was sparked by an incident involving Chinese students in Moscow – and this set a pattern in which the foreign nationals of a succession of different countries, Communist and Western, came under attack in Peking.

The Chinese students, on their way home from Europe where they had been studying, had stopped in Moscow to lay wreaths on the tombs of Lenin and Stalin. They also read quotations from

19

the writings of Chairman Mao and, not surprisingly in view of the delicate state of relations between the two giant Communist nations, Soviet police had intervened. Peking claimed the students were injured and Chinese blood was shed in Red Square, a debt that must be repaid in full. The term 'fascist atrocities' – later applied to British actions in Hong Kong – was used to describe Soviet police methods. An editorial in the Chinese Communist Party newspaper, *Renmin Ribao* or *People's Daily*, addressed to the Kremlin's leaders, employed a mode of address new to the records of relations between Communist states. 'You handful of filthy revisionist swine,' it began and went on to say that the 'atrocities' resembled those of the Czar, Hitler and the Ku-Klux-Klan.

Anyone who had ever doubted China's penchant for exaggerated language before was left with no doubt now. Similar minor incidents involving Chinese students called home because of the burgeoning Cultural Revolution occurred in Paris and Belgrade. And the reaction in thin-skinned, face-conscious Peking was brisk. The French and Yugoslav embassies were also besieged by screaming, militant demonstrators. The demonstrations at the three embassies went on side-by-side. 'Crush the dog's head of Tito!' 'Down with de Gaulle!' 'Hang Kosygin.' It seemed likely that the homecoming students had deliberately got into trouble abroad to prove their revolutionary integrity in response to the mounting pressure of the Cultural Revolution to which they were returning. Those at home tended to accuse students abroad of living a bourgeois-style life.

The West was aghast when Red Guards demonstrating at the French embassy singled out a French diplomat and his wife for particularly vindictive treatment. While driving into the embassy after lunch the diplomat's car had bumped very lightly against a Red Guard loudspeaker truck. The Red Guards dragged M. Robert Richard and his wife from the car and hemmed them in with a 'circle of hate' – a method of treatment all foreigners in Peking soon came to dread. M. Richard, a commercial counsellor, and his wife were kept standing in the street in below-freezing temperatures for seven hours while those pressing around them spat on them and abused them ceaselessly. When it got dark Red Guards brought up a searchlight and turned it on the unfortunate French couple.

Later at the Chinese Ministry of Foreign Affairs when the French ambassador went to protest, the macabre sense of high farce was accentuated when two elderly Chinese supported by nurses were brought limping into the room where the ambassador was attempting to present his case in diplomatic terms. They were the alleged victims of M. Richard. Slogans were later daubed on the walls of the French embassy saying 'The bastard Richard and his bitch must compensate and apologise or bear the consequences.'

Foreign diplomats and journalists in Peking had, up to this point, been disinterested observers of the violence and mass hysteria that came with the Cultural Revolution. But now it had become a very real threat to them and in the succeeding months this sense of unease grew. The apprehension felt by all was eventually justified – especially in the case of the British.

The action against foreigners in Peking had followed on the heels of the 'January Storm', in which workers and Red Guards in Shanghai and elsewhere seized control of factories and institutions from their superiors, it is now known, on instructions from Mao and his supporters in Peking. The Maoists claimed that many people in authority were supporters of President Liu Shaochi who, they said, opposed Mao. The hallmark of the Cultural Revolution, the wall poster, had established itself at the centre of the confusing scene in Peking by this time. Reports of the contents of these unofficial information sheets – unprecedented in Communist countries – reached the outside world daily from the handful of foreign correspondents in Peking.

Outside speculation on the possibility of civil war in China snowballed when one wall poster reported rival mobs hacking and killing each other in Nanking and cutting off each other's ears and noses and tongues. This particular report was later said in other wall posters to be untrue and very possibly was. But as was the case with hundreds of thousands of wall posters put up within the view of foreigners in these months there was no way of telling with certainty.

It was at this point that I was assigned to Peking.

World interest in these strange and seemingly inexplicable events in China was so great that newspapers were voraciously gobbling up every crumb of information from Peking. Consequently I found myself writing about China even from East Berlin. In my office behind the Berlin Wall I received on teleprinter the news services of both the East German and Czechoslovak news agencies. Both had correspondents in Peking, and the Czechoslovak correspondent was a Chinese speaker and a particularly able reporter. From East Berlin I filed reports gleaned from the two agencies and this news was distributed by Reuters around the world, along with reports from our Peking correspondent, Vergil Berger, and reports from Hong Kong, Tokyo, Singapore and any other world centre which had anything valid to say. The volume of information available from wall posters, unofficial Red Guard newspapers and personal observation on the teeming streets of Peking was so great that often every correspondent working there had something unique to contribute to the picture the outside world was receiving each day.

In Peking at that time there were only four Western journalists. In addition to Reuters the French news agency, Agence France Presse, and the West German news agency, D.P.A. (Deutsche Presse Agentur) maintained correspondents there. The fourth was a reporter of the Canadian newspaper, the *Toronto Globe and Mail*. There was also a corps of about a dozen Japanese correspondents whose reports were given world-wide distribution from Tokyo. They had a great advantage over their competitors because of the similarity of the written Chinese language to Japanese. They could also move about more easily without being obviously identified as foreigners.

With the editors of newspapers throughout the world hanging on every word written by correspondents in Peking it can perhaps be imagined with what delight I received the news of my assignment there.

I had been Reuters resident correspondent in East Berlin for twenty months and during that time had travelled frequently in Eastern Euope – Czechoslovakia, Rumania, Hungary, Bulgaria and Poland. Living in, and reporting from, Communist countries is something of an acquired taste and to some extent an acquired craft. Although I had no special knowledge of China or Asia, my experience in Eastern Europe did equip me in a small way for an assignment in Peking. I had cut my journalistic teeth at the age of nineteen on a small weekly newspaper in the Glasgow suburbs, the *Bearsden and Milngavie Chronicle*. I had worked on the Chronicle in the evenings and at week-ends while in the Royal Air Force.

After leaving the Air Force I became a reporter with the *Eastern Daily Press* in Norwich and Norfolk and four years later in 1964 joined Reuters in Fleet Street.

I can remember being asked during my first interview at Reuters why I wished to make the transition from the provinces to national and international journalism. In a fairly inarticulate reply I said words to the effect that I wanted to be 'mixed up in important events'. Looking back over the past two years that remark now has a certain irony.

Nevertheless, one night late in January 1967 I had just returned to my flat in East Berlin after having supper in my favourite restaurant, the Ganymed, on the banks of the Spree just inside the Berlin Wall. The telephone rang and a Reuter executive asked me how I would like to go to Peking.

The non-stop anti-Russian demonstrations were continuing. Chinese in Moscow had called the Russian leaders bastards at a press conference in their Moscow embassy. Relations between the two Communist giants were at breaking point. The Cultural Revolution on the domestic front was becoming ever more confused and sensational. China seemed to be in the grip of a mass mental aberration.

What was it all about? What did it all mean? How would it affect the rest of the world?

How would I like to go to Peking?

It was a correspondent's dream. I made a conscious effort to restrain the enthusiasm of my reply. I was twenty-eight. I didn't want to be thought over-eager and unreliable. Yes, I quite liked the idea. And it was settled there and then subject to my getting a visa from the Chinese.

I put down the telephone and moments later was looking in the bathroom mirror at a face wearing an ear-to-ear grin of delight. The grinning face was told aloud several times that it was going to Peking, and if anything its grin got broader. Perhaps with only a slight inkling of what lay ahead it might have become a little lopsided.

CHAPTER TWO

Getting There

In mid-February 1967 I crossed through the Berlin Wall from East to West at Checkpoint Charlie for the last time and flew to London from Tempelhof airport in a BEA Viscount.

When a Reuter correspondent passes through London between assignments his time is taken up with briefings for his new post. He spends a few hours with the editor of the desk dealing with the area from which he will be filing – in my case the Asian desk. He has discussions with the manager for Asia; with Accounts Department to clear the mind of thinking in terms of sterling/ East German Marks, and to substitute thinking in terms of sterling/ Chinese Yuan; with the editor of World Desk, the unit which receives and processes a deluge of hundreds of thousands of words each day from Reuter men all around the world – the editor usually asks the correspondent to remember the flood of words and bear in mind that his dateline is not the only one with an interesting story to tell on any particular day. He has discussions with people dealing with insurance, with travel arrangements, with tape recorders, with Reuters Economic Services, with the New China News Agency, with staff questions. He talks with correspondents who have already completed assignments in the post to which he's going and meets with, it seems, a hundred and one new problems. Reuter correspondents undergoing the briefing process for new assignments tend, I fancy, to move along the corridors and across the editorial floors with a deliberately subdued sense of elation, trying to appear casual and blasé. But not one, I'm sure, goes through the process without feeling at least a slight sense of exhilaration that he is bound for a spot on the map that holds out the prospect of new excitements and challenges. The last appointment in a departing correspondent's diary is a brief meeting with Reuters general manager, Mr Gerald Long, in his office on the seventh floor of the eight-storey building at 85 Fleet Street. Then he walks out of the front door which looks across to the black tiles-and-glass of the *Daily Express* frontage and the brown stone of the *Daily Telegraph* building. He is ready for London airport and Washington, Paris, Bonn, Lusaka, Singapore, Buenos Aires, Tokyo, Warsaw or wherever he happens to be headed. Perhaps Peking.

Reuters is a world news agency with a history stretching back more than 100 years. It is one of the four great world-wide news agencies, the others being the American agencies, Associated Press and United Press International, and Agence France Presse. I've often found that in England itself many people do not have a clear idea of what Reuters is and does. So I will sidetrack briefly with a background sketch and some statistics. Perhaps some confusion arises because of the very name. Reuters is a prominent British organisation with a German name. Confusion is perhaps excusable. The founder Paul Julius Reuter was a German who was later granted naturalisation. From the time of its founding in 1851 English people had difficulty pronouncing the name correctly. A humorist of the *St James Gazette* in the late 1850's wrote a ditty which might still be of help – and sets out succinctly the principles of an independent organisation still dedicated solely to the collection of factual, objective news from all parts of the world, and its dissemination by the fastest means modern communications, in the shape of cable, radio, computer and satellite, can provide.

I sing of one no Pow'r has trounced
Whose place in every strife is neuter
Whose name is sometimes mispronounced
As Reuter.

How oft, as through the news we go
When breakfast leaves an hour to loiter
We quite forget the thanks we owe
To Reuter.

His web around the globe is spun
He is, indeed, the world's exploiter:
'Neath ocean e'en the whispers run
Of Reuter.

Paul Julius Reuter born in 1816 in Kassel, Western Germany, began publishing a news sheet in Paris in the spring of 1849. It failed. When the Prussian State telegraph line from Berlin to Aachen was opened to the public in the autumn of 1849 Reuter went to Aachen, established a telegraphic office there and supplied local clients, merchants and bankers with financial information from Berlin. In 1850 the French government made its Paris-to-Brussels telegraph line available for public use. Enterprisingly Reuter recognised that by covering the 100-mile gap in the cables between Aachen and Brussels by message-carrying pigeons he could monopolise a fast link between the greatest commercial centres of the Continent, Paris and Berlin. This fact is responsible for the worn old joke sometimes heard in Fleet Street pubs that Reuters still keeps flocks of pigeons on the roof at 85 Fleet Street. A Reuter man returning conscientiously from a brief evening refreshment to his desk by the new, quietly-humming editorial computer might depart to quiet jeers of 'He's got to get back and feed the pigeons.' However, a century ago Paul Julius Reuter established agents in the main European cities to widen his scope of information gathering. But as the telegraph lines moved on, he moved too to London in the year of the Great Exhibition, 1851. He followed the cable, a principle which was soon to make Reuters span the globe and a principle, which, in 1970, Reuters is still pursuing with computers and space satellites.

The development of Reuters was closely bound up with the economic, political and military history of the past 100 years and it became a prosperous family business in the process. Reuter men of the past number Edgar Wallace, a Boer War correspondent, and Ian Fleming, Moscow correspondent in the Stalin era, among their ranks.

In the late 1920s almost all the shares in Reuters were bought up by the Press Association, the organisation of British provincial newspapers, and in 1941 they were joined in ownership by the London newspapers with a circulation covering the whole country. At the same time a trust or charter was set up to guarantee Reuters integrity, independence and freedom from bias at all times. This independence is perhaps Reuters most jealously guarded asset and one which I was at pains to explain to the disbelieving Chinese officials who ordered my house arrest on July 21st, 1967 as a reprisal for the British Government's actions in Hong Kong. 'You know very well what your connections are with the British Government,' was the impassive reply my explanation attracted. I did. None! But the Chinese Communists either did not believe it or did not care anyway.

In 1946 a decision was taken to extend the ownership of Reuters to Commonwealth newspapers outside Britain and by 1951 it was owned and operated in partnership by the Press of the United Kingdom, Australia, New Zealand and India. The Indian connection was later severed and Reuters is today owned by British, Australian and New Zealand newspapers.

Famous examples of Reuters breaking historic news ahead of all rivals began with the assassination of President Lincoln in 1865. The agency reported the news to England two days ahead of all rivals. Reuters American agent, finding the mail boat had left New York harbour, hired a tug, raced after it and threw his report aboard in a canister. *The Times* published the report – and reprimanded its own agent for being beaten by Reuters. The relief of Mafeking was reported to the Queen, the Prime Minister, England and the world first by Reuters. An enterprising correspondent is said to have bribed an engine driver to hide the report in one of his sandwiches en route to the nearest cable office. And even in 1944 the much-joked-of carrier pigeons made a comeback to contribute another chapter in the Reuters story. The birds were used to fly messages out from Reuter correspondents who landed on the Normandy beaches with the Allied invasion forces.

In 1951 Reuters celebrated its centenary – and released a flock of pigeons from the roof of 85 Fleet Street to mark the event!

I was reminded of Reuters historic pigeons when presented with a bizarre set of customs regulations at the border between Hong Kong and Communist China which specifically forbade me to take pigeons in with me to Peking. Perhaps the Fleet Street bar room wags would have liked to imagine me assuring an inscrutable Chinese customs officer I had no pigeons with me, raising my hat politely as I made to leave, and inadvertently revealing a quietly-cooing bird with empty leg-container attached, perched comfortably on my head.

The days of a two day 'beat' on an assassination, however, are long gone. Now two minutes is considered a creditable lead on transcendent news, so fierce is the competition among the leading world news agencies. This was the margin by which Reuters beat the two American agencies in announcing the launch of the first-ever space satellite, Sputnik I in October 1957. In November 1963 Reuters was one minute ahead of Associated Press with the announcement of the shooting of President Kennedy but a fraction of a minute behind the same agency with the news flash of his death. Each agency sells its 24-hours-a-day world news service by contract to subscribers – newspapers, radio stations, television services, governments, clubs, business firms, or indeed any organisation or individual wishing to buy it. Big news media often subscribe to two, three or even all four world news agencies. Therefore to send news clicking quickly and efficiently on to the teleprinters of the world's newsrooms ahead of its rivals is a matter of prestige for the agency concerned and a continuing indication of the value of its news service. So enthusiastic correspondents of world news agencies tend to be on their toes night and day wherever their dateline might be.

Now on the editorial floor of Reuters Fleet Street home a computer has been established at the nerve centre of its world-wide communications network. It receives all cabled news stories and can where necessary re-transmit priority news flashes, untouched by human hand, to all parts of the world in a matter of seconds. A far cry from the pigeons of Paul Julius Reuter!

Each day that the world spins Reuters is gathering news from 183 countries and territories. Between 600,000 and 700,000 words per day – the equivalent wordage of about ten average-length novels – flood into the Fleet Street office giving details of general news, sport and economic developments around the globe.

Some 1,600 men and women abroad including 300 full time correspondents wake up each morning to provide the service and in London it is sifted and shaped to be sent out to 118 countries and territories.

In the London office around the hub known as the World Desk expert journalists tailor news services specifically for the varied interests of newspapers and radio and television stations in the United Kingdom, Europe, Africa, Asia, Australia and New Zealand, North, South and Central America and the Caribbean. Up to two-and-a-quarter million words of general and economic news go out over these services each day to feed the insatiable appetite of the world's population for information. Between 3,000 and 4,000 daily newspapers around the world with a total circulation reaching 328 million copies daily receive Reuters news service. And Reuters serves 400 radio and television networks feeding news to 573 million sets.

It was as one individual cog in the machinery of this long-established and widely-respected news agency that I took off from London's Heathrow airport in a Boeing 707 of BOAC on the morning of Tuesday March 7th, 1967 to fly to Hong Kong en route to China to report on the Cultural Revolution. I was the sixth Reuter correspondent assigned to Peking since April 1956 when an office was first opened there.

CHAPTER THREE

Getting In

Sitting in my room in the Hong Kong Hilton on the day before I was due to depart for Peking, I looked out of the window at the dark outline of the hills of the Chinese mainland. I felt apprehensive. That was China proper and tomorrow I would cut my ties with the Western world and go into it. I wrote of my apprehension in my diary and would reproduce the notes here now if I could. But my diary and other personal possessions were destroyed or stolen by the Red Guards who sacked and burned the British Mission in Peking six months later. The diary was left there inadvertently in my brief-case along with my passport and some other possessions.

It would be easy to say that as I looked out at the hills of Communist China on that day in Hong Kong I felt a premonition that something terrible would happen to me. But I didn't. I felt similarly ill-at-ease and apprehensive when I first caught sight of the grim, concrete-block and barbed wire Berlin Wall as I drove towards it on a foggy morning down the broad avenue in West Berlin that was once called Unter den Linden. And during nearly two years in East Berlin and Eastern Europe nothing serious happened to me. That is if you don't count being held briefly for questioning in an East Berlin suburb by three car-loads of plain clothes State Security men, who closed in on me from different directions when I visited the Ghana Trade Mission, which was being besieged by them at the time in order to make a hostage of one Ghanaian whom the East Germans wanted to exchange for an East German agent arrested in Ghana. Or if you don't count the several times I was followed by car in Poland by Secret Service men in fedoras and heavy overcoats with turned up collars. Or the time they came to my hotel and took away for several hours' questioning a Polish interpreter travelling with me and then told him he must get out of town with me and back to Warsaw as quickly as possible or else. Or the time I was followed inexplicably all evening in the streets of Bucharest by a man who had watched me intently in the hotel bar. Or the strange clicking noises that occurred during telephone conversations in all these countries, almost certainly caused by 'bugging' devices.

But, as I said, nothing serious happened to me. These few incidents are briefly related not in an attempt to dramatise the life of a foreign correspondent but to show the uneasy circumstances in which he lives in a society alien to his own. To balance that I should perhaps add that some Communist correspondents of East Bloc news-agencies whom I have numbered among my friends have related experiences similar to mine – when visiting Britain, the United States and Canada.

But China was a bigger and even more alien environment to me than East Berlin or Eastern Europe. And Hong Kong was a thousand miles from Peking not just the other side of a concrete wall. And the Cultural Revolution seemed to be doing strange things to a people we had barely begun to understand anyway.

On that apprehensive day the sense of elation I'd felt at the assignment while in East Berlin evaporated completely. I didn't want to go into China at all. I made my last telephone calls to London – there is no normal telephone contact between China itself and Britain – with what can best be described as a heavy heart. I had been one week in the Crown Colony of Hong Kong – a tiny anachronistic vestige of the British Empire that was to be the indirect cause of two years' solitary confinement for me in Peking.

Words like 'incongruous' and 'anachronism' spring to mind immediately when trying to define Hong Kong's continued existence as a colony in time and space. But both words are inadequate. Here in 1970 a former imperial power that has declined practically out of sight as far as its former Empire is concerned, still retains possession of a colony on the territory of the most populous and most militantly anti-imperialist nation on earth. China, with a population that might be approaching 800 million now, a quarter of all people on earth, needs only to take a deep breath to push the British out of Hong Kong like a fat man bursting a button off the front of his shirt. The rioting in 1967 which led to the arrest of many Chinese there and my house arrest in Peking by way of retaliation, drew more world attention to Hong Kong than it had received at any time since the Communists took over in China in 1949. Many people must have wondered why Chairman Mao's China had allowed Britain to retain possession and rule so long in this colony of nearly four million people – ninety-nine per cent of them Chinese.

The short answer seems to be because it suits them that way. I shall discuss the reasons why in a later chapter dealing with the circumstances in which Peking decided to make me a scapegoat for British actions in the colony.

Hong Kong is many things to many people. To dissident Chinese on the Communist mainland it is a possible bolt hole from the oppression they feel under Mao's rule. To the Peking rulers themselves it is a lucrative source of hard foreign currency and a financial and banking link with the outside world – there are fifteen Communist-controlled banks there, including the Bank of China. To the British it is a colony administered in an unmitigatedly colonial style to maintain it as a prosperous and dynamic trading centre and port. To American sailors fighting the war off the coasts of Vietnam it is a place for brief spells of 'R and R' – rest and recreation. A walk through the neon-lit waterfront district of Wanchai, immortalised by Richard Mason in his novel and the film 'The World of Suzie Wong', soon dispels the stranger's romantic notions. Instead of the cheongsams, bead curtains and bamboo, the plaintive strings and muted cymbals of the East I found leather-booted, mini-skirted, hip-wiggling Chinese girls crashing out deafening rock music on super-amplified guitars in bars with harsh neon strip lighting, rubber-tiled floors, formica topped tables and a juke box in the corner decorated with white nude female figures. The Mama Sans in the half-empty waterfront bars that shot up too quickly and got ahead of demand make remarks like 'The Korean War was much better business than Vietnam'.

Hong Kong is the home also of a tall white building, allegedly packed with computers and the latest data processing machinery, that must be easily the biggest consulate in the world. In the United States consulate in Hong Kong a small army of Chinese interpreters translate every word in every publication obtainable from the mainland. And a team of keen-eyed political officers collect and interpret every scrap of information from every available source to provide the man in the White House with as reliable a guide as possible to conditions in China and the intentions of its hostile leaders.

Hong Kong is the home of the notorious China Watchers – those journalists who now cannot or will not venture into the jaws of the Communist dragon. They watch and listen and glean and sometimes gaze across at the mainland, often puzzled, sometimes cynical but ever fascinated by their enigmatic subject.

Hong Kong is the place where correspondents stop on their way to Peking – and the place for which some correspondents resident in Peking make a dash every few months for a breath of fresh air and a slice of decadent bourgeois life.

I stayed one week in Hong Kong meeting China Watchers, British officials, some of the keen-eyed political officers from the U.S. consulate and anybody who could tell me something that would help me begin to understand the confusion of the Cultural Revolution. A measure of the ignorance existing among outsiders of conditions in China at that time – or any time in fact – can be gauged from the suggestions given to me by the China Watching Brigade when they learned I was going in by train.

'Look out and see if the factory chimneys are smoking in Wuhan.' (Wuhan is one of China's biggest industrial centres.) 'Keep your eyes skinned to see if there are rice shoots coming through the water in the fields.'

I'd never seen a paddy field at that time and privately doubted my ability to differentiate between a barren and a thriving rice field. I wasn't too bad on factory chimneys but was uneasy at analysing the economic effects of the Cultural Revolution on the strength of smoke or the lack of it. What if they'd secretly discovered smokeless fuels?

I took my golf clubs to Hong Kong meaning to play there every few months during my breaks from Peking. I left them with Lee Casey, the Hong Kong Reuter correspondent, but since I never managed to get away from Peking until two years later they remained unused. Those clubs went right across Asia, came back unopened and got into headlines around the world a few days after my release since they were the first things I asked after when I spoke to the outside world for the first time – to Lee Casey who had by then taken over Reuters office in Tokyo.

Hong Kong is also the place to have suits made quickly. I went to a certain tailor Chang. I spotted his shop as I strolled through the colony's teeming streets. In the window was a blown-up photograph of Mr Chang patting one of his twenty-four-hour suits into place on a smiling Cary Grant. Anything good enough for the suave Mr Grant was good enough for me, I thought. And went in to order two lightweight creations in which to withstand the humid Peking summer. The fittings were admittedly a bit hurried as I was leaving the next day. But when I put them on in Peking the trousers failed to reach the tops of my shoes by a good two inches, giving me a slightly hill-billy appearance. I remember thinking that I bet he wouldn't have got away with that kind of thing with Cary Grant!

Before leaving for China I made what turned out to be an ironic effort to steer clear of trouble with the visiting cards printed for me in Hong Kong. As a courtesy to the Chinese in Asia, Westerners often have their names printed in transliteration in Chinese characters on the backs of their cards and this sometimes leads to amusing translations from the Chinese sounds corresponding to Western names.

I got one of the Chinese translators in the Reuter office in Hong Kong to compile Chinese characters and he came up with three for the sounds of GAY-AN-TUNG, which was the nearest thing to Grey Anthony. Only after 500 had been printed was it noticed that one way of translating the characters might be offensive or even dangerous in Peking. It could have read: 'Record the dying phase of China.' I felt a correspondent going in with a name like that might be in trouble if the Chinese looked at it prophetically, so after much head-scratching the middle character was changed to make it read, 'Record a peaceful China!' Another amusing example was that Lee Casey had a card that could be variously read, according to the translators, as 'Scholarly person', 'Insignificant person' or more simply and colloquially 'Bugger all'.

Early on the morning of Tuesday, March 14th I pushed my apprehension from my mind, had my bags put into a taxi outside the Hilton, crossed from the island of Hong Kong on the Kowloon ferry to the mainland and caught the nine twenty-six train for the border, Canton and Peking.

CHAPTER FOUR

Getting to Work

After an hour's train ride through the farmlands of the New Territories the visitor to China steps down from the train at Lo Wu to get his first tangible view of the People's Republic – a large red star emblazoned on the whitewashed wall of a customs building. The British and Chinese flags fly from masts a few yards apart at the border.

Everybody has to walk on his own two feet into China at this point. The border is marked by a narrow, sluggish, brown river and a small iron bridge carrying two railway tracks spans it. But the Kowloon train stops short of the bridge and after brief British customs formalities a guide from the China Travel Service leads the usually small party across the dividing line. Cases are trundled over on a trolley.

Three People's Liberation Army soldiers stand impassively at the centre of the bridge wearing khaki peaked caps bearing red stars. The stars and red flashes on the collars are the only insignia on the drab khaki uniform since badges of rank have been abolished. Two wear pistols in holsters and one carries a rifle on his back. On the day I crossed only two German businessmen, a Pakistani and a Malay were going in. The soldiers checked our passports with a glance and we stepped into the People's Republic of China.

The station and village on the Chinese side is named Shum Chun. The first impression is of neat, orderly customs buildings liberally covered with slogans in Chinese characters praising Mao Tse-tung.

Hoardings ten feet high stretch along the other side of the railway track, covered in vivid coloured representations of workers carrying tools, peasants toting wheat sheaves and African, Asian and Latin American revolutionaries with burning eyes holding aloft rifles with fearsome-looking bayonets fixed.

At the customs counter I remembered the pigeons and smiled to myself. It was in the Hong Kong office of China Travel Service that one of the staff had drawn my attention to a notice pointing out that live pigeons and opium were among items which the Communist authorities did not allow travellers to take in. I had grinned at the time and prepared to make some joke about it, but the grave, flat-faced reserve of the girl employee nipped that idea in the bud. The comrades clearly would not have found anything I said amusing.

Some other prohibited imports specified were arms, explosives, ammunition, Chinese currency and 'literature harmful to Chinese interests'. China's sensitivity to opium obviously dates back to the Opium Wars of the nineteenth century, when Britain took up arms to force the Chinese to accept the privilege of importing the debilitating drug that would help London balance its payments for tea, silk and other imports from China. Opium-smoking was successfully stamped out by the Communists after 1949.

The ferment of the Cultural Revolution at that time had caused travellers, especially Westerners, to approach frontier entry points into China with some disquiet. But to everybody's surprise traditional Oriental politeness prevailed. A courteous customs man ticked off the items I had declared, murmuring from time to time, 'Yes, Mr Grey, we can pass that'. 'Yes, that's all right, Mr Grey.' Then carefully memorising my name again from the passport, he used it in wishing me a safe journey and a pleasant stay in China.

The few foreign residents in China are allowed to take in most things duty free on entry. But on second or third return trips duty can be as steep as 100 per cent on things like radios, record players and records themselves.

After the customs check, tea is served in a clean comfortable waiting room, then a Chinese lunch eaten with chopsticks follows before it is time to board the train to journey into the hinterland. Many of the people in the border station wear, as part of a health drive, white gauze masks over their noses and mouths – the kind that Westerners associate only with doctors and nurses in hospital operating theatres. Music and songs extolling Mao Tse-tung play almost constantly from loudspeakers. These new impressions greeting Western eyes at the meeting point between two worlds quickly become commonplace in the interior.

From Shum Chun there is a brief train journey to Canton, where I had to stop overnight because there was no connection to Peking that day. I remember stepping out of the station at Canton into the afternoon sunlight expecting to see anything, rival revoluionaries hacking each other to pieces, tearing at each other's throats, parading each other in dunce's caps or whatever. But it was quiet and tedious like the humdrum life to be seen in a station forecourt anywhere.

I was met by Mr Chin, one of the ubiquitous guide-interpreters of China Travel Service who greet and shepherd all foreigners at arrival and departure points in China. Canton was the only city outside Peking that I saw and as it turned out it didn't disappoint me in the department of Cultural Revolution action, colour and newsworthy happenings. Quite the contrary. In fact there was so much excitement that I missed my train to Peking. This I gathered, from the scowl and consternation visible on the face of the China Travel man was the first time a foreigner had missed a train under his agency's guidance in the strictly disciplined history of the People's Republic.

I was driven to my hotel in the hired car provided, and later in the afternoon I steeled myself to go out alone into the crowded streets of Canton. I say steeled because for a European who has never been in Asia before the experience is almost traumatic. Every eye in the crowded street swivels to rest on the stranger. Chinese see very few foreigners and the sight of a pink-skinned, long-nosed, blue-eyed foreign devil is something freakish among them. The steel quarters on the heels of my shoes banged loudly on the pavement and echoed ringingly against the background of the almost noiseless scuffle of their cloth shoes. Having stared at my long nose and pink skin in disbelief all eyes swung down to stare at the cause of the noise on the paving stones. I didn't know where to look, tried to appear unconcerned. Cyclists wobbled by looking back at me as though transfixed and practically fell off or ran into something before turning to face forward again. And Canton is probably more used to seeing foreigners than any other Chinese city with the possible exception of Peking! Never have I felt more alone on a crowded street. When Neil Armstrong took his one small step for man into the unknown on the moon he must have felt only slightly more apprehensive than I did stepping down that Canton street. But grinning children gathered round my legs and it became clearer that the attention I received was more curiosity than hostility.

I became slowly acclimatised. And Canton was soon to give proof that it was maintaining its historic reputation as a city of political ferment. Here the Opium War started, here the Sun Yat-sen revolution had its roots; the Communist movement in the twenties boiled up in Canton and was ruthlessly crushed there by Chiang Kai-shek. It has been a city of secret societies and intrigue.

The everyday streets of this city, the biggest industrial complex in South China with a population of two and a half million, are covered with formal painted slogans praising Mao Tse-tung. A portrait of the Chinese leader hangs above almost every door. I walked a mile and a half along a main street where there were doorways every three steps and not one lacked the small image of the leader. Inside the open doorways there were often two or three larger pictures of him on the walls. The roads were swarming with cyclists and as in other Chinese cities most bicycles bore a small red plate on the handlebars with a painted quotation from the writings of Mao.

My guide said that the average wage was seventy yuan per month (about ten pounds sterling) and that rent accounted for only five per cent of this and food fifteen per cent for the average family. There is still an appearance of poverty and backwardness which the Chinese freely admit. But the people and children of Canton appeared adequately nourished and clean, cheaply dressed but not ragged, which is a great advance over the past.

The streets teem with life and vigorous working activity. Canton is built in such a way that the upper storeys of houses in the city centre project over the pavements providing a covered walk with brick pillars supporting the upper storeys at the pavement's edge. Inside the open doors one sees perhaps a dozen women sewing clothes in a small co-operative, a barber drying a customer's hair with an electric hair-dryer, a tiny woman tending rows of babies in cots packed into a small room or bicycles being repaired on oily floors. Open-fronted shops sell cakes and biscuits, cotton, cloth, vegetables, traditional Chinese medicinal herbs, rice, noodles, cups of steaming tea or oranges and apples in a fast-changing kaleidoscope of sights and aromas.

Dress is fairly uniform in Canton as it is in other Chinese cities and I never saw a skirt being worn by any of the women and girls. All wear blue, black or grey baggy trousers with some kind of blouse hanging loosely outside them. Their invariably dark hair is usually in bunches held together by elastic bands or plastic binding or is cut short enough to hang neatly loose. Like the men they wear rubber-soled cloth shoes or thonged sandals. The men wear blue or khaki denim trousers and tunics often with round peaked caps. Children are often barefoot but almost always more brightly dressed than adults with coloured blouses, shirts and jackets.

Rickshaws have disappeared from the streets of China. Now there are pedicabs which have the same seat for the passenger as the rickshaw but are three-wheeled and are pedalled by the driver instead of run on foot. The number of cars seen in the streets of Canton each day can almost be counted on the fingers. But the more numerous buses and lorries make a greater noise honking their way loudly among the droves of cyclists on every street than can be heard on the congested streets of some Western capitals.

I walked on, soaking up the strange surroundings, and after about an hour my journalistic heart skipped a beat when I caught sight of my first Cultural Revolution demonstration. Children were parading along the street carrying red banners, coloured portraits of Mao and banging drums and cymbals. Other groups came marching along the street and I decided to follow them. They led me to the Sun Yat-sen Memorial Hall, a large building with a blue-tiled pagoda-style curved roof standing in a park. I suppose I thought to myself 'Here's where Grey gets his first scoop' and followed the marchers through the park gates into the hall.

I shudder now at my temerity. Why I wasn't immediately arrested for spying on the Cultural Revolution I don't know. Beginner's luck perhaps. I went right into the hall and sat down near the back in an empty row of cinema-type seats. The stage was lit and draped in red and over it all was suspended on wires a huge coloured portrait of Mao lit by a spotlight. Very 1984.

They began letting off fire crackers at the door as larger and noisier parades of marchers arrived and stacked their tall red flags around the portals of the hall. Then Maoist cheer leaders began to harangue sections of the audience from the aisles, exhorting them to follow in the reading of his quotations. I began shrinking down in my seat. I was as conspicuously out of place as stair-rods in a bungalow.

Then young Red Guards came over and started asking who I was. I can only think that up to that point I had been regarded as an Albanian Comrade – Albanians are the only Europeans 100 per cent safe in China. I tried to say 'Ying Kuo' indicating I was English but they didn't seem to understand. Then one came back with something written on the back of a grubby envelope. 'Dear Comrade, are you good?' it said in badly-written English. I tried to hedge but another note came saying 'What do you do?'

I had been getting more and more edgy and now forgetting all ideas of Grey's first scoop I decided to go out to get a breath of fresh air before I was arrested.

Outside an officious-looking young Chinese wearing spectacles, drab khaki clothes and a haversack slung low round his back accosted me in English, asking what, who and where did I think I was. I said rather weakly I was a British journalist on my way to Peking just having a look round. He translated this to an older authoritative Chinese who had arrived, questioned me a bit further and asked which hotel I was in. When I told him, he enquired what my room number was. I thought this a bit ridiculous since the hotel, reserved for foreigners, was practically empty and I was almost the only guest occupying just one of what seemed a thousand rooms in the great, drab, Stalinist-style building.

When I wouldn't give my hotel room number the young Chinese hurriedly made as if to mount his bicycle and ride away. I thought if I was going to be arrested anyway I'd find out on what account. What was the rally for, I said. To my surprise the older Chinese answered and the younger one translated to me: 'It is to increase production in the textile industry.'

I was not arrested.

But the young man eventually did mount his bicycle and pedal furiously away, haversack jiggling on his bottom, presumably headed for the Public Security Bureau to report the fantastic impudence of the foreign devil.

I returned to the hotel and telephoned a brief story to Reuters office in Hong Kong telling how Canton's textile industry was trying to boost production. I also dictated another piece telling how Canton's food shops were apparently stocked with normal supplies. This counteracted a widely-quoted story of the previous day from Moscow Radio which had reported famine conditions in South China with shops locked and empty in Canton. When I reached Peking, staff of the New China News Agency praised me for the 'objectivity' of the report on Canton's food situation.

Next day Mr Chin took me to a hallowed shrine. It was a museum. Originally a Confucian temple, it later became the National Peasant Movement Institute and Mao himself had taught there in 1926. The simple chair, bed, table and trunk he used had been preserved and were reverently shown to me. I tried to film the tiny room with my cine camera and a crowd of children gathered.

Chinese children are as endearing as any in the world, possibly more so because of an elusive, doll-like quality the young Chinese face has. But they hate being photographed by foreigners. Every time I turned my camera to try to capture them on film they fled squealing like snowflakes before a gale.

After we had played this charming game a few times a grave little girl of about nine approached and my guide indicated she wished to give me something. I bent over and she politely pinned a farthing-sized badge bearing Chairman Mao's profile on my lapel. Gold profile on red background, Chairman Mao, the red sun in our hearts. I straightened up and the children clapped delightedly. Mr Chin smiled a rare smile and I grinned too. If only those who cherish the ideals of Reuters, the objective, independent world news agency, could see me now, I thought. Only one day in China and already going around with a lapel badge saying in effect 'I like Mao'.

It was on the way back to the hotel from the Peasant Movement Institute that the first signs of Grey's much sought-after Canton scoop began to reveal themselves. Army lorries with loudspeakers mounted on their cabs roared by trumpeting slogans that I couldn't understand. There was great activity on the walls. New purple posters were being pasted over those already cluttering buildings in the centre of the city. Eventually I got Mr Chin to tell me what the loudspeakers and posters said. 'Welcome the Military Control Commission in Canton and Kwantung province.' The Army had taken over.

The warring factions of Maoist and anti-Maoist workers, and Red Guards had caused such disruption in the heavily populated

South China region it seemed, that Peking had ordered the People's Liberation Army to step in.

I was quite excited at the coincidence of such a development on the day I was in Canton but tried to conceal it from Mr Chin. I asked if we could drive around the streets as the celebration parades mushroomed all over the city to the accompaniment of clashing cymbals and drums. I tried to sound casual in the questions I asked him but couldn't wait to get back to the hotel to telephone Hong Kong.

When I did the line was bad and there were only Chinese staff in the Reuter Hong Kong office who did not take dictation very well. So I had to shout and spell out every single word of my story ten times into the telephone and when Mr Chin came to take me to the train I was still sweating and shouting frantically into the instrument. But I had to finish.

So we left the hotel with not much time to spare to reach the station. By this time the celebration parades had grown to vast proportions. Lorries and coaches had brought thousands of peasants in from the countryside and they marched and counter-marched in the city carrying red banners and Mao portraits, and banging the every-present cymbals and drums. The loudspeaker lorries with great Mao portraits on their sides were now decked in the darkness with strings of red lights that cast the glow of Hades on the marchers below. A waiter from the hotel ran in front of the car trying unsuccessfully to clear a path through the thickening crowds. We ground to a standstill and the crowds pressed in around the car. Mr Chin sat staring stony-faced ahead of him. We would miss the train and it was my fault, he said without any attempt to be polite.

The red lights glowed eerily. When the demonstrators found there was a strange white face inside the car they pressed round closer on all sides staring in. Mr Chin stared ahead.

It was a weird, macabre moment and it unsettled me considerably. As we edged forward through the crush, new eyes were turned on the car and it was halted time and again. We got to the station at long last to see the red tail lights of the train disappearing up the track. I'd missed the train to Peking.

I was escorted back to the hotel by the disgruntled Mr Chin and eventually left twenty-four hours later for the Chinese capital.

CHAPTER FIVE

Getting to Peking

A trip by train across China affords, from a railway carriage with all modern comforts, a view of a stark landscape that has not changed much for centuries. From the vantage point of a comfortable sleeper or well-appointed dining car, peasants in wide-brimmed straw hats can be seen staggering along with baskets of earth slung from yokes or tilling the land with ancient one-furrow wooden ploughs.

Few Westerners travel in present-day China and the view from the train during the three-day journey from Hong Kong to Peking is still a comparatively rare one to Western eyes. About 1,500 miles separate the Crown Colony and the capital of the Chinese People's Republic. In the well-watered south the rice growing area is green and sometimes lush. In the dry, dusty and often drought-ridden north the wheat fields are hard and gritty. Many of China's 500 million peasants could be seen busily at work in the constant battle to feed the vast population.

On the trip contrasts were immediately noticeable. In the train from Kowloon to the China border, during an hour's ride young Chinese living in Hong Kong played cards in my compartment. They wore elastic-sided Chelsea boots and tight trousers, smoked cigarettes, had long stylishly-cut hair and listened to British pop songs on a blaring transistor radio while drinking Coca Cola through straws.

Once across the border young people and old wore similar baggy blue or khaki trousers and jerkins and many had white gauze face-masks. Uniformed soldiers of the People's Liberation Army were in evidence everywhere on stations and on the train itself. The only music or broadcast to be heard came from relay speakers in every compartment on the train. It was an unending mixture of quotations from the writings of Mao Tse-tung and revolutionary songs.

From Shum Chun to Canton, a two-hour ride, I travelled in a comfortable local train. A smiling Chinese girl attendant in white jacket, Red Guard armband and blue baggy trousers came round serving tea three times in that short time in decorated porcelain mugs. A picture of Mao looked down from either end of the long carriage and a coloured portrait was mounted before the front funnel of the steam locomotive. Every engine I saw on China's railways had a picture of Mao on its front.

After the stay in Canton I found myself seated comfortably in a coach bearing on its side the slogan 'Down with modern revisionism, support Marxism-Leninism' as I waited to begin the thirty-eight hour trip to Peking. The martial strains of China's most popular song 'Sailing the Seas Depends on the Helmsman' boomed from the station loudspeakers as the twelve-coach train slid out. The helmsman referred to in the song is Mao.

I was the only Westerner on the train and had been given a four-berth sleeper to myself.

The carriage exteriors are painted green with yellow stripes and permanent slogans like the one I've mentioned. They are kept very clean. The outsides are washed at longer stops and inside an attendant periodically draws a mop dipped in fragrant disinfectant along the floors of the coaches. My sleeper was panelled with light, veneered wood. Lace curtains hung at the window and a small table under it was covered with a white embroidered table cloth. A glass-stemmed table lamp with a scarlet shade cast a rosy glow in the evening. There was a picture of Mao. A knob under the table allowed the relay loudspeaker in the compartment to be turned down but not off. The loudspeaker in the corridor outside kept up the constant flow in Chinese except during the accepted sleeping hours ending around seven a.m.

As the train began moving an attendant brought in a large coloured thermos flask filled with boiling water, a porcelain mug with a lid and several small bags of tea so I could make my own in the cup when required. The steaming water was replaced at regular intervals throughout the journey.

The dining car to which I was called by a white-coated steward was clean and comfortable with a potted plant on every table. Good Chinese and European food could be selected from a two-language menu, in Chinese and English. There was one curiosity.

After dinner the waiter took the order for breakfast, after breakfast the order for lunch and after lunch the order for dinner. The impression given was that time was required to prepare exactly what I wanted. At meal times there were always six to a dozen soldiers wearing revolvers eating in the dining car or just sitting there reading to each other from their red booklets of Mao's quotations. The rest of the time they patrolled the train. The loudspeaker relay was louder and shriller in the dining car and there was no way of shutting it out.

At stations and along the route, all buildings were covered with slogans praising Mao and his thoughts. Ten-foot high, full-length coloured portraits of him looked down on every platform and most times there were more huge hoardings depicting those same African, Asian and Latin American revolutionaries in colour, marching with eyes ablaze brandishing rifles with bayonets fixed. At most stops passengers embarked and disembarked. Many carried their belongings in string bags dangling from the same bamboo yokes that are used for carting buckets and baskets in the fields. Other travellers on the train got down at most stations to stretch their legs, buy newspapers or a snack of dried chicken on sale from platform trolleys.

After a comfortable first night's sleep in the smoothly running train I awoke at daybreak to find a Chinese troop train standing outside my 'bedroom' window on the south-bound line. Soldiers with red stars on their caps clambered over covered field guns and trucks draining off the overnight rain.

On through the fields, past cattle and pig trains going south to Hong Kong and then the view of China as it must have looked for hundreds of years spread out.

Terraced rice fields cover the plain in which the track is laid. The plain is bordered by bare grey mountains on either side. Ancient but effective irrigation systems nourish the shoots. Bare-footed peasants wade around, plough, plant and carry earth for new dykes, bending, lifting, heaving, pushing, running with their loads, hoeing, digging but all the time working hard. The most striking impression of the journey was this intensity of work and the energetic physical labouring of the Chinese peasantry.

A woman washed clothes in a hollow where rain had gathered, two men pulled a single-furrow plough with ropes over their shoulders where apparently no beast of burden was available, a squad of thirty people hacked at a small dried-up rice field with hand tools, squatting on their haunches turning the soil without the help of a plough. A few slender isolated trees of the kind depicted in traditional Chinese scrolls were just bursting into pink and white blossoms to soften the stark, mostly treeless land-scape. As the train moved northwards the terrain became flatter, drier and dustier and the spring weather became colder. Whereas the southern areas had trouble keeping back the rivers and streams which in parts flooded the land, in the north the land was parched and in need of moisture.

Some saplings by the railway had photographs of Mao nailed to them and in some fields red flags fluttered from bamboo staffs beside the working groups. On one mountainside several miles from the train I saw Chinese characters spelling out the most common slogan 'Long live our great leader Mao Tse-tung'. It had been cut out of the slope in characters that must have been twenty or thirty feet high.

Crossing the mighty, mile-wide Yangtze river at Wuhan pro-vided the contrast of one of China's biggest industrial complexes. Hundreds of chimneys belched smoke – I thought of the Hong Kong China Watchers – and thousands of workers wearing uni-form blue denim trousers and tunics swarmed through the streets to and from the factories. Shanty-type dwellings were packed on either side of the railway emphasising the sudden concentration of population.

The second dawn came as the train sped on revealing troops helping in the dry northern wheatfields. The violent Cultural Revolution activity had been damped down to allow efforts to be concentrated on spring cultivation and the troops were playing an important role helping with ploughing and carting.

This dry dusty picture continued until the train pulled into Peking's modern station just after ten thirty a.m. on Saturday 18th March, 1967, right on time after the thirty-eight-hour journey.

Through the carriage window as the train pulled into Peking station I saw a European man and his wife on the platform. I was on the train only thirty-eight hours but I'd been the sole non-Chinese aboard and the sight of Europeans again was a peculiar pleasure. Since getting home from Peking I've learned that the Americans have coined an amusingly-American phrase for what I was obviously undergoing without knowing it at the time – 'cross-cultural shock'.

Almost immediately I realised the fair-haired young couple were Vergil Berger, Reuters correspondent in Peking for the past two years and his pretty American wife Joyanne. They greeted me and eventually introduced me to a shy, middle-aged Chinese man who had been standing quietly to one side as I stepped off the train. This was Lao Wang who was employed to drive the small beige Volkswagen Reuters had shipped to Peking for the correspondent's use. Six months later Lao Wang – who did his job as driver efficiently and willingly and who, as far as I knew, was as patriotic to his Chinese homeland and as loyal to his government as any other Chinese – was dragged alone and sweating with fear before a 'struggle meeting' of 15,000 screaming Red Guards who accused him of all kinds of ludicrous 'crimes' because he had worked for me.

CHAPTER SIX

Getting the Cultural Revolution in Perspective

To try to say what the Cultural Revolution was and is in a few pages is probably as difficult as that other problem involving a camel and the eye of a needle. This book is not a treatise on the Cultural Revolution. I shall try in a thumbnail sketch to outline the phenomenon briefly, in order to give a perspective to the overall account. No doubt it will suffer from all the drawbacks of over-simplification and the fact that the Cultural Revolution is different things to different people. Also, even now much about its origins, development and outcome are still unclear. What can be said with certainty, I believe, is that the Cultural Revolution was Mao's own brainchild and he remained its guiding light.

Through the movement he set out to instil a new sense of total and selfless devotion to the continuing Chinese revolution in every man woman and child in the country. He seemed determined to realise his vision of the entire population dedicating itself enthusiastically to the building of a Communist China within the framework of his political thought. And his determination to do this by exhortation and 'arousing the masses', the methods he had employed in winning the civil war, was not hampered by the fact that to achieve his ends he would have to attack and destroy large parts of the Chinese Communist Party – those pragmatic, civil service-minded bureaucrats who thought in terms of gradual consolidation of economic growth through such things as material incentives. This opposition to the Maoist way crystallised under the leadership of President Liu Shao-chi, who for nearly forty years had worked and fought alongside Mao to guide China towards the goal of Communism.

Until the Cultural Revolution the Chinese party had undergone none of the vicious purgings that wracked the Soviet Communist Party under Stalin. It has been said that in the West we have elections every five years and in Communist countries they have their purges. In this light the Cultural Revolution became a gigantic purging operation and made up for the lost time of the comparatively purge-free past. But unlike purges in other Communist parties which have tended to take place in the vacuum of the offices and meeting chambers of the Party's leading bodies, China's purge in a sense involved the entire population. Everybody was called on to look into his political soul, to take sides, express condemnation of the anti-Maoists or become an outcast. Mao's legend in China is so gigantic that it would have been impossible for him to suffer total defeat in the struggle. But the movement followed a tortuous course across the vast terrain of China sometimes descending into chaos and anarchy. Government departments in Peking shuddered under its impact. And because the Maoist ideal was staunchly opposed to the Russian style of Communism – the dreaded 'revisionism' – and the Western sin of 'imperialism', many foreigners in China were sucked into the whirlpool of confusion and some ripples of the turbulence spread to Chinese in countries abroad.

The Communists under Mao had won China in 1949 after over twenty years of bitter strife with Chiang Kai-shek – except for time out to join forces with him uneasily in resisting Japan in the Second World War. After a period of consolidation and careful industrial construction Mao tried to send his country catapulting ahead economically with the Great Leap Forward in 1958. Again he employed the exhortatory, self-sacrificing methods of the civil war to arouse the masses, and sent them marching into the fields of massive communes and into factories in regimented columns with drums and flags flying.

Some analysts estimate that the excesses of the much-publicised Great Leap set China's economy back ten years. In 1959 Mao stepped down from the presidency and was succeeded by Liu Shao-chi, although Mao remained in the vital power seat as chairman of the party.

It now seems clear that the germs of the Cultural Revolution were being quietly incubated during the early 1960s in the aftermath of the Great Leap although its symptoms did not become outwardly visible until 1965. In 1962 Mao warned the Central Committee of the need to beware of revolutionary degeneration. The next year he drew up plans for the Socialist Education Movement which was his first concerted effort to prevent China sliding down the same slippery slope as the Soviet Union to what he called 'the restoration of capitalism'. In this he put strong emphasis on the need to rear revolutionary successors.

Liu Shao-chi had always been closely connected with the day-to-day organisational running of the party and consequently was personally concerned with the appointment of leading officials or *cadres* throughout China. Therefore many party men in positions of power owed personal allegiance to him and subscribed to his more bureaucratic way of thinking and working. This was one of the reasons why fierce struggles developed at all local levels between the chosen men of Mao and 'the capitalist roaders in power in the party', as Liu's supporters were called. Later Liu was dubbed 'China's Khrushchev' because of his allegedly revisionist tendencies, and Mao may well have imagined that after his death Liu might make a 'secret speech', similar to the one Khrushchev delivered to begin the de-Stalinisation process in the Soviet Union.

Whether Mao conceived the Cultural Revolution as a means of purging the party of those who did not subscribe to his methods of military romanticism or whether they agreed to some need for a campaign of spiritual regeneration throughout China but opposed its extremes and so incurred his wrath, is still not really clear. It's a chicken-and-the-egg kind of problem.

The first public symptoms of the Cultural Revolution were a rash of unusually severe and persistent press attacks on intellectuals and writers in later 1965 and early 1966. This was followed in June 1966 by the surprising and sudden dismissal of the mayor of Peking, Peng Chen, from his post. Peng, a powerful member of the Central Committee's top body, the Politburo, and a possible later contender for highest office was removed at that time along with other army, cultural and propaganda leaders. It now seems this was part of Mao's plan to secure absolute control of the capital, the army, under his new number two, Defence Minister Lin Piao, and all propaganda media, in preparation for the launching of the campaign proper. The first wall poster of the Cultural Revolution went up at Peking University and was broadcast nation-wide. The president of the University was sacked and later seen heaving coal, as the purge of 'bourgeois rightists' grew.

In August the Central Committee met in some form that was able to approve a sixteen-point Maoist blueprint for the Cultural Revolution. Liu Shao-chi was downgraded in the party rankings from number two to eighth. Then a few days later the first Red

Guard rally was held and over a million of them marched across the Square of Heavenly Peace to be reviewed by Mao. Soon they were roaming the streets and making world headlines with a campaign of terror against 'bourgeois elements'. In their more bizarre moments they renamed streets – the street where the British Mission stands was changed from 'Glorious Flower Street' to 'Assist Vietnam Street' – made passengers pedal the drivers in pedicabs and mounted a campaign to change traffic light regulations so that traffic would 'go' on red because it was a 'progressive' colour and stop at green. They were dedicated to the sixteen-point directive's demand to wipe out 'old ideas, old culture, old customs and old habits' which the bourgeoisie were allegedly using to stage a comeback, and replace them with new ones to change the outlook of society.

The movement intensified and in some schools Red Guards beat teachers to death, and terrorised professors were reported to have jumped to their death from windows of university buildings. Foreigners saw Chinese 'bourgeois and anti-party' people beaten in the street. Some Red Guards were reportedly killed in the backlash that followed. The public hysteria had begun.

Red Guard groups were formed basically from youths who had shown themselves to be dedicated to Mao's teachings and who came from suitably proletarian class backgrounds. They received some para-military training from army men. Bigger Red Guard parades followed during the autumn and Red Guards went on Long March pilgrimages to the capital and all over the country, emulating the historic Communist trek across China in the thirties. Some reports said nine million arrived in Peking. Wall posters proliferated, attacking almost everybody – one which was quickly covered up even attacked Mao himself. In January 1967 the 'January Storm' broke out in Shanghai in which workers and Red Guards 'seized power' in factories, schools, offices and institutions from the alleged capitalist roaders. Then the incidents with Chinese students in Moscow, Paris and Belgrade brought on the demonstrations against the Soviet, French and Yugoslav embassies in Peking.

The struggles to seize power spread violence to the rest of China, and everywhere factions appeared and fought each other while claiming to be true supporters of Mao. It was at this stage that I entered China.

CHAPTER SEVEN

Getting into Trouble

My arrival in Peking coincided with a nation-wide lull in the Cultural Revolution. The prospect of China being submerged in strife and confusion during the vital spring crop-sowing period clearly had its influence on the rulers of a country where history has been haunted by famine. The army was called on to help quell the upheavals and the military takeover I had seen in Canton was part of this general move. So I was able to absorb my first impressions of the city in which I was to become a prisoner, in a comparatively relaxed atmosphere.

From my room in the Hsin Chiao (New Bridge) Hotel, I could see workers knocking down the last remaining parts of the great south wall which surrounded the Imperial City of the Chinese Emperors. It was making way for the building of an underground railway, some foreigners said. Other suggested the excavations were for a nuclear blast-proof shelter.

Peking in March is cold and whipped by dry, icy winds that bring great clouds of sand with them from the Gobi desert. During these dust storms everything, both inside and outside the house is covered with a fine layer of grit. The grandeur of the curved golden-tiled roofs of the palaces of the Forbidden City and the broad sweep of the central Boulevard of Eternal Peace cutting through the vast concrete plain of the Square of Heavenly Peace contrast sharply with the drab uniformity of the blue and khaki cotton clothing of the people.

The entire foreign community in Peking is normally restricted to an area within a radius of about twenty miles from the city centre. There are a few exceptions to this rule and those that make up the foreign community – diplomats, foreign correspondents and their families and the odd visiting businessman – may drive out along clearly defined roads to the Great Wall that snakes across the mountains north of Peking. This huge, ancient barricade, said to be the only man-made work that would be visible from the moon, is a popular attraction at week-ends. Other places that may be visited include the Ming Tombs, dotted in the hills west of the city. Otherwise Peking for the foreign resident is mainly a round of diplomatic dinner parties, cocktail parties and the occasional visit in a group to one of the excellent Peking restaurants.

The Chinese leaders up to the level of premier Chou En-lai appear at the frequent National Day receptions given in turn by the diplomatic missions of the countries represented in Peking.

On March 23rd, five days after reaching the Chinese capital, I was clinking champagne glasses with Chou En-lai and Foreign Minister Chen Yi. But just to correct any impression that I was granted immediate and exclusive access to the Top I should add that I was just one of a crowd of journalists, diplomats and their wives attending the Pakistan National Day reception in the Peking Hotel and that Chou is in the habit of formally clinking glasses with the row of tables nearest that of the chief guests. He didn't look at me directly and certainly had no idea who I was. In fact I noticed as he approached the table glass-in-hand that he said something shortly out of the corner of his mouth to the aide moving at his shoulder. I gathered from a Chinese speaker that he'd said the equivalent in Chinese of 'And who are this lot?' The aide had quietly replied, 'Mainly press'. But Chou En-lai showed two years later that he was not unaware of my name. In an odd series of remarks at public receptions after my release from two years solitary confinement he invited me to stay on in China. I shall discuss this in a later chapter.

But in Peking in March 1967 journalists were not the only people behaving like journalists. Diplomats were behaving like journalists too. Third, second and first secretaries could be seen in the crowded streets elbowing through crowds, going from wall poster to wall poster, notebook and pencil in hand, peering at the latest news reports, scandals, rumours and defamations daubed in black-ink Chinese characters on the pastel-coloured paper. Then they tended to rush back to their embassies to report. And the correspondents who didn't speak Chinese, that is to say all four of the Western correspondents, tended to rush to the embassies to find out what the latest reports, scandals and defamations were. And the diplomats tended to rush to each others' embassies to see if their colleagues had got something different, or better, or the same. Some Russian and East European news agency correspondents spoke Chinese too, so some people would rush to them as well to check. The dozen or so Japanese correspondents who read Chinese almost as easily as their own language spent more time than anybody else rushing around the paper-smothered walls – often late into the night and again early in the morning. They kept their information basically to themselves in Peking. But their often verbatim reports of posters re-published round the world from Tokyo were a large contribution to the dissemination of information on the Cultural Revolution in its early stages.

Friendship between Western and Communist journalists and diplomats thrived in Peking at this time in a unique way. The humiliation of the Russians at the airport in February had involved other East Europeans and Westerners and there was a growing sense of solidarity on an 'Us against Them' basis after the French and Yugoslav embassy demonstrations. These friendships developed with great camaraderie in the weeks that followed. In my experience of friendship with journalists from Communist countries in Eastern Europe and China it has become clear to me that the ideological differences which supposedly divide the world do not necessarily prevent friendship at a personal level and this encourages me to believe that the differences are only as insuperable as the obstinate, devious human spirit – which seemingly must have enemies – chooses to make them.

On April 7th Vergil Berger and his wife departed from Peking and I moved from the Hsin Chiao hotel into the two-storey house at 15 Nan Chihtze, under the high grey walls of the Forbidden City. This was to be my home for the next three and a half months and an isolated prison for two further years.

By this time massive street demonstrations against President Liu Shao-chi had begun and my three Western collleagues – Jean Vincent of Agence France Presse, Hans Bargmann of D.P.A. and David Oancia of the *Toronto Globe and Mail* – and I were busy filing reports on this and the daily revelations of the Peking graffiti artists.

On May 1st I clapped eyes on the living legend that is Mao for the one and only time. And for a brief moment the living face I had seen looking out from a million printed portraits everywhere my glance fell in China did not register although he was passing within a few feet of me.

It was in the Working People's Palace of Culture standing to the east of the Tien An Men – Gate of Heavenly Peace. There, groves of wistarias, pines, willows and cypresses surrounded a group of buildings with yellow-tiled roofs and red walls that were the halls of the Imperial Ancestral Temple in the Ming and Ching dynasties. Now the whole compound is a park with the splendid proletarian name given above. I went there on the invitation of the Foreign Ministry on May Day morning to watch the cultural displays. Usually on May Day there is no formal parade but premier Chou En-lai often strolls casually around the parks with a small group of government and party leaders. Mao has normally stayed at home in his single-storied, yellow stone house, in another compound adjoining the Forbidden City where the top leadership lives.

But on this morning I noticed that among the crowds there were thousands of uniformed soldiers of the People's Liberation Army. If I'd had a jot of sense I would have realised immediately why they were there. Perhaps my judgement was affected by the fact that lots of Red Guards, youths and girls, were lining up along the pathways applauding the foreign visitors, including me. I was about to smile back at them when I looked round to check and found I was leading a group of Albanian fraternal friends. But the smiling faces of the Chinese girls were so pleasant I smiled back anyway and clapped back too like the other Communists behind as I walked. It was pleasant to see them looking happy and the sun was shining. But suddenly the soldiers were moving in a purposeful way. They lined up in ranks three deep along the pathways, linked arms, braced themselves and waited. The crowds behind them thickened in anticipation. And I still expected to see Chou En-lai stroll by.

When the commotion and cheering began out of sight around a bend in the path the penny still didn't drop. And when a jeep rounded the corner into view, for one unenlightened moment I looked at the massively tall erect figure in high-buttoned grey tunic and cap and thought vaguely 'Who's that?' But the teenage girls and youths standing around me in the dense crowd didn't wonder. They just went out of their heads. Jumping up and down, screaming shouting, waving red booklets of the Great Man's quotations. The excited crowd surged in a great rush against the triple barrier of soldiers which bulged forward with the momentum. I was desperately trying to keep my feet in the mêlée. At one time I was practically on my knees, the next being thrust forward in a rush. I had been carrying a tape recorder and the microphone was torn from my hand accidentally and the twelve feet or so of cable wound itself round legs and bodies and I was being hauled around on the end of it. I also had a cine camera but so great was the commotion as Mao went by, massive, impassive, impressive in his stance, that I never even began to focus it on him.

Suddenly he was gone and the still half-hysterical crowd was streaming after the little convoy of jeeps passing out through the park gates.

Outside the crowd formed up again round the Tien An Men and waited expectantly to see if Mao would make another unexpected, unscheduled appearance. But minutes stretched to half an hour and nothing happened. Then a young, handsome Chinese of about eighteen who had been standing quietly in front of me turned and said, to my great surprise in good English, 'Aren't you English?'

I said I was. Spoken English is rarely encountered in China and I racked my brains for something to say to engage this boy in conversation. Eventually I said rather inanely: 'Excuse me but what are you waiting here for?' 'To see Chairman Mao of course,' he said and turned back to continue his vigilant watch on the rostrum of the Gate, like the other thousands around us. 'Why?' I persisted. The boy turned and with a polite expression which contained some pity for one who had to ask, he said quietly: 'Because I love Chairman Mao.'

He clearly did. This left a much more vivid impression with me than weeks of official propaganda.

Reporting from Peking demands one basic quality in a correspondent – he must be a diligent reader. Each day he must read the seemingly endless propaganda-laden reports of the New China News Agency, Hsinhua, which chatter into his office on a teleprinter. He must become used to reading about his own country and Western society generally in insulting, distorted terms. He must accustom himself to reading that the 'broad masses' of his own country love Chairman Mao and are reading his ideological writings in preparation for the day when they will overthrow their bourgeois reactionary exploiters. He must carefully scan the columns of the Chinese official press each day and select what he judges to be meaningful items for his Chinese interpreter to translate.

He must attend National Day receptions of foreign embassies in Peking and hope to get a glimpse of the Chinese leaders and hope that the speeches they make will provide a news story. He must keep his eyes open in the streets and perhaps he may discover material for the odd feature story now and again.

He must ask the Foreign Ministry Information Department for organised visits to factories, farm communes, for interviews and visits to other parts of China – but he must be prepared to be granted none of these things. And he must expect to remain ignorant to a large extent about what goes on around him. He must try to accustom himself to seeing China as a goldfish views the world of humans through the walls of his goldfish bowl. He is there but he is fairly successfully isolated from China by the authorities. To speak to Chinese, even those working in his own house, about anything beyond the prosaic details of their duties is very difficult. But when the phenomenon of wall posters and unofficial little scandal sheets known as Red Guard newspapers burst on to the streets, correspondents and diplomats were presented with a sometimes overwhelming daily deluge of information and mis-information unprecedented in a Communist country.

The millions of posters and newspapers told of an alleged plot by President Liu Shao-chi to overthrow Mao and grab control of China by a military coup d'état, allegedly revealed humiliating details of the private lives of those leaders under attack as anti-Maoists, spoke of fighting and killing in various provinces of the vast country and reported on a thousand and one topics too numerous and irrelevant even to make the news columns of the world's press or find their way into the diplomatic bags going home from the Peking embassies.

A tide of paper slowly engulfed the centre of Peking as the Cultural Revolution went on. Shop fronts, offices, factories and schools merged into an indistinguishable paper-covered blur as the assiduous poster-writers went through their increasingly prolific daily and nightly exercises. None of the Western correspondents in Peking spoke or read Chinese when I arrived and as I knew only a handful of characters myself I felt an overwhelming frustration in the streets in the early days since information was literally growing on the walls, to be plucked at will for the price of a few months spent learning the tortuous Chinese characters. Later in the long isolation of my confinement, unknown to my guards, I managed to learn enough Chinese to translate the poster pasted to my back by the Red Guards when they invaded my house.

One day soon after my arrival I went out to look closely at the wall posters I'd heard so much about outside China. I accompanied a Western diplomat on the rounds of his favourite corners and crannies where, from experience, he expected to find important or well-informed announcements on the gaily coloured sheets of pink, yellow, green, purple, red and blue paper. I could only stare uncomprehendingly at the jumble of black brush strokes as he scribbled intently in his notebook. Thick crowds of Chinese in cotton drabs were invariably gathered to read and digest the contents. The posters and Red Guard newspapers were as much a revelation to the Chinese as to the foreign community.

The impression left in the mind is one of elbowing gently through the crowds of Chinese, ignoring the almost overpowering smells of garlic and the acrid sweet-sour body scent that rises when any crowd of humans gathers closely together in a hot sun.

The Japanese correspondents adopted mass production-line methods on the posters. They went out in groups at night. One sat in a car cruising at the kerb-side typing furiously as colleagues with flashlight torches read off the texts through little megaphones.

Later in the year as the turmoil got out of hand throughout China, the government held out the threat of trial on spying charges to anyone reading wall posters or buying Red Guard newspapers. Until that time I frequently bought the unofficial papers from young Red Guard sellers in the street and took them to friends who would scan them for interesting items. The translators working for correspondents generally refused to translate anything but the official press.

In the early days of the wall posters some foreign diplomats had the temerity to remove surreptitiously whole posters from the walls under cover of darkness, roll them up and send them back to their European chancelleries to give their desk-bound colleagues at home a first-hand view. They shuddered at the thought of these rash acts in later months when the atmosphere in Peking's streets became so tense and hostile that foreigners did not dare to be seen even glancing at the posters.

In Communist countries all foreign correspondents wishing to file news to the outside world have to be accredited to the Ministry of Foreign Affairs. This involves prior submission for approval of a brief personal description and background information on one's career and education. Photographs must be provided and one is pasted into an identification card that the correspondent must carry with him at all times. Shortly after my arrival on March 18th I paid my first visit by appointment to the Chinese Ministry of Foreign Affairs Information Department. It was the first of three such visits during two and a half years in China. Each time I saw the same official, a Mr Chi, who had been in London as a diplomat and who spoke faultless English with an Oxford accent, an uncommon feat for a Chinese. These brief interviews live on in my mind as cameos of the non-comprehension, the artificiality of contact, the latent hostility and the frightening lack of common ground existing between Western and Communist Chinese minds. At this first interview, Mr Chi, immaculate in his cadre's uniform buttoned high at the neck, was formally correct in welcoming me to China. He politely took notes of my requests to be granted interviews with Lin Piao, Defence Minister and Mao's chosen successor, Chou En-lai or Foreign Minister Chen Yi. He noted my desire to visit schools, factories and communes. He also gave me the first example of the Information Department's elusive, ambiguous terminology that seemed calculated to leave foreign correspondents ill-at-ease.

I asked if I could legitimately use a cine camera I had brought with me to take news film. The reply was accompanied by the sharp, frozen smile that during the interview flickered across the narrow, handsome features of Mr Chi's face like the flashes of a faulty neon-tube.

'That is not what you have come here for, Mr Grey.' The smile was so sharp, I remember thinking rather melodramatically, you could have cut your fingers on it.

I asked for a yes or no and the ambiguous phrase was repeated.

At two later meetings separated by two years solitary confinement a stony-faced Mr Chi was first to tell me that my freedom of movement was being restricted because of 'fascist atrocities' committed by the British in Hong Kong; then finally the brittle, humourless smile was back again when I was informed I was free and that 'What we say counts! '

Troubled times for foreigners in Peking that had begun early in 1967 with actions against the Russian, French and Yugoslav embassies boiled up again at the end of April when the Indonesians came under pressure. It was a continuing series of events that was to be climaxed in the late summer by a Red Guard invasion of my house and my solitary confinement, the burning and sacking of the British Mission, the beating of British diplomats and sexual humiliation of British girls. Indians, Burmese and Mongolians, Japanese and Italians were also to feel the fury of Red Guard demonstrators.

Trouble that has waxed and waned for years in Indonesia between Indonesians and Overseas Chinese living there erupted afresh in late April and consequently the Indonesian embassy in Peking became the object of demonstrations. Effigies were burned at the doors, windows of a car were smashed, loudspeakers were hung over the compound walls directing an ear-splitting barrage of sound day and night at the unfortunate diplomats and their families.

After a week of demonstrations in which half a million people took part the chargé d'affaires and an attaché were expelled in retaliation for the expulsion of two Chinese diplomats from Djakarta. The Indonesian diplomats were surrounded at Peking airport in a 'circle of hate' for over an hour. In the throng they had to endure the humiliation of Red Guards screaming slogans at them and dashing paper flags in their faces. I watched Red Guards paste a paper slogan saying 'Kill Suharto' (Indonesia's president) on the briefcase of the chargé d'affaires as he held it in his hand in the midst of the crowd. Slogans were painted at his feet on the floor of the airport lounge. To get to the plane he had to make his way slowly through a narrow passageway between hundreds of Red Guards drawn up two feet apart across the tarmac. They jostled the two diplomats and their families, shaking their fists and red booklets of Mao's quotations in their faces and screaming 'Get out of China' and other abuse. In Canton the Indonesians were subjected to further indignities. Communist and Western diplomats and journalists who had gone to see them off were held back by linked-arm cordons of Red Guards around the mob and its victims.

It was the turn of the British next. In the first week of May a labour dispute arose in a Hong Kong plastic flower factory. Hong Kong Communists got involved in demonstrations and arrests by the Hong Kong police followed. On May 15th after a week's silence on the subject, the Chinese Foreign Ministry called in the British chargé d'affaires, Donald Hopson, and read a protest statement demanding that Britain accept the leftists' demands in Hong Kong. The British police action in the colony was described as a 'bloody fascist outrage'. Demonstrations began, as expected, that night at the British Mission in Peking.

About a week earlier a British diplomat had intimated to me that it was suspected the Hong Kong trouble might come home to roost in Peking and perhaps I ought to be ready for possible difficulties along with the diplomats and their families. I remember thinking rather illogically there was little likelihood of a single British journalist being the target of demonstrations.

But that night slogans proclaiming 'Down with British Imperialism' were pasted on the Mission walls and on the homes of the British diplomatic families a quarter of a mile away. Next day hundreds of thousands of demonstrators chanting 'Hang Wilson', burned and strangled the premier in effigy before the gates. In Shanghai a mob broke into the home of the British diplomat resident there, frog-marched him around for several hours and smashed everything in the house.

Slogans were pasted on the courtyard walls of my house at 15 Nan Chihtze saying 'Crush British Imperialism – only the people are really strong' and 'We strongly oppose British fascist authorities in Hong Kong – the Chinese people will not stand idly by.' When I asked who had pasted up the slogans a policeman outside said, 'The revolutionary masses'.

I gave a description of the week that followed in a letter to my girl friend, Shirley, in London, and reproduce it here because the account is more immediate than a two-year-old recollection.

'Monday, May 22nd Peking.
'... Your cable arrived as I was having breakfast on Thursday morning and those few words were very cheering to me when I

was feeling low and the pressure was beginning to tell. At the time I was faced with constant demonstrations and people shouting in the street and sometimes surrounding me.

'The demonstrations stopped today. The main storm lasted three days from Tuesday until Thursday night. But even now the children and youths in Nan Chihtze don't willingly give up the entertainment of shaking their fists at me and shouting '*Ta tao Ying-Kuo-la*' (down with the British limey).

'I still have a four-feet long "paper tiger" made from straw – quite well made with four dangling legs, a long tail and wearing a John Bull top hat – hanging on the curved roof of the courtyard gate on the street side. The gates themselves and the front wall are still plastered with slogans. Also we had a heavy rain at the week-end turning the steps – where yellow paper posters are pasted saying "Wilson must be fried" – into a gooey slippery mess of paper and glue.

'A rather splendid effigy of Harold Wilson some eight feet tall with top hat and a long red tongue hanging out, striped jacket and painted black shoes was also "hanged" on my small gateway so that when I opened the gate on, I think, Thursday, the two straw legs dangling from above confronted me. I had hoped to keep him, not thinking they would burn it since it was too close to the house. But on arrival home around one a.m. on Friday night/Saturday morning, I found a group of fifty or so Red Guards waiting for me. They had been waiting hours I think, since I discovered next day that other effigies had been burned outside the British office about eight or nine o'clock. But I went out to the cable office around nine and then visited David Oancia, the Canadian correspondent until the early hours.

'As I put my car away they put a flaming torch to Wilson whom they had cut down and propped up on a cross a few yards in front of my door. As I walked to the door they shook their fists at me and screamed, over and over, "Down with British Imperialism, long live Mao Tse-tung," in Chinese. I stood in the doorway and watched the burning, which lit up the whole of the narrow street, until the head and top hat fell off, then walked inside and got Moscow on the phone (Reuters office there that is) within some ten minutes. I phoned a story saying "as I dictate my story to Moscow, the smell of the smoke from the burning effigy is seeping into the house and every time I look out of the window,

Red Guards scream their slogans with renewed intensity", or words to that effect. In fact they hung around until about three o'clock and I finally fell asleep fully dressed, not feeling inclined to retire in the normal way. They had pasted a slogan on the road in front of the figure saying "The end of British Imperialism".

'I don't know how many of my stories were published as I wrote them, so forgive me if I am repeating things you already know. If it would be possible for you to get hold of the London evening papers during the bad days and also any cuttings from any of the other national papers I would be very interested.

'The incidents involving me personally began really on Tuesday when as you saw in the cutting you sent me, I was surrounded and had flags stuck in my face coming out of the British Mission. I managed to keep moving and reached my car. That night as I was racing out to the cable office to send an urgent rate cable direct to London at huge cost on the sacking of the Shanghai diplomat's house, I saw some of my Red Guard "friends" just beginning to stick posters on my walls. So I added that to my cable when I reached the office.

'The next morning I invited David Oancia, who is a nice fellow, over to help me take photographs of my plastered house. As we were doing so a crowd gathered, mainly youths. We carried on taking shots of me going in the slogan-smothered doors, etc.,* then a young gentleman wearing a Red Guard armband arrived on the scene to rouse the rabble. He stuck his fist in the air and shouted "Down with British Imperialism" and they all took it up. The crowd quickly grew to two hundred or so, so we whipped back inside. David thought he would try to leave after a bit, but as he reached his car the crowd closed round him. I tried to take a shot of him with my still camera but they stuck their fists up in front of the lens. There was ... (excuse me, got to write story).

'Since that last paragraph two hours has elapsed. Donald Hopson rang me to say he had been summoned to the Foreign Ministry and told the Shanghai office is being closed and Peter Hewitt, the diplomat there, was being given forty-eight hours to get out. So now I find myself very tired again, and with not much of the letter written. My tiredness has been cumulative – a mixture of long tense hours every day and strong demands on

* This was the cine film often shown on television news during my house arrest.

nervous energy, too. I was in bed just after ten thirty last night but still don't feel fully rested.

'I shall probably finish this tomorrow now. Anyway I was saying . . . there was nothing I could do so I went back inside my house and went up to the roof (just pausing now to get big whisky and soda and ice going – my favourite drink these days) to photograph the scene in the street in still and cine. They rocked David's little blue Volkswagen pressing around it, shouting and waving their fists. Pretty awful experience for him. Every time I aimed my camera they became more agitated, screaming at me and rocking poor David more wildly. Finally they had the idea of driving me off with stones and I, being nothing if not discreetly valorous, got down out of the way behind the roof parapet. David got away after about half an hour, but meanwhile a call from Tokyo I had asked for the day before from our office there, came through in time for me to do another "as I write Red Guards outside are . . ." type of story.

'After that it was unpleasant going out of the door at any time. There would always be a crowd reading the insulting posters which said things like "Crush Wilson's dog's head" and "Down with the British Imperialist bastard" or it could have been bastards. I adopted a habit of approaching the door across my courtyard at a fast silent walk, wrenching open the door and moving fast at small groups outside, who parted in surprise at my sudden appearance. Reluctance only spurred them on.

'My staff of five Chinese filed up into my office on the first day, said there was something "we must do" and disappeared until next day to attend demonstrations outside the British Mission. Left to fend for myself mealswise was suddenly difficult. They reappeared next day some surly, some embarrassed, then went again the next day to a big rally against Britain.

'One sign of the pressure I was under was that I did not comb my hair for nearly a week. I lost my comb at the week's beginning and never had time to buy another and employed finger-combing with odd strokes of the clothes brush I have. Today I spoiled the whole appearance by going out and buying a comb.

'The next day I almost got caught in a crowd outside the British office. I was doing some cine work outside in the deserted street when suddenly a column of marchers appeared with placards, portraits of Mao and big red banners. I swung my camera on them and they marched at me trying to surround me. They almost succeeded. One hung his red banner over my face so I could not see, while the others crowded round screaming in my face. They deliberately tried to block my way, flinging up their arms and standing in my path. Some hit me lightly on the head from behind with placards and hustled me. But I managed to keep changing direction and inching forward till I made the gate of the British office and turned and photographed them again from inside.

'The next day when the demonstrations had really cooled off, David and I were doing a few pictures of each other against the walls of the British Mission. Then we got in his car so I could film. As we drove out of the gate some youths took it into their heads to throw stones at us. We drove away and came back from the other end of the street, and the gang of youths galloped along the street again. I was standing outside the car filming Hopson's residence as they approached, and swung the camera on them to get them hurling stones. Then one thudded against the windscreen with an almighty crack; it was about the size of my fist, so I leapt into the car and we beat a retreat. One more story.

'By this time David and I began to feel we were bad medicine for each other together. By this time we were also becoming very nervy.

'It is strange to be surrounded, shouted at and have fists waved under your very nose without being physically hurt and always to feel hostility against you. It is difficult to explain to others and hard to recall yourself after it is over. It is a subtle and nasty form of aggression...'

My house became the object of Red Guard demonstrations in Peking because Reuters was the only other British organisation with premises there. The British Mission demonstrations lasted several days and the Chinese reported that a million demonstrators took part. This scale of political demonstrations befits a country of over 700 million people. A million past the gates of an embassy in three days became a criterion by which foreigners measured the intensity of protest. I shall describe these massive, strictly-disciplined demonstrations in detail in a later chapter. A mass rally in a sports stadium of 100,000 people roaring slogans against the victim country often topped off the million-in-three days treatment and this happened with the initial Hong Kong demonstration. Chou En-lai attended and Britain was accused of colluding with agents of Nationalist leader Chiang Kai-shek in the colony to oppose Peking.

The intensity of the demonstrations meant that for long periods the Mission was besieged and diplomats and their families were harassed going in and out; some were held up for half an hour or so. Harold Wilson was given a new epithet in effigy on the walls of the Mission – 'The Vile Saxon.' The loudspeakers blaring constantly outside made work difficult and created a constant sense of tension. When the Chinese Government ordered the closure of the Shanghai consular office which looked after the interests of the British nationals living in Shanghai, it was for China the removal of a final reminder of the days when imperialist Britain was dominant in Shanghai. The diplomat's office and home had occupied prominent, colonial-style premises in the centre of the city.

After a lull of about a week an inflammatory New China News Agency report from Hong Kong was published saying 'at least two hundred Chinese compatriots were killed or seriously wounded in Hong Kong and Kowloon as British authorities sent thousands of riot police into the streets to slaughter workers and staff of Chinese organisations'. In fact only one man had died in dubious circumstances. But the anti-British demonstrations started up again in Peking and the Chinese press made threats that Britain's 'head would be smashed' if she continued on her current course in Hong Kong.

In an editorial the *People's Daily* spelled out the kind of emotions that remain buried deep in the Chinese mind from the nineteenth century. British Imperialism owed the Chinese people a blood debt from a period of more than a hundred years, it said. Every hatred, old and new alike, the Chinese people kept alive in their memories. There would certainly be a day for the Chinese to settle their general account with British Imperialism.

Then a scuffle involving Chinese in Ulan Bator, capital of Outer Mongolia, increased the hysteria in Peking and the demonstrations turned on the Mongolian embassy, the sixth foreign embassy of the year to become the target of demonstrations. It stood just around the corner from the British Mission and the marching demonstrators carried on from one to the other killing two diplomatic birds with one demonstrator's stone.

Two British diplomats leaving Shanghai were kicked, punched, spat on and smeared with glue by Red Guards who also tried to put dunce's caps on them.

In Peking the Chinese staff of the British Mission went on strike and staged a sit-in around its doors attempting to get Donald Hopson to come out to receive a petition in a humiliating fashion. They were joined by my household staff, my interpreter and driver. The flats of British families were turned into a kind of diplomatic slum by Red Guards pasting paper slogans over the outside windows and papering corridors and landings with posters, smearing whitewash on outside doors and corridor walls. Paint was thrown at British vehicles.

As the trouble in Hong Kong rumbled on into June the Peking press issued a call intended to inflame emotions. Kowloon and Hong Kong Chinese were ordered 'to mobilise and organise themselves to launch a vigorous struggle against the wicked British Imperialists'. Peking demonstrations were mounted again to support this.

Then came the Six-Day War between Israel and the Arabs to add fuel to the flames. Accusations from the Arab world that Britain and America helped Israel in air attacks provoked another million-in-three days march past the gates of the battered-looking British Mission. Pro-Peking Arabs living in the Chinese capital smashed their way into the Mission itself, tussled with two British first secretaries, Anthony Blishen and Raymond Whitney, tore down the Union Jack and smashed a portrait of the Queen. Two days later they came again, set fire to a car and pelted second secretary John Weston with eggs when he tried to reason with them from the steps of the Mission.

Donald Hopson lined up his staff across the gateway of the residence to prevent a break-in there and in another scuffle Blishen was struck on the head by a heavy placard on a pole and his spectacles were smashed. All Chinese employed by Britons in Peking went on strike again.

When Donald Hopson gave a champagne reception on the lawn of his residence on June 9th to mark the Queen's birthday, hundreds of thousands of demonstrators blocked off the area and Red Guard cordons were flung across all possible approaches to prevent any guests arriving. A bizarre prospect ensued. Immaculately-suited European and Asian diplomats with their ladies in gaily-coloured cocktail dresses were stopped in their shiny black cars or on foot by the lines of drably-attired Chinese youths wearing red armbands and expressions of arrogance and contempt. They repeated rudely that it was not possible to go to the British Mission 'because there is a demonstration going on'. No amount of reasoning or arguing could move them. They simply began reading in unison from their little red booklets of Mao's quotations in aggressive fashion.

On the lawn of the residence the British Mission staff and their wives sipped champagne rather forlornly as the noisy demonstration roared like a boiling sea round their tiny island. Only one diplomat, a Dane, reached the reception – arriving in a most undiplomatic manner by climbing over a back garden wall before the cordons were put in place. The reception took on a belated air of gaiety about two hours after it started when Jean Vincent of Agence France Presse and some French diplomats and I managed to break through two tiring Red Guard cordons in a car by pretending to be en route to the nearby Polish embassy.

Outside the Mission, grotesque, life-sized clay figures of President Johnson, Harold Wilson and Moshe Dayan roped by the neck were set up in the gateway.

Then the Bulgarian embassy, the seventh diplomatic mission to attract Red Guard attention in 1967, was demonstrated against after three Chinese students were expelled by the Sofia Government.

Side by side with the anti-foreign demonstrations in May and June, all foreign correspondents in Peking had been filing reports on the increasing violence and confusion in the provinces. Those allegedly killed or wounded in clashes were numbered in hundreds and thousands. It seemed clear that anti-foreign sentiment was being whipped up deliberately by the Peking leadership to provide a unifying focus for the warring elements and to counteract the spreading lawlessness of the Cultural Revolution which seemed to be fast getting out of hand. Strict decrees were issued to the population from Peking calling for order throughout the country but they seemed to have little effect if wall poster reports were anything to go by.

When in mid-June an Indian diplomat was accused of spying, stripped of his diplomatic status and expelled amid ugly scenes of violence, the sense of unease among foreigners reached new heights. Even those from countries who appeared to have nothing to fear from China were worried about the possibility of the violence being turned against them.

On the evening of June 12th I was at home. As I was getting a cold beer from the refrigerator in the basement, the teleprinter of the New China News Agency which I kept there began to chatter out a news item. It accused two of my friends in the diplomatic corps, Khrishnan Raghunath, second secretary at the Indian Embassy, and P. Veejai, a third secretary, of spying. I ran out to my car and quickly drove to the embassy in Legation Street parking my car in the quiet street outside. As I talked in the embassy with Khrishnan Raghunath, Red Guards began mounting a demonstration outside. Loudspeakers opened up, glaring floodlights were trained on the embassy gates and the besieging crowds began their now-familiar pattern of slogan-chanting and abuse.

Raghunath, a young and able Chinese speaker and a respected expert on the Cultural Revolution among Peking's China-Watchers-from-the-Goldfish-Bowl, had been taking photographs with Veejai at a legally permitted area for foreigners outside Peking in the Western Hills. They were accused of photographing military areas.

As I left the embassy to file the story to London I got into trouble with the demonstrators although the affair was nothing to do with me. I had paused inside the gate, listening to the demonstration outside, then quickly asked an embassy guard to open the small wooden door in the wall at the side of the main gates so I could slip out.

When I did it was a nightmarish moment. The door opened, I stepped out from darkness into the totally unexpected glare of a spotlight and a wall of hysterical demonstrators surged forward screaming unintelligible sounds and thrusting paper slogan flags on sticks under my nose. Their wild faces in the blinding glare and the struggling motion all round me as they tried to hustle me away from the door into the midst of the crowd to isolate me in their 'circle of hate' was horrifying. I lunged desperately back towards the door in the wall yelling at the top of my lungs for the guard on the inside to let me in again. After frantic moments it opened and I fell gratefully inside.

After a rest I was shown to a side door in the face of the building that opened onto Legation Street about seventy yards along the street from the hullabaloo outside the gate. It seemed quiet outside. The door was opened – and normally I would have expected to find in its place a space through which to pass.

But instead the space was covered with paper stuck to either side of the door frame. I decided to go anyway and launched myself through arriving in the street amidst a bursting gluey mess of paper. Wall posters and slogans had been pasted up along the entire frontage of the embassy labelling it 'Raghunath's Spy Headquarters'. I walked hurriedly away in the opposite direction attracting startled glances in the dark street from odd Chinese not connected with the demonstration. When I got to the cable office I noticed my jacket and trousers were covered in wet yellow glue stains. I had burst into the street rather like a tiger going through a paper hoop in a circus, I thought, now able to smile about it. Perhaps Mao Tse-tung had something like that in mind when he coined his famous phrase 'All reactionaries are paper tigers' – a description the Red Guards were to apply precisely to me later when they invaded my house.

A demand that Raghunath be brought before 10,000 people at an indoor sports stadium for trial as a spy was presented to the embassy next day by the Public Security Bureau – an unprecedented demand to a representative of a foreign government enjoying diplomatic immunity. But the Foreign Ministry had declared his diplomatic status void. Slogans saying 'Hang the international spy' were added to the others at the embassy.

A Chinese deputy Foreign Minister later called in the Indian chargé d'affaires to inform him the mass trial had taken place despite Raghunath's remaining in the embassy and had sentenced him to deportation and Veejai to expulsion.

The next morning very early at Peking airport, diplomat and journalist friends of the two gentle, likeable young Indians, who had gone to see them off, watched aghast as they were punched and kicked and dragged around helplessly among a crowd of several hundred Red Guards on the airport runways.

Veejai was dragged past the railed off area where I stood. His shoes had been torn off, his shirt was half ripped from his back and he was bare-chested. His head was forced almost to the ground and he was dragged by the neck and arms, stumbling, falling and ashen-faced among the crowds. Raghunath suffered a similar fate although he was entirely lost to view in the milling Red Guards until the airliner took off for Canton. Embassy staff members who tried to go to their assistance, including bearded Sikh embassy guards, were punched and kicked. Indian cars at the airport were covered in wall posters and several Westerners who had come to see them off were involved in scuffles and incidents before the Red Guard leaders blew their whistles, formed their groups up into neat columns and marched them proudly away with red banners flying.

Two days later, after outraged Indians in New Delhi had attacked the Chinese embassy there, the entire staff and their families were ordered into the Indian Embassy and besieged there. Streets were cordoned off so nobody could reach them. Legation Street was the scene of the Boxer Uprising siege of 1900 and memories of this were suddenly aroused when Chinese began climbing on surrounding rooftops and taunting the beleaguered Indians in the embassy compound. This went on for four days before the siege was lifted.

In the middle of all this on June 17th China exploded her first hydrogen bomb and the streets of the capital overflowed with the marching millions again celebrating this event. It seemed to correspondents there that it was just one cataclysmic thing after another in the long summer of 1967 in Peking.

I described the tension in another letter to Shirley:

'... The fact is that several British wives are preparing to return to London to spend their holidays there with their children rather than have them come out here. Some people have got pretty low during the last few weeks with constant demonstrations and the uneasy uncertainty of what might happen next. You have, no doubt, read about the Indians being beaten up before our eyes at the airport.

'There was also the smashing up of the British office, the blockading of those trying to get to the Queen's birthday reception, houses have been daubed with slogans and even the windows covered over with posters. One woman came upon a Chinese actually inside her hall putting whitewash slogans on the front door. The Shanghai beating and glueing and wrecking and now the siege of the Indian embassy has made the entire foreign community feel on edge.

'I don't want to exaggerate the situation but unless there is a fast improvement it's going to be an unpleasant summer here. I have been very edgy sometimes myself. My cables on the beating up of the Indians were held up for thirteen hours and I spent a worried day expecting trouble from official quarters. I telephoned the story to Tokyo to beat the deliberate cable delay, when I discovered it by accident. Jean Vincent had the same experience. Nothing had arrived in Paris or London by ten thirty p.m. by cable and we spent the whole evening sitting around drinking Scotch and trying to make weak jokes about being tried as spies or at least being beaten up at airports around China on expulsion. What I am trying to say without making myself or anyone else sound like heroes in a beleaguered city, is that it is unsafe to invite you. Hong Kong is now in the throes of a long campaign of trouble which can have repercussions here any day.

'It would be terrible to have you make a long journey here then have to go back on the next plane because of the decision to evacuate all British women and children. I don't know if it will come to that but it has been mentioned as a possibility in private conversations. And I also have strong doubts whether you would get a visa now. There have been wall posters saying tourists are to be stopped coming to China but I don't know whether this was either true or made effective.

'On the explosion of the hydrogen bomb my own personal group of Red Guards and Revolutionary Rebels came along to give my house a new covering of wall posters. In black Chinese characters three feet high on pink paper, one slogan said "Explosion of our hydrogen bomb has given you British and American Imperialist bastards the hump". My front steps were covered with others saying "Down with Wilson" and "British and American Imperialists opposing China will come to no good end". These were signed by revolutionaries of the Peking Photo Machine factory – the same mob that did my house with posters and effigies and have been renewing them at suitable intervals since. They have clearly been designated to "look after" this imperialist bastard, as you so endearingly refer to me in your last letter.

'My translator has just announced his resignation to me "for health reasons" so I am trying to get another. I don't remember whether I told you but they were on strike ten days during last month – all my household and office staff – along with those at the British Mission. Relations have been very strained. I often saw my driver, cook, amah and translator demonstrating at the doors of the Mission and they joined in chanting at me when I went in and out. Makes life very difficult . . .'

CHAPTER EIGHT

Getting Deeper In

Diplomats who for a year had been going around peering at wall posters with notebook and pencil in their hands stopped this journalistic practice abruptly in mid-June. And so too did journalists. They stopped because a scarcely-veiled official threat was made to try as spies any foreigners who sought information from posters or Red Guard newspapers. The threat was formally made in a statement by the Chinese Foreign Ministry the day after the beating of the Indians at Peking airport.

It was issued as a stern warning to 'foreign reactionaries' and implied that Western, Communist and other uncommitted countries had directed their diplomats and correspondents 'to engage unscrupulously in all kinds of illegal activities, trying to steal by every means, political, military and economic intelligence'. They were snooping around with ulterior motives surreptitiously photographing, copying and stealing wall posters and resorting to all kinds of sinister methods to collect papers and leaflets put out by revolutionary mass organisations, the Ministry said. In an apparent allusion to Japanese correspondents the statement referred to those who sought information 'posing as Chinese', in a list of what it called crimes. The case of the Indian diplomats should serve as a warning, the statement said.

Next morning at nine o'clock the tennis courts at the International Club, normally deserted at that time on a working day, were packed to capacity by the entire corps of Japanese correspondents energetically playing tennis and being seen energetically to play tennis.

It seemed that if Peking's leaders couldn't stop the fighting and killing in the provinces at least they could stop it being reported to the outside world from wall posters. The foreign 'reactionaries' in Peking glanced uneasily at each other across the diplomatic dinner tables and grew more uncertain of their safety.

74

At the end of June the Burmese embassy had become the ninth diplomatic mission of the year to feel the fury of Red Guard demonstrations following anti-Chinese riots in Rangoon. Families were moved inside, windows were smashed, effigies were burned and a million people marched past in three days. Like a weary old war-horse no longer stirred by the smoke of battle I made no attempt to go to see it. I confined myself to rather tired telephone calls to the beleaguered embassy. The voices of the unfortunate diplomats were barely audible above the deafening din of the demonstrations and a million Peking demonstrators were old hat, it seemed now, and didn't make much impact in the world's press.

A few days earlier I had felt the first unsettling effects of official action against me personally by the Chinese Government that was to lead eventually to two years imprisonment in my own house.

The occasion was the state visit to China of President Kenneth Kaunda of Zambia. The trouble in Hong Kong was continuing and Britain had shown no signs of meeting the exaggerated demands made by Peking in the May statement. So it seems a little more insidious pressure or insult was thought desirable. All other Western, Communist and Japanese correspondents were invited officially by the Foreign Ministry Information Department to see Kaunda arrive. But I was not. I went to the airport anyway and was ordered rudely to stay alone in the passenger lounge and watch through the window while other correspondents were led to a press enclosure on the tarmac outside.

The British chargé d'affaires was the only head of foreign diplomatic missions not invited and when he arrived at the airport he was rudely prevented from entering and ordered to return to Peking.

The other correspondents had been invited to attend a welcoming banquet that evening but I was excluded. When I asked an Information Department official why I was being discriminated against I received the stock reply given insolently to questioners to whom the Chinese have no wish to be polite: 'You know very well why.' I was excluded from all events connected with the Zambian president's visit, and was not handed the final communiqué.

It was at this stage that I decided, at the suggestion of my London office, to seek some relief from the tension-charged atmosphere in Peking and try to go out of China to Tokyo for a break until the pressure eased.

Then an unpleasant Chinese version of the cat and mouse game developed over my attempts to get out of China – and eventually the Chinese cat got the better of the mouse and I didn't manage to leave.

In normal times forty-eight hours is required to secure an exit visa. A correspondent must apply to the Foreign Ministry Information Department and this department in turn informs the Public Security Bureau which issues the visa. I applied on June 29th to depart five days later on July 3rd. Result: silence. I renewed my request on July 3rd for departure July 6th. No reply. When I enquired by telephone the answer was in the best inscrutable traditions of the Information Department: 'We will let you know.'

The cat and mouse game was tentative up to this point. Then unexpectedly an official called me on July 7th to say I could apply that day for an exit visa with re-entry valid up to one month. I got my visa, bought my air ticket and was ready to leave on Monday, July 11th. And to be fair it seemed nothing would have prevented my reaching Hong Kong that day. But an external factor of fate took a hand in the game. On July 8th five Hong Kong police were shot dead from across the border by Chinese Communists in a tragic incident at the border village of Shataukok. And in response to a request from my London office I delayed my departure to cover any repercussions of this deterioration in Sino-British relations from Peking. And when I renewed my application for an air ticket on July 12th it was too late.

On the evening of July 11th – the day I should have safely reached Hong Kong – a reporter of the New China News Agency, Hsueh Ping, had been arrested in the colony in connection with the rioting there, and accused of unlawful assembly. So with their strict attention to reciprocity, the Chinese government, it seems, then gave instructions to China Travel Service to prevent my leaving. From that moment on I was confined to Peking.

The conversation at the China Travel Service office in the Boulevard of Eternal Peace is worth recording.

'I would like to book an air ticket to Canton.'

'Name please?'

'Grey.'

'There are no seats available.'

'But I know your planes fly three-parts empty every day.'

'There are no seats.'

'What about next week?'

'No seats.'

'Next month?'

'No seats.'

'At Christmas?'

'No seats.'

'What about a train seat?'

'No seats on the trains either.'

'You mean up to Christmas?'

'That's right.'

'How about next year?'

'No seats.'

'I don't believe this. I think there must be seats.'

'How could you know Mr Grey, you don't work here.'

I had an idea and drove quickly to the offices of the state airline a few miles away on the other side of Peking. At the counter a clerk was booking a German onto a flight for Canton.

'Are there seats to Canton,' I asked blandly without giving my name.

'Yes, plenty of seats,' the clerk replied.

I gave my name and he booked me a seat and changed my old ticket. I knew I'd never get past the airport controls if orders had been given from the Foreign Ministry so I asked him to check carefully that there was a seat.

Ten minutes later he came back. 'The flight has been cancelled,' he said, put a cross through my ticket and handed it back.

The cat, confident of final victory now, lifted its paw and I went back to my car. The twenty mile radius from the Gate of Heavenly Peace was now the size of my area of free movement and it would get smaller yet.

The day after the ludicrous conversation with the China Travel Service man, the first demonstration at the British Mission for about a month was held. About a hundred members of the staff of the New China News Agency marched to the Mission gates with flags and banners. They read out a petition demanding the release of Hsueh Ping in Hong Kong, describing his imprisonment as a 'fascist outrage'.

'You must release Hsueh Ping, apologise to him and compensate him for all losses,' the petition said. If the Hong Kong authorities continued on their course they would be held responsible for all the grave consequences, it added.

Hsueh's trial had been opened and adjourned for a week the previous day. I waited through that week knowing that what happened to me depended on what happened to Hsueh at his trial.

Shortly before this Donald Hopson had been called in by the Chinese deputy Foreign Minister Lo Kuei-po to hear 'a most serious and most vehement protest' against what were called 'the frenzied provocations and fascist atrocities' carried out against Chinese workers in Hong Kong. Seven workers had been 'barbarously murdered', he said. The situation had reached a grave stage now, Mr Lo added. I, for one, as a private individual likely to get caught between the two wrangling governments, tended to agree with that estimation.

My spirits sank further when on July 17th another New China News Agency demonstration at the British Mission was laid on after two more of their Hong Kong reporters were arrested. Several hundred Chinese hurled rotten tomatoes and stones at the two British diplomats who went to the gate to receive their petition.

On July 18th I wrote the last entirely private letter for more than two years to Shirley.

'... The reasons why I've not written for so long are complicated. Mainly for some three weeks now I have been hoping to surprise you with a telephone call from Hong Kong or Tokyo or both. You see, due to some unpleasant discrimination against me by the authorities here and due to the sort of rough time I have been having these past few months it was suggested I get out for a couple of weeks to Tokyo.

'This has proved impossible. It has been a series of trying and annoying inconveniences ending with the refusal to grant me a ticket on any airliner this year to get to Hong Kong. This appears to be in reprisal for the arrest of a Hsinhua correspondent in Hong Kong. Now two more have been arrested.

'Apart from the psychological effect, which is not really too great of course, I am fine. My spirits have been going up and down like a yo-yo in recent days because of the situation. I hope you won't be alarmed by this letter. I expect it is only a temporary inconvenience. But damned annoying just the same. I hope it won't be too long before I get out for a break and can talk to you by telephone . . .'

On July 19th Hsueh Ping was sentenced to two years imprisonment by a Hong Kong court.

Donald Hopson immediately invited me to be his personal guest at the residence adjoining the British Mission to avoid the possibility of my being set upon as a reprisal or to avoid any other unthought-of eventuality in my own remote house by the Forbidden City. After a day and a half spent quietly reading in the comfortable lounge of the residence, a call came through for me from the Information Department of the Foreign Ministry. It was Mr Chi.

'We would like you to come to the Ministry at six o'clock.'

'What is it about?'

'It is about your work.'

I put down the phone and prepared to go to the Ministry.

I had no alternative. I had already been a prisoner in effect in Peking for nine days. I was just about to discover that even this comparatively free time had run out.

Part 2

CHAPTER NINE

Arrest

High on the crest of Liupan Mountain
Our banners idly wave in the west wind.
Today we hold the long cord in our hands;
When shall we bind fast the Grey Dragon?

from a poem by Mao Tse-tung.*

Since the sentencing of the Chinese journalist, Hsueh Ping, in Hong Kong both I myself and the British Government had been expecting a reprisal against me.

After the telephone call from Mr Chi a friend from the British Mission drove me to the Foreign Ministry and on the way I turned over in my uneasy mind what form the reprisal could take. I feared the worst – trial on completely fictitious spying charges and a jail sentence. I hardly dared hope I would be expelled from China. This had usually been the severest form of action taken by governments against foreign correspondents in other parts of the world and in China too, up to that time. Expulsion from the country he is covering is normally the last thing a correspondent wants, but on this occasion I hoped against hope this would be the outcome so that I could return to the safety of London.

On arrival at the Ministry, housed in the spacious tree-lined compound of the old, pre-Communist era French embassy in Legation Street, the friend who had driven me there, second secretary John Weston, was told to leave. He had hoped to stay to discover the outcome of the meeting.

* The Grey Dragon is the ancient Chinese name for a constellation of seven stars in the eastern sky. In the poem Mao was referring to Japan attacking from the east and attempting to exhort his countrymen to resistance and victory. But I could not resist the temptation to apply the final two lines as a title to the discussions that must have been going on in the Peking Foreign Ministry in mid-July as they thrashed out when and how to act against me.

I sat alone in an armchair in the comfortably furnished reception lounge – the same armchair in which I had talked to the smiling Mr Chi shortly after my arrival four months earlier. Two officials had entered. The first a woman, wearing the baggy, faded-blue cotton trousers seen on all men and women throughout China whatever their occupation. She wore a crumpled blouse of a light colour hanging loosely outside the trousers. She was bespectacled and unsmiling.

But she walked briskly towards me and put out her hand for me to shake – the first incongruity of this strange meeting. I shook it. Mr Chi came behind. I shook hands with him too. The officials seated themselves and as they did so the door opened and incongruity number two came in – a man with a tea tray. The tray with three large Chinese cups with lids and a pot of pale yellow tea was set on the low table between me and the Information Department officials. Handshakes and tea. Things can't be too bad after all, I thought, and began to breathe more easily.

The woman official, who was apparently a superior of Mr Chi, began reading from a flimsy sheet she held in her hand. Her Chinese words meant nothing to me and I looked to Chi for a translation. He read in turn from his own sheet in his clipped, well-modulated Oxford accent.

'We have asked you here to discuss one question,' he began. I pulled a sheet of paper across the table from the small pile put there for the use of visitors and took a sharpened pencil from the jar beside it. It was practically a reporter's reflex action. I began writing in shorthand the text of the statement read to me.

'It is regarding the repeated serious warnings to the British Government and the British authorities in Hong Kong who are becoming more savage and frenzied in their fascist suppression of our patriotic countrymen in Hong Kong. They have gone to the lengths of unreasonably kidnapping, brutally beating and illegally trying Hsueh Ping and brazenly and unreasonably sentencing him on July 19th to two years on totally groundless charges.'

Pause. Another flow of Chinese from the woman. Another translation. My hand was shaking slightly as I scribbled the words. The preamble was a familiar part of all Chinese vituperation. I tried with difficulty to breathe normally as I waited for the woman to reach the heart of the matter.

She went on: 'The British Hong Kong authorities brutally persecuted correspondents Chen Fen-ying and Chen Teh-mu and five other patriotic Chinese correspondents by unreasonably kidnapping them and subjecting them to illegal interrogation. This is a gross political provocation by the British Government and the Hong Kong authorities that the 700 million Chinese people will not tolerate.'

Mr Chi was glaring at me and emphasising his words vehemently in a fashion calculated to convey revolutionary antagonism towards the class enemy – a show, I reflected later, designed as much to impress his superior of his correct political orientation as to impress me.

But they were coming to the crunch.

'I am now instructed to declare as follows: In view of the illegal persecution and the fascist atrocities in Hong Kong against Chinese correspondents, the Chinese Government deems it necessary to adopt measures to restrict the freedom of Grey of Reuters in Peking. From this moment onwards you must remain in your residence and not depart from it. The visa for exit and re-entry issued to you is declared withdrawn from today. You must immediately abide by this decision or you yourself will be held responsible. That is all we have to say to you.'

While continuing to write, my first reaction, oddly enough, was one of relief. I was not accused of spying and not to be put on trial – at least immediately.

I looked up and the two Chinese stared back impassively. I told them that since neither I nor Reuters were connected with the British Government the affairs referred to in Hong Kong were nothing to do with me and their action was quite unjustified.

Through Mr Chi the woman official replied: 'Do you think the atrocities are justified?' A reply to that seemed pointless and then she appended the habitual Information Department remark of total ambiguity. 'You know very well what the relations are between you and the British Government.' Another pause and she continued through Mr Chi: 'We are expressing the greatest indignation and adopting measures against you.'

I asked how long the restriction on me would last. 'There is no need for me to answer you now. The British authorities in Hong Kong should release the correspondents immediately without conditions.' Although the Chinese Government cleverly stopped short of saying it in so many words so as to keep all their options for future action open, I was now clearly a bargaining counter for the release of Hsueh Ping from his Hong Kong cell.

I was a hostage in Peking.

I put one more question to the poker-faced officials. Would visitors be allowed to come to my house? Again I got the deliberately rude ambiguity. 'We have dealt with your main points. You can think it over for yourself.'

I sat looking at them unsure of the next move. The woman gestured towards the door with a faintly contemptuous movement of her chin indicating my presence was no longer required. The tray with its three lidded tea cups remained unoffered and untouched on the low table. There was no offer of a handshake now. I folded my shorthand notes, put them in my pocket and walked to the door. Unthinkingly, I expected to go out to John Weston's car to drive home. But in the carpeted corridor outside a small, bespectacled Chinese in the khaki jacket and cap of the Public Security Bureau was waiting. He put a hand on my arm.

'Come this way please Mr Grey,' he said using, surprisingly enough, the 'Mister' the Information Department had dropped as an added sign of disrespect. He led me outside to a dun-coloured Polish Warszawa saloon car. Another uniformed Public Security Bureau man appeared and I was motioned into the back seat. They got in on either side and I sat squeezed uncomfortably in between them as we were driven out of the compound. July in Peking is very hot and very humid and the heat is accompanied by torrential monsoon-type rains on many days of the month. It had begun raining while I was in the Ministry and now a downpour swept streets jammed with marching crowds of demonstrators.

They were yelling slogans against President Liu Shao-chi and dissident army leaders in Wuhan in central China who had recently kidnapped and held hostage the Public Security Minister, Hsieh Fu-chih, and another Maoist leader who had gone south from Peking to try to iron out factional troubles. The Cultural Revolution had reached a climax of confusion and unrest and my house arrest was, I believe, the result of several complex factors reaching crisis point simultaneously. I shall outline them in a later chapter.

The car was held up for many minutes by the endless columns of marchers who had been ordered onto the streets despite the downpour. I was reminded again of getting caught in demonstrations in Canton. At 15 Nan Chihtze six other Public Security Bureau men waited, sheltering under the curved roof of my gate that stuck out over the street. They wore waterproof cloaks to their ankles against the weather. I was escorted into the courtyard and the small bespectacled one, who turned out to be an interpreter came to the door of the house and said, 'Show me the room in which you are going to sit'.

I was horrified at the prospect of them coming to watch me sitting in the house and I refused for a while to go inside. Eventually I surprised myself by saying to the little man that he was exceeding his orders. The Ministry had said I was restricted to my house, not that the guards should come inside. He looked puzzled for a moment and then went outside to the permanent police box, apparently to phone for instructions. He returned shortly afterwards to say the guards would stay in the courtyard. I asked for an assurance that they would not come inside the house but he just said: 'That depends' and left.

The six others remained sheltering under the gate and I ran upstairs to my office to see if the telephone had been cut. It was working and I called the British Mission to tell them I was under house arrest. The news was conveyed to Whitehall and later that evening the Chinese chargé d'affaires was called in and the Foreign Office made a protest against China's action. I turned on my Zenith portable shortwave radio and heard of this on the B.B.C. World Service news. I called Jean Vincent so that he might file a story to Paris. He and several other friends tried immediately to visit me but were turned away from the gates by the Public Security Bureau men.

None of the Chinese domestic staff working for me were in the house and, being hamfisted in the kitchen, I fortified myself for the first of what was to be two years of evenings alone with a bowl of cornflakes and milk.

Several friends called by telephone during the evening as they were to do during the next month and I went to bed wondering what lay ahead.

The entire action against me can perhaps be thought of as the application, with traditional Chinese subtlety, of a kind of mental thumbscrew, tightened progressively in an attempt to bring an answering twitch of pain and submission from the corporate body of Britain and the British Government in London. In late June and early July the obvious and deliberate delay in the eventual granting to me of an exit visa was perhaps a reminder that the thumbscrew existed and my thumb was in it. On July 12th when the Chinese journalist was arrested in Hong Kong the screws were tightened up in the act of refusing to allow me to book a flight to leave Peking. The obvious intention was to influence the British in Hong Kong to deal very leniently with Hsueh Ping. When this had no effect and Hsueh was given a two year sentence the Chinese clearly felt a further tightening of the screws might bring the British to their senses. So I was put under house arrest. And when it didn't bring results the pressure was really put on one month later with the invasion of my house, my confinement to an eight-feet square room and the cutting of all contacts between me and the outside world. They perhaps wound up the torture device as tightly as they dared with the burning a few days later, of the British Mission, the terrorising of the British diplomats and their families and the restrictions on their movements in Peking.

I think the Chinese responsible for these measures must have been surprised that although they were hurting the bodily extremities in Peking, the Whitehall nerve centre did not twitch or submit as they had expected.

If there is any explanation except good fortune that no British people in Peking during that summer were killed or maimed then perhaps it is that somewhere somebody had given strict orders that it should be remembered that a dead or permanently damaged hostage is no hostage at all. That if you torture too hard then the subject is unlikely to remain in a state to go on suffering. It was this carefully calculated and continuing cold-bloodedness towards myself in solitary confinement and other British hostages in China that eventually aroused such widespread popular indignation in Britain and other countries. This indignation possibly became something of an embarrassment to China's more pragmatic leaders. But I believe that despite their embarrassment, they felt that what had been done in China's name hotheadedly could not then be undone without risk of losing face before the West. And possibly could not be undone without risk at home to the more moderate leaders themselves in their own positions.

*   *   *

In the days that followed I became used to the frustration, boredom and depression of being a prisoner in my own home. From being active, busy and absorbed with my work I was suddenly faced with total inactivity. Friends telephoned constantly to try to help me in my isolation. Britons, Frenchmen, Italians, East Germans, Poles, Russians, Yugoslavs, Indians, Pakistanis, Canadians, Swedes, Danes, Norwegians and people of all countries and all shades of the political spectrum in Peking telephoned to sympathise, express concern and simply to be friendly.

Meanwhile the guards in the courtyard found a rhythm. Two remained in the courtyard all the time, the others outside in the street. They brought chairs with them and sometimes I would surreptitiously watch them from behind a curtain upstairs. They moved the chairs around the courtyard as the day wore on. In the morning they sheltered from the hot sun in the shade of the east wall, moved under the south wall as the sun got higher, moved on again under the courtyard's west wall in the afternoon and by evening had moved their chairs back to the morning's position. I was reminded very much of K, the character in Kafka's haunting novel, *The Trial*, and his strangely illogical jailers in the next room of his house.

At three-hourly intervals at nine a.m., midday, three p.m., six, nine, midnight and so on the shift changed. This was marked by the drone of voices which reached me in the upper part of the house where I lived. The guards stood in the middle of the yard, facing each other, each man at the corner of a small imaginary square, holding their red books before them like prayer missals. They intoned the quotations ritualistically, and the two departing guards left and the two new arrivals took over the chairs. If ever at night they caught me watching their little ceremony from a darkened upstairs window they stopped, turned off the light in the yard and shone their flashlights up at the window. And I always retreated. My dining-room was on the ground floor and at night as I ate in isolation the guards peered in through the uncurtained windows, shadowy figures in the gloom outside. If I went downstairs to the ground floor during the evening either in order to reach the basement kitchen to get a drink from the refrigerator, or to put my cat Ming Ming in his sleeping place, they shone their torches through the windows or through the glass panels of the door at me. Or they appeared silently against the windows and stood looking in. It was unpleasant and un-nerving and made me move about the house quietly so as not to attract this unpleasant attention. This led on the hysterical night of the Red Guard invasion to a charge of having 'sneaked around' in my own house.

Most evenings I played chess with John Weston by telephone. We each set up our own board and indicated moves to each other by numbers. This was a very pleasant distraction. I left the board set up during the day and when Ming Ming the cat discovered this it became a favourite game of his to knock the pieces around. My opponent was suspicious of this explanation when I claimed I could not go on in a losing position because of the cat's inter-ruption of the game! At first I gave Ming Ming a sharp reprimand and dumped him back on the floor. But he persisted and dabbed so charmingly at the chess pieces that I eventually spent an hour one afternoon shortly before I was invaded, photographing him at this game.

During that first month of my house arrest I became very firm friends with Ming Ming. I had inherited him from Joyanne Berger who had left him behind reluctantly when she departed from Peking with her husband, Vergil, after I took over the Reuter assignment. Ming Ming was a young brown and white cat of which Joyanne had become very fond. I teasingly told her that she had coddled and spoiled him and promised her that although I would treat him well when I became his owner I would turn him into a man's cat, treat him with rough affection and overcome what appeared to be his nervous disposition.

But so busy was I in the first three months of trying to under-stand, report and interpret the Cultural Revolution, I left Ming Ming very much to his own devices. I fed him regularly and chased him firmly out of the bedroom, where he had previously been accustomed to sleep, and gave him the odd friendly pat but not more. I have always liked cats and admired their disdainful pride and firm independence in not becoming subordinate to people in the way dogs do.

When I was put under house arrest I had time to get to know Ming Ming, and we became good friends. He was a friendly little animal and an expert at clearing the house of geckos – the little Asian lizards that infest ceilings and walls of all Peking houses in hot weather – and cockroaches. In the long humid evenings I would knock the geckos from the high ceilings with the extended aerial of my shortwave radio, Ming Ming would pounce on them and having played sadistically with them for a while pick them up in his mouth and gobble them up, seemingly enjoying the squeaking noises they made meanwhile. He did the same with cockroaches. He also liked to play with a table tennis ball, knocking it gently to the top of the stairs, pushing it and watching it intently as it went bump, bump, bump to the bottom. Then he would come back into my office, stand looking up as if to say 'Well go and get it and I'll do it again.' And, like most foolish animal lovers, I would and he did. I would also play a kind of hide and seek with him around the furniture at night, which he invented in his devilment when he came to know I was about to pick him up and carry him down to his sleeping place on a chair in the dining-room.

Ming Ming in fact turned out to be an intelligent and endearing pet and in my total isolation I became very fond of him. It was an enduring regret that I did not think to throw him out of the window on to an adjoining rooftop the night the Red Guard mob came in.

To add to my sense of unease during that first month, Chinese living in the surrounding low-roofed single-storey houses would climb up at night, shine their torches in through the uncurtained windows of my office where I sat playing telephonic chess, or reading, and repeatedly shouted pleasantries like, *'Ta tao Ying ti huai tan!'* – 'Down with the British Imperialist bastard'.

After a few days of house arrest my driver, Lao Wang, went off for his annual two weeks' holiday. For several days he had sat around the office on the ground floor, obviously ill-at-ease since he had no work to do. I never saw him after he went off for his holiday and although I had an indication that he was later in hospital, no longer able to drive and had suffered possibly serious mental trouble, I did not discover until I was released two years later that he had been treated harshly at the hands of 15,000 Red Guards because of his employment with me. I will describe later the way he was terrorised. My cook, Sao Kao, the man who looked after the boiler and general household jobs, Lao Chiao, and my wash amah, Mrs Hou, continued to work in a distant and remote manner.

I often feared invasion by demonstrators but never anticipated the eventual further restriction of my living space. I remember saying to a caller on the telephone one day that I was a 'sitting duck' for further violent action. Sometimes I hid important personal papers under carpets for a day when I heard demonstrations in the streets but took them out again later since it seemed futile.

The teleprinter bringing the New China News Agency reports into my basement continued to function and this allowed me, to a degree, to keep abreast of the tempestuous events in China at that time. I wrote 'ghost' stories of the events with the help of my telephone contacts with diplomat and journalist friends to occupy my mind and keep my records up to date. I began keeping a diary recording my moods and feelings.

My record player had broken and one evening I telephoned a good friend, Noeleen Smyth, the British Army nurse assigned to Peking to look after the minor medical needs of the British diplomats and their families. I asked her to put on her gramophone my long playing record of the Beatles' 'Sergeant Pepper's Lonely Hearts Club Band' and to leave the telephone receiver next to the speaker so that I might sit and listen to it. I like the Beatles and had lent the record to Noeleen to play a few days before my house arrest began. Sitting quietly in a chair with the telephone to my ear I had listened to one or two tracks when, without warning, the line went dead. I replaced the receiver and tried to dial the number again. The line was still dead. It was not until two hours or so later that I was able to get through to Noeleen to find out what had happened. It seems both our telephones had been deliberately cut off. Clearly the British Hostage was not going to be allowed to listen to decadent bourgeois music over the staunchly revolutionary Peking telephone service.

I amused myself dreaming up an imaginary explanation to this. I saw one of the team of men who possibly sit somewhere in Peking with headphones on, listening to all the telephone conversations of the foreign community. I saw his face growing nervous with dismay as he twiddled the knobs on his tape recorder to record what was passing between Grey and the British nurse. The prospect of having to face his shift supervisor at midnight might have appalled him. 'What have you got tonight, comrade?' the supervisor might bark. And the hesitant monitor would stammer that he had transcribed and written out the words to six of the latest Beatle numbers and would immediately be banished as politically suspect. Obviously not daring to risk that situation, he had cut us off!

After a week without mail or newspapers from England my deliveries of mail were restored and Peking friends sent me paperback books and magazines in the post. But I found myself becoming very idle and slothful in the humid heat of July and after about two weeks of this tried to work out a strictly-disciplined programme for myself. I got up early and went up to the flat roof which looked out over the rooftops of the Forbidden City. There I skipped with a rope for five minutes, trying to keep fit and sweating profusely in the sun, which was hot even in the early morning.

On July 24th I had had my last contact with the Information Department. I had rung to ask for a clarification on whether I could still file news, by sending my driver to the cable office with what I wrote. Mr Chi replied in a not entirely unexpected way: 'We have made all points clear. You should know the answer.' I said the answer had not been made plain and he repeated his previous statement, adding, 'This is our answer.' I then asked if some belongings in a briefcase left at Mr Hopson's residence could be brought to me along with a large packet of laundry which the Norwegian correspondent, Harald Munthe-Kaas, had collected for me. After a further pause the voice of Chinese officialdom told me: 'That point should be clear to you. Think it over for yourself, you should know.'

Fresh poster-slogans were pasted on the outside walls of my courtyard saying 'Down with British Imperialism. We strongly support the strenuous measures taken by our government.' From the roof of my house, which was the only place I could comfortably go out into the fresh air, I was able to hear the hubbub of demonstrations across the rooftops in the Square of Heavenly Peace – like the one in which the Maoists wildly celebrated the release and return to Peking of the kidnapped Public Security Minister.

Time passed slowly for me. Then the tempo of anti-foreign feeling began to build up afresh. On August 9th a crowd set fire

to the car of the Mongolian ambassador in Peking after the driver
had refused to accept a portrait of Mao that people in the street
tried to force on him. The car was left a gutted wreck because
the demonstrators regarded the refusal as 'an insult to Chairman
Mao'. Demonstrations at the Mongolian embassy followed. New
demonstrations against the Indonesians were mounted outside the
embassy and part of it was burned.

Border incidents in Hong Kong continued and Gurkha troops
had to draw their jungle knives in a show of force against the
Communist Chinese. China accused Burma and India of foment-
ing border troubles. On August 14th demonstrators besieged the
Soviet embassy again following trouble with a Soviet ship in
Dairen harbour.

On August 17th Chinese demonstrators broke into part of the
Soviet embassy in Peking breaking furniture and windows and
setting fire to documents. Earlier a Soviet diplomatic car had been
set on fire, rather ironically, outside the 'Friendship Shop' for
foreigners – the same spot where the Mongolian car was burned a
few days before. Japanese businessmen were roughed up by Red
Guards for reading wall posters.

On August 18th Italy's Peking trade mission was attacked and
the head Italian official was dragged out of his office by Red
Guards and put on a 'mock trial'. This followed trouble with
Chinese ships in an Italian port where the Chinese sailors refused
to remove militant slogans from the vessels at the request of the
Italian authorities.

It seemed Chinese demonstrators were being ordered to lash
out hysterically at foreigners. A frenzied climax was being
reached, and on August 18th this new tide reached me and from
that day on I ceased to know much about what was happening
in the outside world for nearly two years.

The outburst of anti-foreign outrages in Peking was an abrupt
reversal of official policy. Only a few months before the first
demonstrations against the Soviet embassy in early 1967 a Chinese
had run amok in a shop for foreign diplomats, stabbing an East
German and an African. He was publicly tried and sentenced to
death and all foreigners' houses were from that time guarded by
uniformed Public Security Bureau men standing by red sentry
boxes. In a rare reference to the subject it was officially stated
that xenophobia was not the cause. Then came the Cultural

Revolution and this carefully-correct attitude of the government was swept aside.

A Reuter correspondent on foreign assignments writes not only the hard, fast-breaking news but also background features about the country in which he operates. These are news stories of a more or less timeless nature, telling of interesting aspects of a country's cultural life, its sports, institutions, its personalities or any unusual human interest stories – in fact anything which might be expected to find its way onto the feature pages of a newspaper. They enable a correspondent to give a picture in greater depth than he can project into the more immediate and expensive news cables he files each day which have an element of urgency. These features, which in Reuters parlance are called by the contrived name of 'Situationers', are sent to London by airmail and distributed to subscriber newspapers throughout the world by airmail too, allowing the correspondent to spread his words a bit more generously than cable charges and teleprinter time allow.

To capture some of the atmosphere of Peking and China at the time, I followed my programme of discipline in that first month of house arrest and wrote of Peking's famous restaurants, the unexpected dangers for Western motorists lurking among the swarms of cyclists on China's roads, about toy Red Guard dolls on sale for foreigners, about army officers who darned their men's socks in a spirit of proletarian unity, about the growing legend of Mao Tse-tung, and about Peking's international airport which is silent for most of the day because of the scarcity of air traffic. On the last day of my contact with the outside world, August 18th, I was writing a Situationer about Peking's non-stop demonstrations. A supreme irony was to become apparent to me two years later when I read again the words I had been writing then.

As I wrote I was still hoping that perhaps I would be expelled soon from China and could return home. The features could then be published. Two years later, in May 1969, when I was first allowed to go to the upper part of my house alone again, I found the typescript of that same story splashed with blobs of Red Guard glue which had been dashed everywhere as numerous portraits of Chairman Mao were pasted up on the walls of every one of my rooms and corridors. It had remained in the typewriter which had been flung to the floor.

I had been trying to draw together the stray ends of the anti-foreign violence and give it perspective. The typescript read:

Situationer

Demonstrations

By Reuters Correspondent.

Peking, August 18. Reuter – Battered and defaced embassies and diplomatic missions throughout Peking, their number now in double figures, bear witness to the vehemence of Chinese protest demonstrations in all political directions during the year of the Cultural Revolution.

From June 1966 to August this year eleven missions were sub-jected to the now-familiar demonstration pattern unique in a world in which political demonstrations are becoming increasingly rampant.

The Soviet Union, Yugoslavia, Bulgaria, Mongolia and Czecho-slovakia – the revisionists – Britain and France – the imperialists – Indonesia, India and Burma, – the reactionaries – and Italy, so far unclassified have all experienced the sound and fury of the massive Chinese crowds.

Now, long after some of the demonstrations have finished the embassies stand with their walls covered with a mess of posters, some have broken windows and stained walls and the Soviet and Indonesian embassies were burned in parts.

The thing that distinguishes Peking demonstrations from those anywhere else in the world is their sheer size and iron discipline. Ever since the Soviet embassy became a target for the newly-formed Red Guards in August last year – the link was that the Cultural Revolution opponents of Mao Tse-tung were accused of the Moscow crime, revisionism of Communist ideology – the pat-tern had been unfailingly the same.

First come the poster stickers and road painters. They arrive to deface the embassy compound walls and the road outside usually late at night before the main demonstrating day. Some sporadic groups march by shouting slogans against the appropriate 'ism'. The next day in the morning school-age Red Guards and students begin streaming by with portraits of Mao, slogan placards and coloured paper flags bearing the same slogans.

Canvas-walled toilets are set up by the roadsides near the embassy concerned – certain evidence of a protracted demonstration – and often carts come along selling tea and buns. As the day wears on factory workers and peasants finished with their shifts begin moving into the picture.

All concerned march in neat ranks chanting slogans read off a piece of paper by cadres marching alongside the columns. The basic slogans chanted at every demonstration in this order are 'Down with U.S. Imperialism, Down with Soviet Revisionism, Down with British Imperialism'. Others involving the appropriate name of the country concerned and its leader are inserted as necessary. Fists and paper flags are waved at each shout. Effigies are burned before embassy gates. I have watched Brezhnev and Kosygin, Harold Wilson, Mrs Gandhi, General Suharto, General Ne Win and Mongolia's Tsedenbal go up in smoke and blazing straw in Peking in the last few months.

For a really angry protest the highly efficient organisers can get a million people marched past the gates of an embassy in three days. Those that have been accorded the doubtful distinction of a million or more demonstrators are the Soviet Union, Britain, Burma, Indonesia and Mongolia. The campaigns have been triggered mainly by incidents in the various countries involving Chinese diplomats and students or Overseas Chinese. Britain caught a double dose of the 'million' treatment over Hong Kong and the Middle East War.

The crowds are brought into the capital's centre by lorries from factories, communes, offices and schools at fixed times in remarkably well-organised schedules. The marching throngs usually spread for miles along the central Boulevard of Eternal Peace approaching or leaving the two main embassy quarters. Red Guard groups wearing paper badges of authority line up across road junctions to re-direct traffic and point the way to the marchers among what could be a confusing cluster of missions.

If it rains they carry waxed paper umbrellas and plastic macs, if it's hot they carry bamboo leaf fans. The same demonstrators must have taken part in many of the different demonstrations. Cartoons carried in the parades or stuck on the appropriate embassy walls show mighty workers' fists crushing the revisionists, imperialists or reactionaries.

Groups of actors perform skits before the embassy gates depicting the enemy lunging around in futile fashion and usually finishing with the Chinese victors leading the vanquished away with ropes around their necks. China's official news media broadcast abroad

D

the facts of the size and duration of the demonstrations. The campaigns have a dual effect. The news goes around the world and those taking part receive an object lesson in China's policy towards the country concerned. Until the British Mission was broken into during the Middle East War . . .

As I wrote the words 'Until the British Mission was broken into during the Middle East War . . .' I heard a commotion in the street outside and soon the Red Guards were inside and dragging me downstairs. The sentence that was never completed would have read: 'Until the British Mission was broken into during the Middle East War, the demonstrators had never intruded into the premises of foreigners.'

CHAPTER TEN

Solitary

On August 18th, 1966, it will be remembered, a million representatives of China's militant young Red Guards marched across the Square of Heavenly Peace for the first time. They became the heroes of the Cultural Revolution and were dubbed the 'little generals' by their creators, the party leadership.

On August 18th, 1967 a celebration rally was held in the massive Great Hall of the People, which flanks the Square of Heavenly Peace on the western side, to mark the first anniversary of that momentous day in China's revolutionary history. It went on late into the evening attended probably by some 10,000 Red Guard representatives. For some of those attending, the evening was spiced with the prospect of new heroic deeds to be done that night. The house of a lone foreign imperialist was to be invaded and 200 of them were bravely to manhandle him and his pet cat. Posters had been prepared and wooden slats and hammers and nails for barring doors were in hand too. And there was enough black paint to coat window panes to keep out the light of day.

In the office on the upper floor of my house I sat at my typewriter unaware of all this. I had been under house arrest for exactly four weeks. I was wearing only a pair of tennis shorts and a yellow towelling shirt because of the heat. The thermometer in my office had shown ninety-eight degrees Fahrenheit at one o'clock in the morning a few nights before and it was not much cooler on the 18th.

I was engrossed in my writing and only vaguely noticed the noise in the street outside at first. I went on typing. Although I had realised I was a 'sitting duck' in my confinement I suppose on that irrational basis common to us all, 'nothing-serious-can-ever-really-happen-to-me', I never in fact expected further trouble. So it was with a slight feeling of annoyance at having my concentration interrupted that I finally stopped typing to see what the cause

of the commotion was in Nan Chihtze. I walked through my bedroom to the bathroom where a window looked down over the
fifteen foot high wall into the darkened street. It was about
eleven p.m.

Immediately my eyes fell on the crowd in the gloom I knew
what was happening. People blocked the entire street and my angle
of vision allowed me to see only those on the far pavement. All
were looking towards my gate and the excited shouting and banging were coming from there.

I ran back through my bedroom to the office to telephone the
British Mission to tell them I was being invaded. It wouldn't
help but the only thing I could do was try to tell somebody. But
even as I crossed the landing from my bedroom to the office I
heard the mob breaking through the door of the house from the
courtyard and beginning to mount the stairs. I dialled the number
with the sound of things breaking and yelling coming nearer up
the stairs. But the number didn't ring out. I think the line had
been cut before the attack began. But I was never really sure
because the second I'd finished dialling the first excited, wild-
eyed Red Guards had rushed the top of the stairs and were in the
room.

I remember stupidly adding to the din by shouting 'Get out of
here!' as they grabbed the telephone from my hands, ripped the
wires from the wall and frog-marched me out and down the stairs.
I was pushed and pulled outside to the courtyard. I stumbled
down the steps of the house into the thick crowd packing the
small yard. Black paint was sloshed on me, soaking through my
shirt and shorts and running down my bare legs into my socks and
shoes. Glue was daubed on my back and a pink paper poster was
slapped on it. I was tugged around with my head forced down
among the crowd while they shouted and screamed slogans and
pummelled me. A kind of tar-and-feathering, modern Peking style,
I suppose.

I was dragged back to the top of the short flight of steps leading
down into the courtyard from the door of the house. There I was
placed into what they regarded as the correct position for the
rest of the arranged proceedings. I was 'jet-planed'. This is the
Chinese expression describing the painful doubled-up position into
which victims are forced at 'struggle meetings' to punish them for
anti-Maoist crimes. My head was forced down to within a foot or

two of the ground and my arms thrust back straight behind me and upwards and held there. The position is an exaggeration of the posture adopted briefly by a racing swimmer at the brink of the swimming pool before he flings himself forward in a long shallow dive at the start of a race. The 'jet plane' designation arises from the similarity of the arms to the swept-back wings of a modern fighter aircraft.

The posture is immediately uncomfortable and eventually painful. The crowd which had been yelling wildly quietened as one Red Guard began to read out a 'list of crimes'. A translator shouted them in English but due to my position and the angry jeering which greeted each announcement I was unable to hear very much. My back quickly became stiff and painful but whenever I tried even slightly to straighten up to ease it, the Red Guard posted at my side yelled incoherently at me, struck me hard in the stomach while forcing my head down with a hand gripping the back of my neck. A very effective method of persuading someone to double up. He did it so economically and efficiently I fancy he must have been very experienced. Struggle meetings were taking place day and night during the Cultural Revolution.

Another zealot was holding my arms straight up behind me and I remained in this undignified position as the crimes list was read out. From time to time I caught the shouted words through the din.

'You have drunk alcohol in your house.' Pandemonium. 'You have *even* despised the paper tiger hung on your gate by the revolutionary masses.' More frenzied shouting. 'You have sneaked around in your house! ' Even greater uproar.

I was referred to constantly as 'reactionary newsman Grey'.

After a while I could see the reflection of my face in a pool of sweat on the stone step just beneath my nose. The sweat ran down from my face, neck and shoulders. The only thing I can remember thinking is whether I would be able to avoid vomiting since the heat, rendered more intense by the bodies pressing around me and the pain in my front and back, began to affect my stomach.

I have no idea how long I was in this position. But I had been interested to notice another of what I fancy was a reporter's reflex action. Newspapermen get used to timing things. In my days on provincial newspapers I had timed goals scored in football matches, kept an eye on my watch as audiences applauded first nights for several minutes and so on. When my head was being forced down I had stolen a quick glance at my watch to see, I suppose, how long the action against me was to last. But I have no recollection of what time the watch showed. Afterwards, when I looked at it again the inside of the watch glass was completely obscured by condensation on the inside – an indication perhaps of the heat of the ordeal. I would guess it was around half an hour. I also have little idea of how many demonstrators invaded my house. Some days later reports of 200 filtered through to the foreign community in Peking. All I can say with certainty is that the house and yard were crammed with yelling Chinese.

The shouting and screaming of slogans was supplemented by the noise of other Red Guards rampaging through the house. Pictures were being flung to the floor and smashed. Typewriters, radios and ornaments were hurled around, books were being scattered, curtains and furniture were being daubed with thick black slogans both in Chinese characters and English. Glass was breaking, nails were being hammered in and glue was dripping on me from a portrait of Mao that was being stuck up above the outside door of the house on the glass fanlight.

Then the crowd suddenly quietened. There was some cheering and some applause. I felt the attention directed away from me for a moment as I remained bent double with only the grey step in my field of vision. Then my chief tormentor was roughly urging me to straighten up. I did so and found dangling before my eyes the body of my cat Ming Ming. He was hanging from the balcony or flat roof above my head at the end of a rope linen line. The noose had bitten deeply into his neck and was concealed by the ruff of fur at his throat. His back legs hung straight down stiffly and there was no sign of movement from him. He was already dead. I felt a great helpless anger at the mindlessness of what was happening.

Cats and dogs were decreed by the Red Guards to be bourgeois-style pets not consistent with the proletarian-pure way of life in China in the early days of the Cultural Revolution and many had been killed and destroyed in attacks on the Red Guards' Chinese victims.

Ming Ming's body dangled motionless against the background of a sea of faces in the dim light of the courtyard. I fancied all were watching for signs of grief on my bourgeois face and I gritted my teeth and stared, I hope, expressionlessly ahead. Then I was forced double again as the mob, noisy again after the brief silence, began shouting 'Hang Grey! Hang Grey! Hang Grey!'

Then the translator's voice again: 'We could kill you Grey but...' and the rest of the sentence was lost in the howls of the mob. Then incongruously they began shouting 'Hang Wilson, Hang Wilson.'

Then there were more accusations. 'You have unjustly arrested newsmen and today closed three newspapers'. This was a reference to actions taken in Hong Kong against Communist news media and personnel. Three long statements were read out without translation. I tried to bend one knee to ease my stiffening limbs and back but another of my guardians, posted on the other side from the stomach-puncher, shouted out this detail excitedly and with his hand forced my leg straight again. I tried to pull my arms back and support my elbows on my thighs to ease the strain but they were pushed away.

After a while whoever was holding my hands up behind me let them go and I tried, still bent double, to rub my aching back. But my hands were knocked away from the painful area. Somehow, after what seemed a long while, I managed, by bringing my head almost between my knees, to get my arms round from behind me and rest them on the top of my thighs seemingly without anyone noticing. Or perhaps with their experience of the 'jet-plane' my supervisors knew exactly how long one could remain stiffly in the original position without collapsing.

I am able to write of the contortions in such detail more than two years later only from notes I made secretly just two weeks after it happened. They had otherwise faded from my memory. Of the last-mentioned manoeuvre I wrote: 'This saved my back considerably and I was pleased with this.'

Both arms were covered in black paint, I was then able to notice. The sound of hammering above and all around me increased and I later discovered this was the process of constructing my 'cell' – nailing wood across the outsides of doors and windows in the part of the house to which I was to be confined.

While I was still kept bent double various leaders in the crowd began reading lengthily in turn from the red booklet of Mao's quotations and the crowd stopped yelling, got out their books

and followed suit. It was rather like the final devotions of a
Maoist mass, I thought later.

Then with my back seemingly almost breaking I was ordered to
straighten up and was led back inside the house. I was pushed
towards the staircase lined all the way up on either side by glaring
Red Guards. I noticed that the Red Guard on the bottom step
at the left was a girl – and with her short jet-black hair pulled
back in bunches from proud regular features she looked to be
one of the most beautiful girls I had seen in China. I was curious
to see the expression in the eyes of a pretty girl who had taken
part in the rough humiliation by 200 of one foreign man and
looked at her as I went by. She stared straight ahead at the opposite wall avoiding my glance. I would like to think that she did
not glare because she had not enjoyed taking part in such an
unlaudable action and that like many other Chinese caught up in
events outside their control, was only there because she had to be.

The sight that greeted my eyes up the stairs was nightmarish.
Black paint ran down every wall. Every square foot had been
daubed with slogans in Chinese and English. 'Long Live Chairman Mao,' 'Down with Grey' – a flattering juxtaposition. The living legend and the unknown, insignificant foreign reporter.

The slogans covered the staircase walls, the landing, my bedroom and bathroom. These rooms were filled with jeering Red
Guards. Even the sheets of my bed had been daubed with black
Chinese characters saying *'Ta tao Ger-lai'* – 'Down with Grey!'
The same poster that was stuck on my back was pasted on walls,
beds, my wardrobe, by the bathroom mirror and many other
places. The doors to my office and lounge were closed and sealed
with wide strips of paper bearing Chinese characters and official
stamps – the same kind of device I had seen pasted across the
sealed doors of Chinese houses in nearby lanes after the occupants
had been banished, presumably to do enforced labour somewhere,
because they had failed to pass scrutiny in the frantic purging of
the Cultural Revolution. I was led around by the Red Guards who
took an aggressive delight in showing me the mess they had made.
Large portraits of Mao occupied pride of place in every room.
The paint ran down the walls, glue and paste dripped everywhere.
The smell of paint, glue and the press of excited bodies in the
house compounded the nightmarish atmosphere.

The bathroom mirror was covered with slogans and there was

one added refinement. The bristles of my toothbrush had been carefully painted black with slogan paint, rendering it unusable. It was held up for my inspection with expressions of particularly malicious glee. The inside of the bath had been painted black too, putting it out of action. I was led downstairs and shown into a part of the house I had rarely previously entered – the downstairs washroom where my amah did the laundry and the tiny adjoining room used partly as a store room and where my driver had a small bunk on which to rest from the heat at midday. The same filthy mess had been made on walls, doors and windows with paint and posters.

Back upstairs again and an interpreter standing by a senior-looking, uniformed Public Security Bureau man told me to 'take what you require for your daily needs' to the small downstairs room.

I hauled the sheets, still wet with black paint, from the bed, gathered together a spare shirt, some clean underclothes, handkerchiefs and a pair of pyjamas. I asked to be allowed to go into my office and lounge to get a few books and writing materials but my attention was drawn rudely to the seals. It was taboo. There were four books on my bedside table and, without much hope, I picked them up and indicated I wished to take them with me. Harry Golombek's Penguin book *The Game of Chess* passed muster, *True Yoga* by William Zorn met no objection, *The Theory and Practice of Communism* by R. N. Carew-Hunt was approved very quickly apparently because the cover bore the heavily-bearded likeness of Karl Marx with the outline of a hammer and sickle superimposed. But the fourth book *Doctor Zhivago* by Boris Pasternak was flung back on the bed with a contemptuous snort of refusal. There had recently been Chinese press attacks on this Russian work of revisionist heresy.

I reflected later that the arbitrary decision on the books I should or should not be allowed mirrored the pettiness of Communists in general towards such things. Carew-Hunt's *Theory and Practice of Communism* is a scholarly exposition, objective and lucid which lays bare the inequities and fallacies of the doctrine. But because the symbol on the cover was right the Public Security Bureau man allowed it. He had clearly heard something about the dreaded *Doctor Zhivago* which allowed some signs of humanity to show through the Russian Revolution but which probably in its entirety was less unfavourable to Communism than the Carew-Hunt book.

I had a similar experience at Checkpoint Charlie once. The East Berlin border men suddenly took exception to a book I'd had with me in my East Berlin flat for several months *The Rise and Fall of the Third Reich* by William L. Shirer. It bore a huge red Nazi swastika on its cover and this was like a red rag to a bull for the East German border man. He practically frothed at the mouth in telling me it was impossible to take it into the Communist precincts behind the Wall. No amount of explaining that I'd had it with me there for several months and was simply taking it back again having carried it through with me earlier that day to the West to read, would move him. Nor would the fact that I was a bona fide accredited foreign correspondent and that I had permission to have all my own books with me and they were only for my own use. It had a swastika and was taboo. The fact that it was a shattering indictment of the Nazis and Hitler and echoed everything the East German Communists said about the past and any prominent West Germans associated with it, made no difference. The swastika in Berlin and the Marx and hammer-and-sickle symbol in Peking were ironic examples of how large parts of the world think, or fail to think, only in terms of mindless symbols.

I had also been allowed to take the blue hard-cover exercise book from my bedside cabinet in which I had been keeping a diary. The interpreter flicked it open and caught sight of some notes I had made on simple Chinese characters – 'Down with British Imperialism' was one – and it was allowed. But all my requests for a pen or pencil were refused. The only other articles permitted were a manicure set in a leather case and a wallet with a few Chinese yuan in it.

I carried my bundles downstairs to the little room and the more rabid leaders of the mob who had seemed to get impatient during the collection of my 'daily needs' quickly got to work on me again.

They crowded into the small washroom urging in with them two photographers with cameras and flash equipment, who had been present throughout the action. They started yelling in Chinese at me and the voice of the interpreter came from the back: 'Bow your head, bow your head!' All started to take up the cry in English imitating the sounds the interpreter had made. Since I seemed to have a choice I simply stood with my hands on my hips looking at them. I remember having difficulty breathing and was shaking with emotion at the helplessness of my position. When I did not bow as required two of them came and knocked my hands from my hips and forced my head down from behind while the photographers fired their flashes. I remembered then that there had been flashes in the courtyard while I was doubled up. Now to add to the collection to show future generations of Red Guards in their family albums, the 'little generals' had shots of a paint-stained reactionary newsman with his head bowed in shame – if they could erase the hands holding him by the neck.

Then the interpreter appeared again to give me clear instructions. I later discovered that he summarised the contents of the poster stuck on my back. It was in effect the 'sentence' of this peculiar form of 'trial' which had been cyclostyled on pink paper beforehand and brought along in great quantities to paper the house and me. He spat out his words: 'One: You must obey the guards. Two: You must remain in this area defined by the masses. Three: You must respect the posters, portraits and slogans put up in the house. Four: You must await further notice from the government. The organisations represented here are the Red Guards and Revolutionary Rebels of the Peking No. 1 Photo-Machine Factory and the Red Guards of the city's Middle and Primary Schools and all proletarian elements in Peking.'

So my own personal group of proletarians from the Photo-Machine Factory, who had been decorating my courtyard walls all summer, were still 'looking after' me.

But still they hadn't finished. A Red Guard came through the crowd dragging the body of Ming Ming along the floor on the linen line. I was slightly dazed and exhausted by this time and only half noticed that he was dragging the cat's body around in the little room. The brown and white fur of the cat was dirty and discoloured with dust and dirt. Another Red Guard was painting the window panes of the little room with black paint to keep out the light. I noticed vaguely that he was dipping his brush into a German beer stein with the 'H.B.' crest of the Hofbräuhaus brewery in blue letters on its side. It was a souvenir 'borrowed' from a West Berlin beer hall for me during a farewell celebration with friends before leaving for Peking. The Red Guard who used it as a paint pot must have 'borrowed' it from me in turn as a souvenir because I never saw it again. On the small, rickety bunk I found a damp bloodstain that could only have been from the body of Ming Ming. Nearly two years later when I was able to return to the upper part of the house I found a large pair of desk scissors in a drawer encrusted to their hilt with a thick brown rusted substance. It seemed to me that it was dried blood and that these scissors were used to stab the body of the cat to make the blood flow after it had been hanged. And to dribble it on the bunk I was to sleep on was designed, I believe, as a final touch of horror for me.

But I was seeing these things just described as though from a distance. Everything had taken on an air of total unreality. Eventually I was left alone and dazedly took a handkerchief to the sink in the washroom to get off some of the paint from my legs and arms. I had remembered asking the interpreter how long I was to remain in 'the area designated by the masses' and he had simply repeated the fourth part of the order: 'You must await further notice from the government.'

I remember standing for a long time in the middle of the little room feeling exhausted but unable for some reason to sit down. My mind was almost blank. The Public Security Bureau guards kept watch from the next room.

Eventually I put the paint-daubed sheets on to the lumpy uncomfortable bunk, crawled under them and despite the heat, the tiny room and the ordeal fell into a deep sleep which lasted until morning.

CHAPTER ELEVEN

Claustrophobia

On July 12th when I was refused an air ticket by China Travel Service I realised I was confined to Peking. To be exact to the area within a twenty mile radius from the Gate of Heavenly Peace. On July 21st after I was escorted home from the Foreign Ministry this area was narrowed abruptly to the limits of my own house. When I awoke on the morning of August 19th I became fully aware for the first time of how restricted my living area had then become. For nearly three months I was confined rigidly to the eight-foot square cell and the adjoining washroom. I was not allowed one minute of exercise outside it.

The bunk on which I had slept just fitted into the room with a few inches to spare either end. At most it was eight feet square. I could walk into the adjoining washroom and lavatory. When I paced up and down in agitation as the full realisation of my plight dawned on me, I found I could take eight and a half paces from one side of the tiny room to the far wall of the washroom between the lavatory and the bath. The tiny room which I came quickly to think of as my 'cell' was hardly a room at all. It was a space between an outer door leading into the courtyard and the washroom which was used only by the amah for washing my clothes. In it was a bunk on which my driver took his siesta and piled around in the room were spares for the car and various pieces of junk.

Later when I was able to keep a diary I described the cell as I sat in it and I reproduce the note here: 'The cell is interesting. It is about eight feet square. It was indescribably dirty and I have had to clean it myself with an inadequate brush made of fine twigs. Whenever I sweep it the dust rises and settles again.

'On the wall which I face when lying on the bunk are the well-worn Chinese characters for the slogan "Long live Chairman Mao Tse-tung". On the door and wall on the other side of it two slogans proclaim "Down with British Imperialism". On the opposite wall is a portrait of Mao with the English words under it "Long Live Chairman Mao". On the door into the washroom and on two walls are copies of the poster stuck on my back on the night of of the raid. Two large pink-paper posters above my bed in English say "People of all countries unite and defeat the U.S. aggressors and all their running dogs".

'The implication of this is that I am a running dog. The other poster says: "Lifting a rock to drop it on one's own feet is a Chinese saying describing the behaviour of certain fools. Reactionaries of all countries are fools of this kind". In other words reactionary newsman Grey is a fool.

'More slogans against British imperialism are on the walls above my head and on each side. The window on the east side is painted entirely black and both that one and the one facing into the court-yard are nailed up. Both windows in the washroom are painted black, nailed up and have wooden slats nailed across them outside. The black paint gives the rooms a dim, gloomy atmosphere. For the first two days I had no fresh air at all. On the third day the small top section of one washroom window was opened a few inches and this is my only fresh air supply. There is no fresh air getting into the cell itself. Sometimes I quietly stand on the chair in the washroom trying not to attract the guards' attention, and bring my mouth and nose as near to the slightly-open window as possible to breathe the fresh air. But I can't quite reach it. On the wall low down alongside the bunk is a blue painted slogan in English "Those who oppose China will come to no good end". All the walls in the washroom are daubed with slogans too. The mirror was also daubed at first but I was allowed to clean it off.

'The lavatory seat was painted black as was the bowl of the lavatory. The bath was painted black on all its inside surfaces and I have made no attempt to clean it and do not intend to. Two more copies of the four-point order poster are pasted up in there – one at eye level beside the mirror so that my gaze falls on it con-stantly. Another slogan on the washroom wall in large characters says 'We warn you Grey you must always be "reliable".'

The new pattern of my daily life soon became clear. Breakfast at around ten – a small amount of scrambled egg on a piece of dry toast and another two pieces of dry toast and some black coffee. Lunch at one – all vegetables, some cooked, some raw, some soup and dry bread, no meat or fish. Dinner at six – a small amount of fish or meat and vegetables and soup. Three screw-top bottles of water a day. No butter, no fruit, no cheese, no milk. When I asked the cook why I was given such food, he pointed to the slogans on the wall and said: 'They say!'

The guards ordered me to keep the door through which they looked into the washroom open all night and they kept the light in there switched on so they could see me immediately if I left the cell. To make it dark enough to sleep I had to close the cell door to shut out the washroom light. It was stifling in the eight square feet with all doors and windows closed.

The guards set up an office in what was once my dining-room and on the second day installed a telephone and camp beds. A coloured portrait of Mao in a gilt painted frame was hung up in pride of place there. The guards changed shift at nine in the morning and nine at night, each time gabbling Mao's quotations in a little ceremony, reading from their red booklets. Sometimes the guards came in and stood in the washroom to look at me in the cell. I had to take my meals hunched on the edge of the low bunk eating from a tray placed on the low seat of the only wooden chair in the cell. I was not allowed a table.

On the walls in the corner of the washroom immediately above the lavatory cistern were painted the Chinese characters 'Ta tao Ger-lai huai tan.' 'Down with Grey the bastard!' I had no flannel in those first days and to keep myself clean had to stand undressed at the sink and wash myself down with a handkerchief.

Since I had nothing to write with at first and in case I should forget how many days had passed I made a mark each day on the wall with a nail I found in the dust under the small radiator in the cell. I made six marks in a line and crossed them through with a seventh to make a neat week and then repeated the pattern underneath for the next week. I was to mark off eleven weeks in this way in the cell. Eventually the plaster crumbled away, as can be seen in the photograph.

When I eventually got a pen and could make notes I wrote of those first agonising days of isolation in that confined space. Although I did not suffer from claustrophobia in the true medical sense I quickly found that I had to direct my mind to thinking of things beyond that small space in order to be able to live sanely in it. In my diary I wrote: 'I can't remember clearly what I have done in the intervening days, but I have performed all kinds of feats of memory to keep myself occupied. I have taken up Yoga. I have thought about my sporting performances, I have recalled thoroughly my school days and all the names of members of my classes at all the schools I have attended. I have recalled where I was on certain days going back many years, I have gone through my life in the Air Force and my career in journalism in great detail and have tried to recall all the pubs I have ever been in. I have read *The Theory and Practice of Communism* one and a half times and am constantly reading the chess book.

'I sometimes play a rather silly game of trying to look at the guard on watch without him looking into my eyes as I walk back and forth past the door through which he watches. Often he is reading the *People's Daily* or *Red Flag* and doesn't always look up at me on each crossing. I have devised a points basis for this game in which I compete against myself and have called it Pass-Look. I wash some of my clothes. People often gather on the roof of the restaurant next door to look in at the small unpainted top section of the window of the washroom at me. The only other piece of furniture in my cell apart from the bed and the chair is a canvas fishing-type stool on which I keep my few belongings (one shirt, pants, vests, socks, a spare pair of shorts, manicure set and wallet). I do Yoga exercises morning and afternoon and sometimes three times a day. Sometimes a guard takes a chair into the courtyard and climbs on it to peer in through the unpainted window at me to see what I am doing.'

The game Pass-Look I devised is perhaps an indication of the mental poverty brought on by the lack of stimulation normally provided by companions and reading materials. I remember I would become in turn team A, team B, team C, and team D, and arranged knock-out competitions among them. To remember them better I made the four teams America, Britain, Canada and Denmark.

Being stared at by crowds of Chinese from the top of the adjoining restaurant was an unnerving experience. I would pretend I did not notice them but they would lean towards the window and suddenly clap their hands or snap their fingers and call out to attract my attention, rather like people do outside cages at the zoo. From their expressions of curiosity and even puzzlement it wasn't difficult to imagine that they thought of me rather like we think of some exotic zoo animal. I used to imagine I might be advertised on the restaurant menu, so frequent were the little groups of spectators some days. Perhaps: Rice and Noodles 10 fen, Steamed bread with cabbage 8 fen, A look at the Imperialist Reactionary Newsman Next Door 15 fen. Or something.

But even though the isolation was unpleasant in those first days I did not really imagine it going on indefinitely. It may seem strange but I remember briefly feeling some elation as the Red Guards dragged me struggling down the stairs on the night of the invasion. After a whole month of inactivity something was happening. Perhaps it might lead to my expulsion from China, I had thought. In that tiny room in those first days I thought that such treatment was so bad that it could not possibly last long and I still hoped for expulsion.

But as time dragged on I began to be more despondent and more hard pressed to find ways of whiling away the time. In recalling all the pubs I had been in for example, I tried also to arrive at a decision as to which was the Best-Pub-In-The-World in my experience. After remembering all that I could, I drew up a short list of ten. I spent practically a whole day on this and reached the conclusion that the test of a good pub is really those people with whom you go to it, or those you meet there. The one I chose as top of the list eventually was The Iron Bridge in London's East End where I enjoyed many carefree evenings with a large crowd of boisterous friends, listening to the jazz singing of the proprietress and the terrible jokes of the compère.

In order to try and keep my mind sharp I learned by heart the list of Yoga postures or asanas I practised each day. There were eighteen elementary postures in the book I had and each one was named after the kind of figure it represented. They were Corpse, Fish, Easy, Thunderbolt, Posterior, Hands, Cobra, Bow, Inverted, Complete, Plough, Twisted, Spine twist, Eagle, Tree, Dancing, Dancing, Locust. I then tried to recite this list from memory faster each day. I raced through the list time and again checking the time against my watch and often was sweating with the exertion of this after several minutes. I believe I reduced the time it took me to gabble them softly to myself to around three seconds after several days.

I renamed the days of the week each morning to give myself

encouragement that something would turn up. I noted them in my diary and looking back at them I realise that subconsciously I had adopted the lyrical Chinese style of proper names. They were: Monday – Day of Optimism, Tuesday – Day of Possibility, Wednesday – Day of Hope, Thursday – Day of Expectation, Friday – Day of Probability, Saturday – Day of Indomitable Will, Sunday – Day of Inexhaustible Confidence. As the weeks passed I added new adjectives to these basic day-names. And in my diary I noted: 'This device helps a little.'

My four months of normal life in Peking had been a frantic daily round of scanning the teeming streets for evidence of what was happening to Cultural Revolution China and rushing to cocktail and dinner parties in embassies and the homes of diplomats to compare notes. This was a seven-days-a-week occupation but I had still occasionally found time to relieve the tension with a game of tennis at the International Club, or a quick dip in the swimming pool, either at the British Mission or in the grounds of the Polish embassy. There were volley ball matches between the embassies into which I was sometimes drawn and occasionally on Sundays there would be a few hours to spare for a walk around the Ming Tombs or the Summer Palace outside Peking. In my twenty-nine years I had been a keen sportsman, turning from soccer to rugby football in my mid-twenties and had always led an active life. The daily demands made on the time of a foreign correspondent makes participation in regular team games impractical but I had managed to keep up my golf, often going out alone to play in West Berlin when a few free hours presented themselves. So the abrupt change from an active life to solitary confinement in a room eight feet square came harder to me than it might have done to somebody of more sedentary ways. But I developed one surprising new interest in that cell. As I sat listlessly on my bunk one morning a slight movement in one gloomy corner caught my eye. I watched as the long, thin, triangular shape of a moth's wing fluttered on the stone-tiled floor. For a moment I thought the moth was in its death throes. Then looking more intently I saw the wing was detached from the long-dead body of the moth. It must be moving in a slight draught, I thought. But there was no draught. Then as I watched, the wing slowly stood up on its tip and, describing a slow arc, wheeled over like the sail of a tiny windmill and lay flat again, but still shifting and turning slightly. I got up from the bunk and squatted on my haunches in the corner to look more closely.

To my surprise I saw a tiny black speck at the apex of the wing that was responsible for its movement. An ant. The little creature was tugging and heaving, pushing and pulling, lifting and shoving the wing across the cracks and crevices of the patterned stone tiles. I watched fascinated. Across the mountains and ravines of the uneven floor he went, for several feet, with unwavering fixity of purpose and eventually arrived in the corner next to the nailed up outside door. He left his load and disappeared into a crevice and moments later several friends emerged with him. Rather like a gang of furniture removers, they each took an end and very busily manoeuvred the wing into the entrance to their home. Gradually it was hauled into the narrow crack, disappearing in short jerks until only the last fraction of it was visible sticking from the crack. Then a final jerk and it disappeared altogether – no doubt after ant-like shouts of 'Heave' for the last big effort.

I rose suddenly from my crouched position, realising I was stiff and cramped. I had been watching the ant's labours, completely absorbed and to my joy noticed from my watch that an hour had passed. To have spent so much time not thinking about myself and my plight was a surprising pleasure. After that I spent many hours watching the ants in my cell. Several times each day small scouting parties of ants fanned out from the hole in the corner and rather like teams of methodical water diviners searched back and forth across the stone floor in organised sweeps to pick up and drag back any articles of antworth.

Moth's wings were clearly seasonal items of great value. Whether they were used for food or for carpeting and furnishing the ant homes beneath my floor I don't know but the following year when walking in the courtyard outside, I also noticed ants dragging the wings of dead moths and butterflies back to their lairs. Sudden and enforced isolation from the hustle and bustle of living brought the focus of my attention to small things around me that passed quite unnoticed in the normal course of life.

The ants in my cells, I quickly found, were bread eaters. Each morning after my sparse breakfast of dry toast and scrambled egg the eager scouts casting tirelessly back and forth across the floor seized on minute fragments of crust and began dragging them homeward. I watched them so closely that I began to fancy I could recognise some of the ants each day. Some seemed more proficient, purposeful, fitter even, than the others. Some dragged their burdens by the shortest route to the communal home in double quick time while others seemed to get bogged down in crevices, constantly changing their grip on the breadcrumb, sometimes pushing, now running to the front and pulling, and often going round in small circles.

Before long I was taking a hand instead of just observing. And perhaps my sporting instincts took a hand to test out my theories of which were the stronger and fitter ants. I took care not to drop crumbs haphazardly. I took shreds of crust and set them out in a line several feet from the hole and waited for the scavenging ants to find them. Then I watched and compared performances as three, four or sometimes five ants 'raced' back across the cell floor to their home, propelling their loads. I made mental bets on them – and got annoyed if one I selected as an early front runner failed to live up to his promise.

I remember one day watching with increasing annoyance as the fellow I had put a lot of faith in early in the race repeatedly dragged his crumb into a crevice between two tiles. He would heave and sweat – if ants sweat – and get it out again but then failing to appreciate fully the physical laws governing the movement of a lever-shaped breadcrumb, find himself swung round by the momentum of the effort put into moving it and tumble back in again. The others I had not fancied so strongly were making steady progress homewards. 'I can't stand stupidity,' I remember muttering fiercely to the unheeding ant through gritted teeth as my annoyance increased. Quite oblivious of the mountainous shape hovering above him watching, the ant continued his fruitless exertions in and out of the crevice. 'If you don't show some sign of learning from your mistakes I shall have to kill you,' I told him, quite unreasonably incensed by his behaviour. He continued unsuccessfully to try to get out of his impasse. I rose suddenly from my stiff, cramped position on my haunches, jammed my foot down on the unfortunate ant and began pacing back and forth again, my mind filled with depression at the wretchedness of my circumstances. But as I walked back and forth over those eight and a half paces my irritation cooled in the emptiness of everything and I suddenly felt an intense regret at killing the ant. The ants I realised were the only non-hostile beings within the bounds of my existence. I had a conscience about being so unreasonable. How on earth could I expect reasonable and considerate treatment from the world when I was so sadistic towards my ants? For several hours I was quite overcome with remorse that I had caused the death of the luckless ant.

I continued to organise my ant races but from then on controlled my annoyance at the less gifted or the less strong. Whenever I swept the tiny room I took care not to fill in the mouth of their hole with dust. I had done this inadvertently at first and for a couple of days no ants had emerged. So I unblocked the mouth carefully and kept it clear after that. When I put down my folded blanket on the stone floor to do my yoga exercises each day, instead of squashing the ants underfoot I got down carefully on hands and knees and placing my cheek next to the stone tiles blew the ants gently back towards their home in the corner. Even so I doubt that they liked being propelled violently in great gusts, arms and legs squirming, towards their hole but they quickly took the hint and scurried unharmed out of sight. It seemed a kinder thing than total annihilation. I must confess, if I am going to be honest, that later I did kill one or two more in cold blood. But I managed to persuade myself I did this in the interest of scientific investigation.

After watching the obviously intelligent and industrious creatures who clearly worked carefully together as a team or integrated colony, I became fascinated to know whether they had any personal regard for each other. I wondered what they would do if one of their number were killed. Would they remove the body back home for burial? So, not without some misgivings I one day despatched two of the scouts in a fairly busy area and settled back to watch the reaction of their companions. But as they cast back and forth across the stones, noses or antennae or whatever they have close to the ground, they displayed no reaction at all to the bodies of the dead. If they ran into the corpses they simply turned aside and carried on searching and would drag away a nearby crumb without turning a hair.

During this time I used to spend perhaps half an hour each morning folding my sheets. I folded them with great exactitude, trying with intent concentration to crease them geometrically at the exact centre, then fold them over again finding the exact centre and finally making neat squares of them both. I would fold my blankets too and pile them all up, in the fashion that was compulsory during my basic training as a recruit in the Air Force. Then squatting and squinting and looking at them from all angles I would judge whether the first sheet folded was in fact more neatly folded than the second. I repeated the process each day remembering the score in my mind. Another odd little competition. No doubt the psychiatrist could explain to me the deep significance of this act but to me it was a time filler.

One afternoon feeling on the edge of desperation for something to occupy my idle hands and brain I seized on the idea of carving something out of a bar of soap with a nail file. I had found an old piece of hard yellow washing soap behind the bath and was very pleased that I had thought of anything at all new to do. I am no artist or sculptor, but with infinite care I tried to fashion the shape of a female figure from the soap. I sawed away with the nail file for an hour or two. I had given her a curved Siamese hat and succeeded in adding the likeness of a small naked bosom. It was with the derrière that I ran into trouble. Trying too hard, perhaps, to give a firm voluptuous sweep to this portion I broke off one of her none-too shapely legs and was quite distressed for a few moments. Then remembering it was soap I ran some hot water in the basin and submerged her, sticking the leg back in place. These hasty repairs proved quite successful and I was ridiculously pleased with this little image, although I settled for a fairly flat-bottomed version to avoid the likelihood of further mishap. It brightened the whole afternoon for me and I tucked this objet d'art away in a pocket of a dressing gown hanging on the door. After a time I forgot about it and it was not until near the end of my imprisonment that I came across it again. For a while I considered bringing it home as a souvenir but it reminded me so vividly of the mental poverty of the time in which it was made, that while still undergoing the final weeks of my solitary life I didn't wish to be reminded of it. I broke it up and washed my socks with the pieces.

In that eight-foot cell little jobs like cutting my finger nails became important because they provided some active way of passing the time. I cut them very carefully, manicuring and caring for the nails and quicks with greater care than I'd ever been accustomed to employ before in my life.

I spent a large part of one day trying to recall exactly how all the people I knew said my name. I realised that everybody had a different inflection, a different accent, a different intonation. Some spoke it quickly, others slower, some drawled. I closed my eyes and softly tried to imitate the exact pronunciation of my name as rendered by members of my family, friends and colleagues. It was especially pleasing to recall how past girl friends of different nationalities had spoken it in their charming accents!

Meanwhile the Public Security Bureau guards had brought blackboards with Mao's quotations chalked on them in English and propped them up on chairs in the doorway where I could see them constantly. But instead of being disturbed by them as they must have hoped I would be, I learned them in order to give my memory practice.

The first one they propped up read: 'Make trouble, fail ... make trouble again, fail again ... until their doom. This is the logic of the imperialists and reactionaries of all countries in dealing with the people's cause and they will never escape this logic. This is a Marxist law.'

Having learned this I passed on to the second: 'The enemy will not perish of himself. Neither the Chinese reactionaries nor the aggressive forces of United States imperialism in China will step down from the stage of history of their own accord.'

All the quotations put up before me were, it seems, designed to confront me with an ever-present statement of the rightness of their cause. The third week I was told in another chalked message, this time in the words of Mao's deputy Lin Piao, that: 'Mao Tse-tung's thought is Marxism-Leninism in an era when imperialism is heading for total collapse and socialism is advancing to world-wide victory. It is a powerful ideological weapon for opposing imperialism and for opposing revisionism and dogmatism. Mao Tse-tung's thought is the guiding principle for all the work of the party, of the country and of the army.'

I also carefully committed this to memory. Perhaps there was one thing they didn't realise. Learning Mao's thoughts by heart helped stave off claustrophobia too!

CHAPTER TWELVE

Sacking

As I sat on the bunk in my eight-foot square cell in the days following the Red Guard invasion I often wondered what the British Government was doing about my plight, wondered whether the Office of the British Chargé d'Affaires in Peking was making representations to the Chinese Foreign Ministry about me. I envied my British friends living in what I thought was the safety of the diplomatic compound in the eastern suburbs of Peking. But unknown to me, instead of pursuing their diplomatic tasks according to the protocol of their profession, my friends and their wives were about that time themselves struggling in the hands of Red Guard hordes, terrified and at bay, as the Peking Foreign Ministry continued to use mob violence as a cold-blooded instrument of policy against foreign residents.

The determination of the Hong Kong Government to clamp down on the colony's Communist press and its journalists as part of their effort to stamp out the rioting and lawlessness had boomeranged on unfortunate Britons in Peking. The increasing pressure on me had done nothing to influence the Hong Kong authorities over the case of Hsueh Ping, the New China News Agency reporter. And they continued to pursue their uncompromising policy towards Communist newspapermen who broke the colony's laws after my house arrest. On August 17th three Hong Kong Communist newspapers were ordered to be closed down and lawsuits were instituted against two others and the firms printing and publishing them. If any one thing immediately prompted the Peking Foreign Ministry to order a Red Guard invasion of my house, then I believe it was this. The closures were mentioned by the Red Guards in their shouted accusations against me.

On August 19th further arrests of journalists followed in Hong Kong and on August 20th the British chargé d'affaires in Peking,

Mr Donald Hopson, was summoned to the Foreign Ministry and given an ultimatum. In the form of a protest note the ultimatum read: 'The British Government and the British authorities in Hong Kong must within forty-eight hours cancel the ban on the three newspapers, declare the nineteen patriotic Chinese journalists and thirty-four staff members of these three newspapers innocent and set them free, call off the illegal lawsuits against the two newspapers and two printing firms and make it possible for them to resume normal operations. Otherwise the British Government must be held responsible for all the consequences arising therefrom.'

Mr Hopson was summoned to the Ministry at ten thirty p.m. on Sunday, August 20th, and the ultimatum expired at that hour on the 22nd. The uneasy British diplomats and their families had spent the Tuesday on the alert for trouble. Already in the morning the Chinese staff of the Mission, drivers, clerks and translators, had surrounded Mr Hopson on the terrace outside the door and harangued him for nearly three hours trying unsuccessfully to get him to bow his head and admit the British Government's 'faults'. In the afternoon a crowd of about two hundred demonstrators gathered around the closed Mission gates and when any of the diplomats tried to leave, the Public Security Bureau guards at the gates told them their safety could not be guaranteed. Thus those already in the Mission were, in effect, under siege.

Difficulties confronting the remaining correspondents in Peking at that time made it impossible to report anything more than the bare facts of what happened in the next few hours. Only after my release in October 1969 did I learn the full story from Western and Communist diplomats, journalists and other friends who were in Peking at the time. From their accounts it became clear that the terrorising of the British men and women by the Red Guards surpassed anything done to me on the night of my invasion. Some preparations for a siege-type emergency had been made; food supplies and mattresses had been taken into the office so that staff could spend the night there. During the afternoon a gramophone was produced and loud dance music was played to drown out the noise of the demonstrators' loudspeakers. There were twenty-three people in the mission – eighteen men, including diplomats, Mission guards and communications staff, and five girls. Four of the girls were secretaries in the Mission and the other was the wife of one of the diplomats.

Those inside the beleaguered Mission felt on balance that with the burning and sacking of the Indonesian embassy, the burning of the Mongolian ambassador's car and the incursion into the Soviet embassy the summer's violence had reached its peak and that a siege similar to that experienced earlier in the year by the Russians was most likely.

An impromptu meal of sausages and vegetables was prepared in the main hall and beds were made up in the diplomats' offices. To while away the evening hours the office film projector, used to provide weekly entertainment in normal times, was produced and a Peter Sellers film, 'The Wrong Arm of the Law', was shown in the main hall.

Towards ten thirty p.m one diplomat went out to peer into the street through a small hole in the front wall of the office compound and saw that the crowds had swelled to very large numbers. But uncharacteristically they sat quietly in serried ranks in the road listening to a loudspeaker harangue from one of their leaders. Still it was thought the ten thirty deadline might bring another summons for Mr Hopson to the Foreign Ministry or an attempt to present a petition at the gates as had often been done before. The possibility of a sacking was not excluded but thought unlikely.

Shortly after ten thirty the film was drawing to an end. Some of those watching were even dozing gently in their chairs. The next move would have been towards the makeshift beds. Upstairs in his office, Mr Hopson and three colleagues were playing bridge. The chargé d'affaires had just declared his bid 'three no trumps', but paused to glance out of the window before playing his cards. At that moment he saw the crowd outside rise to its feet and with a great swelling motion move towards the gates of the Mission. Those watching the film downstairs heard his shout, 'They're coming in!' Very loud, very urgent.

Mr Hopson had seen that the line of soldiers, ostensibly there on guard, was obviously going to give under the onslaught of a crowd of some 10,000 – this figure was later published by the New China News Agency.

Downstairs, everybody began moving towards the secure part of the Mission. Embassies and diplomatic missions abroad invariably have built into them an area of maximum security. Only members of the Mission staff are allowed into it. There are usually iron grille doors and a strong-room at its heart with a heavy, solid metal door. In this secure area confidential files and items of value are kept. Most diplomatic missions have some equipment for burning confidential papers quickly to prevent them falling into the hands of the host government in the event of an attack or some other danger to the premises.

Outside the Peking Mission that night other foreign diplomats in their homes in the embassy quarter nearby had seen something the British did not – a military flare, fired into the night sky as a signal for the start of the invasion.

The mob surged over gates and walls of the compound wielding crowbars, mattocks, hammers, poles and other heavy weapons. Some had been seen carrying oil drums through the streets towards the Mission. East European Communist diplomats who saw this tried to telephone the British Mission to warn them but the telephone wires were cut some ninety minutes before the raid began. Fire engines were also seen parked in the vicinity beforehand. A command post with tables and electric lights was set up at the roadside near the Mission and appeared to be co-ordinating the joint operation by several different Red Guard organisations. Afterwards a scarlet Red Guard armband of the 'No. 1. Peking Foreign Languages Institute' was found in the compound. This Red Guard group built itself a reputation as one of the fiercest and most militant in Peking in attacks on foreigners. They were involved in the humiliation of the Indian diplomats at Peking airport and the smashing up of a car in the centre of Peking in which two Western journalists, Harald Munthe-Kaas of Norway and David Oancia of Canada were involved.

At the shout 'They're coming in' the twenty-three people had moved behind the first door leading to the secure area – a wooden door which was bolted. The Minister and his bridge partners had come down from upstairs and everyone then moved behind an iron grille which was locked after them. The whole building was soon resounding to the onslaught of the Red Guards who were attacking doors and windows from all directions simultaneously with their heavy implements. The noise of breaking glass was heard above the tremendous din. It became obvious from the amount of noise that the outer defences were not going to hold and the twenty-three moved behind another iron grille into the part of the Mission known as the registry. They pushed large metal cupboards up against one of the iron grilles as an added defence and extinguished most of the lights so as not to attract attention from the attackers. At the same time wireless operators working at emergency transmitters in the darkened Mission were sending radio messages to London informing them that the mob was breaking in.

The sounds of the attack continued – then there were signs of fire being put to the building outside. One of those involved told me after my release: 'The noise was fantastic, the attackers were shouting and working themselves up into a frenzy. We on the inside were looking at one another, smoking cigarettes, doing any last-minute work which we could in the circumstances and trying to reassure one another that everything would be all right in the end.'

It was afterwards found that two external aerial leads on the Mission wall had been carefully and cleanly cut with wire clippers so contact with London was lost. In Whitehall, the last word received over the Mission's radio link was, 'They're coming in!' Silence followed this dramatic message and for many suspense-filled hours the fate of those in the Mission was not known.

Soon a large part of the building was well on fire. The crowd had brought effigies and inflammable material to put against the windows of the room which the twenty-three were in on the ground floor. They set fire to them and the glass of the windows went, although the iron bars held. As time went by the shutters of the windows caught fire from the material put against them outside. The small beleaguered group was now in a room about twelve feet wide and twenty-five feet long, in total darkness, with fire beginning to loom on the outside of the windows. The mob just the other side of the thin wooden shutters hammered fiercely on them and shouted in Chinese, 'Sha! Sha!' – 'Kill! Kill!'

'None of us in that room who understood Chinese was willing to translate this for our colleagues,' one of the twenty-three told me. During the Boxer Uprising more than half a century before, exactly the same cry was raised in the streets of Peking against foreign diplomats and more than sixty foreigners died then. 'People were frightened, it would be futile to pretend anything else,' he added. 'But they were very calm and doing anything asked of them quietly. A hose was inserted through a window and liquid squirted in. We all feared petrol but one of the girls quickly tasted it and pronounced it water to the relief of us all.'

The fire took hold and smoke began to fill the room in which they were penned. Breathing became difficult and it was obvious that they would have to get out through the steel-plated emergency escape door, as the only other way out was through the fire. They could see that even if the steel door itself held, the surrounding brickwork would not. The attackers were getting to work with sledge-hammers and chisels on the outside and had already made a hole through which they seemed likely to pour into the room. The chargé d'affaires decided that owing to the danger of being trapped in there by the fire an attempt should be made to leave the building. The attack had been under way some forty-five minutes. Mr Hopson finally gave the order to open the escape door and led the way out.

'From that moment on our memory of events is slightly confused, owing to the fact that we were undergoing a considerable physical beating up at the time,' said one of those who followed Mr Hopson out. 'The general effect was of coming out of the darkness into the violently lit area of the compound with great areas of solid burning matter on all sides and a very large frenzied crowd all around. I have a mental image of the Minister lurching off to one side with blood streaming down his face from a blow. And then it was more or less everyone for himself. Most of us were completely on our own. Hands seized us from all sides, punches rained down on us from all directions.'

Some of the girls were seized by the hair and the Red Guards tore off the underclothing of at least one of them. They wrenched their dresses up around their necks and interfered with them as they dragged them struggling around the compound. All the girls were subjected to what one diplomat called the 'lewd attention of prying fingers'. Some Red Guard girls took a malicious delight in causing pain to the men by grabbing their testicles as they were frog-marched around.

'There was a terrible noise, a feeling of real fright and we realised that somehow we must manage to get through this,' a friend told me. 'For what seemed like an eternity, we half rode on the movement of the mob, half struggled in the direction of the gate leading out of the compound. We pressed on through the inferno until at last we got out of the gate into the road.'

There one of the diplomats grabbed a Chinese People's Liberation Army man and shouting at the top of his voice in Chinese told him that since he was a soldier he had to help him. The soldier seemed to become aware then of what must have been his instructions and tried to dissuade the Red Guards from beating the Britons and to rally other soldiers who were there at the time to help. Gradually the soldiers gained the advantage. The exhausted little group was put up against a wall of the adjoining residence and surrounded in a semicircle by soldiers who kept off the crowd pressing in on them.

One of the group recalled the moment: 'At this point we were a pretty awful sight I should say, clothes hanging off us, perspiration pouring down our faces and having had perhaps quite the most severe fright we had ever experienced in our lives. We leaned on the wall like drunkards or hunted animals while the soldiers managed by constant fisticuffs with the crowd and by shouting at them, to get them to lay off.'

Although authority in its peculiar Chinese form, for at least some of the twenty-three, was beginning to get the upper hand, the crowds still pressed around the exhausted group shouting 'Lower your heads!' and 'Filthy imperialist dogs!' Flashlights were shone in their eyes and they were vaguely aware that photographs were being taken. A heavy flagstaff was flung at the group striking one of the girls a nasty blow on the forehead. 'Don't cry' one of the diplomats encouraged her. 'Cry in front of these bastards, not likely!' was her reply.

Most people who have never been in China will probably find it difficult to understand the seemingly inane division of authority between the mob on the one hand and the soldiers of the People's Liberation Army and the men of the Public Security Bureau on the other; why the soldiers intervened outside the gate but not inside it. To those accustomed to Western style law and order it is totally illogical. But in the Cultural Revolution this phenomenon of the forces of law enforcement not intervening in the actions of 'the masses' became commonplace. The ideal of the arch-revolutionary, Mao, expressed in its most simple form is: 'To rebel is justified.' And the army and Public Security people risked the mobs turning against them and accusing them of being anti-Maoists if they tried to stop a 'revolutionary action'. For several days in April I had watched the main shopping street in Peking jammed with warring Red Guard factions fighting over possession of China's biggest department store which was closed and shuttered because of the strife. The opposing groups faced each other from rooftops on either side of the street, running fights were common and the city centre was disrupted for several consecutive days. And the army remained patiently on the fringes trying quite ineffectively to direct traffic around the maelstrom. The army and Public Security forces were eventually told to help the 'left' throughout China and since one faction was often as good or as bad as the other this probably compounded the strife. In the case of actions against foreigners there were probably strict instructions to the security forces to intervene only at a certain stage and not to interrupt or prevent the 'revolutionary activity'. So it seems likely that their role in the planned sacking of the British Mission was to see that not too much revolutionary harm came to the Britons. The horror of the situation, however, lay in the fact that there seemed little they could have done to prevent further excesses by the 10,000 strong mob which seemed frenzied and out of control.

As the twenty-three struggled through the crowd to the gates one by one they were ordered to sit down on the pavement in a protective circle of soldiers so that the mob could not see them. The fire brigade eventually moved in to work on the huge blaze which could be seen in the sky all over Peking. The entire top storey and most of the ground floor were gutted by the blaze. The little group of people grew to about fourteen by one thirty a.m. and they sat on the ground, dazed and severely shaken by the punching, kicking and mauling in the hands of the mob. Some of the soldiers offered them water to drink.

One of the last to join the group was Donald Hopson himself and he appeared to be the worst injured of all. Blood was streaming from the wound on his head, covering his shirt and jacket, and a rough bandage had been fixed around his scalp. The bandage seemed, ironically, to be old United States P.X. stock captured perhaps by the Communists many years before in the civil war with U.S.-supplied Chiang Kai-shek. Later it was seen that on the *outside* of the bandage were the words in English: 'Apply this side to the wound.'

During the action after he had been injured a Chinese had approached Mr Hopson in the crowd and whisked him away, clearly on instructions, to a nearby guardpost and kept him there until the mob's fury abated. Perhaps somebody in the Chinese Government had last minute doubts about the wisdom of allowing something worse to happen to the chargé d'affaires. Mr Hopson, a commando captain in the Second World War, who had been awarded the Military Cross in Normandy, was later knighted in recognition of his services in Peking.

The soldiers eventually brought up an army truck and formed themselves up in two lines, making a rough avenue leading to it. Then they ordered the exhausted members of the little group to walk bent double between their ranks so they would not be seen by the mob still milling around them. In this way they reached the truck without the mob knowing and were told to lie down inside it while the soldiers stood around the tailboard, again preventing outsiders from learning of their whereabouts. The fourteen were subsequently driven back to the diplomatic compound, Wai Chiao Ta Lo.

Some of the twenty-three who had been in the Mission had managed to take refuge in the Finnish embassy opposite, others had struggled the quarter mile back to the residence compound on their own, others had been frog-marched there by the Red Guards. It was around two thirty a.m., four hours after the attack began, when the last ones arrived back. During this time other wives and families of the British Mission staff living in the compound had been taken for safety to the homes of friendly diplomats from other countries on seeing the flames from the burning Mission in the sky. Some did not know until next morning whether their husbands in the Mission were safe.

For a time there had seemed to be a danger that the homes of the British might be burned down too. A group of Red Guards had marched to the flats in the compound where families of the twenty-three waited for news of them. They were heard discussing among themselves whether to burn down the flats as well. Diplomats from other countries living in the compound, despite the risk to themselves, went to reason with the Red Guards to try to dissuade them. Eventually an Army contingent arrived and the Red Guards called off the idea. While the discussion was going on one British wife found herself only a few feet away,

hidden behind an outside door at the entrance to the block of
flats. She held her baby daughter in her arms and while listening
to the discussion – she knew enough Chinese to understand it –
she was having great difficulty in preventing the little girl from
singing 'Twinkle twinkle little star' at the top of her voice.

In the sacking of the Mission one first secretary was beaten so
badly he was confined to bed for two weeks in a prone position
suffering from concussion and 'commotion of the brain', and
was not allowed to move. A fifty-nine-year-old Mission guard who
had a weak heart was frog-marched bent double for a long time
and suffered weals and bruises, as did everyone involved. Wrist-
watches had been torn from those wearing them and stolen. The
Minister's residence, a similar building to the Mission about 100
yards away was ransacked and the contents of all its rooms
burned. But it was not gutted as the Mission was and eventually
it was refurbished and, at the time of writing in early 1970, the
charred hulk of the Mission stood untouched and the refurbished
residence still served as the Mission in Peking.

One interesting feature of the attack indicates how carefully it
was planned. The first Chinese to break through the hole knocked
in the registry wall paid no attention to the group inside but
rushed off quickly and purposefully to other parts of the building,
as if to carry out previously appointed tasks. The Mission archives
remained safe within the steel strong room but the rest of the
building was searched systematically and the contents stolen or
destroyed where they were not burned.

The next day in London, the British Government reacted by
placing restrictions on China's representatives in Britain, compelling them to seek Foreign Office permission before leaving the
country, confining them to a radius of five miles from Marble
Arch instead of the normal thirty-five-mile radius – and keeping
them under police surveillance wherever they went.

Six days later there followed one of the weirdest offshoots of
the Cultural Revolution that occurred abroad. Chinese diplomats
in London suddenly emerged from the Chinese Mission in Portland Place armed with axes, baseball bats and broomhandles to
attack bewildered unarmed London bobbies in what came to be
known as 'The Battle of Portland Place'.

At four a.m. on the next day, August 30th, in Peking, Mr
Hopson was summoned to the Chinese Foreign Ministry where the

E

deputy foreign Minister Lo Kuei-po protested against the 'fascist atrocities' of the London bobbies and imposed restrictions on the freedom of movement of the British in Peking. They could move only between the Mission and the Wai Chiao Ta Lo compound and were constantly followed by Public Security Bureau men. To go shopping, to go to a sauna bath in the Finnish embassy or visit other diplomats for dinner, forty-eight hours' notice had to be given to the Ministry and they approved or refused at will. In addition to extra visas, 'permission' had to be sought from the Ministry to leave China. Lo Kuei-po made no reference to the burning of the Mission at the meeting with Mr Hopson. During the next three months no exit visas were granted except for one sick family and the British lived virtually under compound arrest. In their own press the Chinese, perhaps vaguely aware of the un-praiseworthy nature of the attack on the Mission reported only that 'strong action' had been taken by the masses.

Later, on August 30th, a fresh Red Guard demonstration began at the diplomatic compound ostensibly because of the Portland Place 'atrocities' and the British were called on to come out and face the masses. Mr Hopson was again grabbed by demonstrators who forced his head down by pulling his hair. It was an attempt to make him 'bow his head and admit guilt'. Other foreign diplomats looked helplessly on from their apartment windows. The Chinese Foreign Ministry Protocol Department in surely one of the greatest travesties of its named function tele-phoned to advise the British 'to come out and face the masses or take the consequences'.

In late November Whitehall relaxed the restrictions on the Chinese in London and a few days later Peking responded by relaxing movement restrictions too, but played cat and mouse over exit visas for the next seven months until in July, 1968, conditions returned more or less to normal for British diplomats in Peking.

As I sat in my cell at 15 Nan Chihtze I was not aware of these events. Only when I was released was I able to fit my experience into the general background of the anti-British campaign. In a later chapter I shall analyse the internal political convulsions that gripped the Foreign Ministry in those weeks, leading to one of the strangest chapters in the unhappy history of mutual non-comprehension between the West and China.

It seemed certain that mass organisations of Red Guards and their factory worker counterparts, the Revolutionary Rebels, had been told that at a certain signal they should go in and sack and burn the British Mission as a direct act of reprisal against the British government for failing to bow to the ultimatum over Hong Kong. It seemed also that the security forces had been instructed to make themselves responsible for the ultimate safety of the diplomats. But the chances of them being burned alive in the building or being otherwise harmed by the hysterical mob were great since the security men remained outside the walls of the Mission compound. However the reprisal was planned, a strong impression was left that it got out of control, that mob hysteria took over. The raging fire and the frenzy of the physical attack on the building seemed to overshadow any kind of discipline which might have been intended originally. Several Chinese who were afterwards responsible for rounding up the twenty-three showed anxiety that there might still be someone in the building and questioned the others closely about how many there were altogether and whether they had all got out.

The demonstrators shouting 'Sha! Sha!' as they invaded the British mission were not the only link with the Boxer Uprising of 1900. By an odd quirk of fate a silver cigarette box that survived the Boxer siege was one of the few things to survive the Red Guard sacking of 1967. John Denson, British chargé d'affaires in Peking when I was released in October 1969, showed me the box which stood on a table in his apartment. It was originally inscribed 'Tennis Tournament, Peking, September 1899. Presented by H. O. Bax-Ironside Esq. Won by A. D. Brent'.

Mr Brent Hutton-Williams, a nephew of the winner of that tennis tournament, told me that he sent the cigarette box to Sir Donald Hopson in July 1967 'as a symbol of resistance'. After the Mission fire the silver box was found trampled flat among the ashes and wreckage and Sir Donald had it repaired in Hong Kong and added another inscription. It reads: 'This box having survived the Boxer rebellion was damaged by Red Guards when they sacked and burned the Office of the British Chargé d'Affaires on 22nd August 1967.'

Another relic of the Boxer period did not fare so well. It was a great brass lectern in the shape of an eagle which was inscribed

and presented to the British Embassy by the American community
in Peking. The Americans were sheltered by the British in their
compound during the siege. I had seen the lectern in the chargé
d'affaires' residence at a Whitsun religious service. On the night
of August 22nd the magnificent eagle lectern along with a piano
was used to barricade a communicating door. It was afterwards
found charred black with the eagle chopped from the stand. It
was beyond repair.

At the beginning of this chapter I recalled how I sat on my
bunk wondering whether representations about me were being
made by Britain to the Foreign Ministry in Peking. They were.
But the state of confusion in the Foreign Ministry itself in Legation Street had reached such a pitch of hysteria that the representations were futile.

Sir Donald Hopson told me after my release that on August
20th, when he was called in to receive the ultimatum that led two
days later to the burning of the Mission, he was prepared to take
up the question and did so to the best of his ability. But the meeting had not started well. On his arrival at the gates of the Foreign
Ministry there was such a commotion and hubbub of 'revolutionary activity' going on that the somewhat harassed Chinese
official who had summoned him asked Sir Donald to go with him
to the nearby International Club for the meeting as it was not
possible for it to take place in the Ministry. At the International
Club where Peking's foreign residents normally play tennis, bowl-
ing or sip drinks in the quiet bars, the ultimatum was given to
Sir Donald – and he rejected it. At the meeting he told the Chinese
official he was very disturbed at reports that my house had been
invaded by Red Guards two days earlier and that since then
there had been no word of me and my telephone was cut. The
Chinese official replied that the masses had decided to give me a
dose of 'struggle' and had concluded that the conditions of my
confinement should be made more severe.

Sir Donald, in his own words, protested hotly, but at this point
Red Guards began climbing up the outside of the windows and
looking in. His host left hurriedly in a state of considerable
anxiety and confusion, and the British chargé d'affaires returned
to his Mission to prepare for a state of siege.

CHAPTER THIRTEEN

Diary

I was kept almost three months in the eight-foot square cell from August 18th to early November. Then I was moved to an adjoining room, slightly larger, in which I spent the remainder of the two years. The period in the tiny room, although short in comparison with the total confinement, was one of harsh discomfort, both physically and mentally. But since there was never any definition of the term I was likely to serve in it I think perhaps I was more hopeful of release from it than I was later when I had to grapple with the mental burden of seemingly unending months alone without prospect of release or easing of the conditions.

The period in the small room – and indeed the later term in the room twelve feet square – was not days and nights behind bars with the clank of iron doors being slammed and keys grating in locks as might be expected in a prison proper. But I was confined as surely as if the bars were there. Instead of the bars the eyes and the very presence of the guards contained me. For the first three months they constantly watched the door leading into the washroom twenty-four hours a day from a few feet away and whenever I walked near to it they motioned me back with quick contemptuous gestures. They frequently walked into the cell to look at me and sometimes stood on a chair in the courtyard to peer in through the window at me.

I detested being stared at by the guards as every prisoner must do. And early on I made it my policy to keep my gaze on any guard that came to look at me. I did this so as to do what little I could to keep any guard from feeling at ease in my cell and so poke around in it or feel inclined to stay longer.

I learned a lot about staring and being stared at in my two years in Peking. It is an unusual human being that doesn't eventually feel slightly uncomfortable under the hostile gaze of another. And this works both ways. So I looked as levelly as I could at anyone that intruded into my cell to cut down the unpleasant time they were there. And I also made it a policy to be doing absolutely nothing when a guard came in. I reasoned that the more boring it was for a guard to do an inspection the less often it would be done. I bristled and became tense, my breathing became a little tight on most occasions when the guards came near me during the whole time of my confinement. It was a mixture of the anger, resentment, helplessness and the humiliation of my position that caused this. But I endeavoured fairly successfully to show no outward emotion whatsoever.

At first I had nothing to hide of course, but after a couple of weeks in the cell a small stroke of luck enabled me to have the satisfaction of putting one over my guards in a small way.

On the morning of August 31st breakfast was brought – two slices of dry white bread and nothing else. I pointed to it and asked the cook why. 'No money,' he shouted rudely and walked out.

His reply was consistent with the 'revolutionary' way the Chinese who worked in the house were treating me. Clearly under the circumstances in which I was held the polite and friendly manner in which they had previously done their work was inappropriate. They shouted my surname, 'Ger-lai', in an insulting way before using the few words of English they knew that were necessary to do their jobs. In normal circumstances they had addressed me as Mr Grey and had worked in the house in a pleasant manner and with dignity. All foreigners in Peking were careful to treat their staff politely and with respect knowing past sensitivity to the way some foreigners had behaved in their Concession areas. Not that this had required any special effort in my case since I had found my Chinese staff agreeable and likeable people.

When I had breakfasted off two slices of dry bread I told the cook I had no money to give him to buy food. This was conveyed to the guards and a few hours later a group of Red Guards and Revolutionary Rebels arrived at the house. They conducted me upstairs and broke the seals on the door leading into my office and allowed me to get the cheque book to my bank account at the Bank of China. They crowded into the small room and watched me as I searched my drawers for the cheque book.

I found it and was ordered to hand it to the cook but could

not find a fountain pen. All cheques must be written in ink in China. During the long search for a fountain pen I managed to turn away and slip a ball-point pen from my desk into my pocket unnoticed since I guessed that I would not be allowed to keep the fountain pen when one was found. And I was right. No fountain pen was found and the Red Guards resealed the office doors and led me back to the downstairs cell. The cook would keep the cheque book, lend me his pen to write a cheque with and it would be taken away from me immediately each time I had finished writing, I was told. I wrote a cheque which the cook could cash to buy food and the Red Guards and Revolutionary Rebels left. But I was elated. I had, unknown to them, secured a ball-point pen and began immediately to keep a diary. The first thing I wrote was a detailed account of the night of August 18th.

I took the precaution of writing in shorthand. I did this firstly so that if it was found I could claim it was an old notebook I had been using when doing my job as a correspondent. It would make the job of discovering what it said so much more difficult, though I always felt that if they really wanted to know they would probably have produced a shorthand writer to read it.

I didn't write my diary every day. There was not enough in my empty life to warrant it. But it did help immensely to express my feelings, however wretched, although only to myself. It was a risk, I felt, but one worth taking when I had nothing else. And the idea began to form in my mind that the diaries might become useful material on which to base an account of my experiences. As the time lengthened and the diary grew it became more valuable to me and I became more worried about it being discovered. But I only wrote in it when I felt it was safest and kept it concealed as best I could. Somehow the diary survived and I managed to bring it out of China with me.

Looking back to my shorthand notes now from the early days of 1970 as I write this book, I read almost as a stranger some of my thoughts and deeds in the late summer of 1967 in that tiny cell – so remote from reality does it now seem.

I shall quote liberally from it in this chapter because it recalls the awful atmosphere of those days vividly. Sometimes it makes pathetic reading. I don't wish to gain sympathy by reproducing it. I have been strongly tempted to cut out parts of it that show me as anything but strong, self-possessed. determined and all-powerful in the struggle to endure the isolation. But that is not the way it was. The diary brings back the feelings of desolation I experienced and if this illustrates accurately the effect of such treatment on a man then perhaps it is relevant.

The diary of those first three months shows my mood fluctuating swiftly from optimism and determination to deep depression bordering on despair. If it seems illogical, contradictory, disjointed, tedious or inconsequential it is because that is how it was written. It does show how from hoping every day in the early stages for something to turn up in the next few hours I gradually learned to throw my hopes and expectations further forward so as to avoid the bitter disappointment of nothing happening over and over again. It will trace a pattern with heights of confident self-control and depths of near-hopelessness and anguish. But it will remain an accurate account of what I wrote at the time – not always with the hope or expectation of it ever finding its way into a book like this. Some parts I have edited out for their sheer inconsequentiality, and decency precludes my setting down in print all the cursing I did to my diary, both about myself and my captors.

A friend said to me after my release that he had tried to spend a day alone in his own home in Norfolk without the television on and without going across to the pub for a drink to try to get some idea of what isolation was like. By mid-evening he had given up and said that no matter what I wrote in my account it would be very difficult for anybody else to understand what twenty-six months absolutely alone was like. I told him that I had often thought in Peking that if and when I got out of it I would not be able to remember and understand how I had endured it. And already I find it difficult to imagine how I might again endure being alone for a similar period. After the first few weeks I rarely looked back in my diary to what I had written earlier. Transcribing it from the shorthand, safely back home, it came off each page as a detailed account of emotions and thoughts which without pen and paper would have never survived in the memory.

I make no claims for its literary quality. The outlines were written in a state of unease with one ear cocked to hear if the guard was coming. If the style sometimes seems biblical, or that of the insurance policy, pretentious, lyrical or ungrammatical or all five, or none of these, nobody is responsible except myself and the Chinese government.

I 'hid' my diary many times a day. Every loud noise in the street, the sound of the courtyard gate opening suddenly, the noise of drums and gongs in a street demonstration sent me catapulting from my bunk to the window-sill where my few books and hard-cover diary were. I dropped them down behind a tiny radiator in a dusty recess in one corner. These few possessions were very precious to me and they were all I had to lose. Later during my time in that tiny cell I was allowed to read the *Selected Works of Mao Tse-tung*, and in one of his earliest writings 'An Investigation of the Peasant Movement in Hunan', Mao wrote of the terrorisation of landlords by peasants in his home province and one part struck a chord deep in me.

Of the Hunan peasants in 1927, he wrote: 'At the slightest provocation they make arrests, crown the arrested with tall paper hats and parade them through the villages saying "You dirty land-lords, now you know who we are". Doing whatever they like and turning everything upside down they have created a kind of terror in the countryside . . . One ingenious township peasant association arrested an obnoxious member of the gentry and announced that he was to be crowned (with a paper hat) that very day. The man turned blue with fear. Then the association decided not to crown him that day. They argued that if he were to be crowned right away, he would become case-hardened and no longer afraid and that it would be better to let him go home and crown him some other day. Not knowing when he would be crowned, the man was in daily suspense, fidgeting about and starting at every sound.'

And so for many months I went on 'in daily suspense fidgeting about and starting at every sound', and for all the 806 days of my confinement this was true, although I did to a large extent later conquer the extreme jitters of the first three months in the eight-foot cell. But for most of the time I kept my diary – which was an exercise book with a hard blue cover and looked like a text book – among my reading books and hoped it would not be detected. Occasionally in later months I kept it under my mattress or under a pile of *Peking Reviews*, the official English-language propaganda weekly of the Chinese Communists I was allowed to receive. That I was able eventually to get it out undetected was a great satisfaction to me. When, near my release date, I was permitted to go upstairs for a short period each day, I took my diary under my jacket and hid it among other old notebooks in case the house should be searched finally before I was released. That the diary was able to survive was due only to good luck and perhaps also to my tactics of concealing it and never appearing to be doing anything.

The guards were changed frequently and they were supervised directly by the Foreign Ministry. As far as I know nobody from the Foreign Ministry knew that in the confusion of the August 18th invasion I had been allowed a book with some writing paper in it. For six months the guards did not know I had anything to write with and later they believed they saw everything I wrote – my once-a-month letter and the household accounts which were taken away to the Ministry for inspection. Sometimes the guards would enter my twelve-foot room and poke around among my belongings but miraculously they never happened upon my diary. It caused me many anxious moments and sometimes I dared not hope it would survive.

Here are some of the entries from the early days in the eight-foot cell.

'Tuesday, September 5th, three forty-five. Today I rose at nine fifteen and after washing and exercises and yoga I walked briefly until breakfast. Then after breakfast, for the first time, I sat and sang songs softly on my bunk. They were "Maria" from *West Side Story* and "There's a place for us" and "If I had a hammer". I sang melodically and well, I thought. It was a happy-making experience. Then I walked back and forth for about two hours until lunch. I played an exciting game of Pass-Look on the guards, in which Denmark beat Canada fifty to forty. After lunch of Chinese soup and cucumber slices, I read about Burma's Communists in the *Peking Review*. The *Peking Reviews* for three weeks were delivered on Saturday and came to me almost immediately and provided me with the first news of the outside world since August 18th. I found that the Chinese Government had protested to Britain on August 20th over the arrest of newspaper people and there had been a demonstration on 21st at the British Mission here. It also said some thirty-four workers of the various papers had been arrested. This didn't help my case I thought. But the simple gaining of knowledge after such a long time in the dark was encouraging.

'One interesting fact that emerged was that on August 18th a celebration of the anniversary of the first Red Guard parade was held in the Great Hall of the People. So it seemed that my invasion came after the rally in the Great Hall of the People. Quite an honour! !

'On Monday (yesterday) I became very depressed and did a lot of head in hands stuff. I had knelt at the side of my bed and prayed to God for help. One of the reasons for this may have been that in the morning while doing yoga I started swallowing and couldn't stop. There was nothing to take my mind off it. This may have undermined my nervous well-being for the day. Anyway in mid-afternoon it became very bad and I was suddenly in the deepest depression of the six weeks. Today it is six weeks and four days altogether.

'Last week when I felt the need to do something to keep up morale, I began each day naming the days. Monday was the Day of Optimism, Tuesday the Day of Possibility, Wednesday the Day of Hope, Thursday the Day of Expectation, Friday the Day of Probability, Saturday the Day of Indomitable Will and Sunday the Day of Inexhaustible Confidence. Monday, yesterday became the day of Imperturbable Optimism. Today is Distinct Possibility. This device helps a little. The guards changed on Sunday night and the new set are very keen and keep coming and looking at me more often. One came into the washroom today looking for a place to put a second Mao quotation board.

'Monday, September 11th, three thirty. Feeling not bad today, rose at nine, washed, shaved, etc., did exercises and yoga, named the day "Day of Unshakable Optimism". (Sunday was the day of Inexhaustible Confidence in the Future, Saturday was the day of Permanently Indomitable Will, Friday was the day of Constant Probability.) After breakfast I walked and played Pass-Look in which Denmark won fifty to forty-seven in the second game of a three game final. After lunch I read the boring portions of *Peking Review* and walked until three thirty.

'The arrival yesterday of the *Peking Review* gave me my second dose of information since I was put into solitary confinement. It revealed that on August 22nd Red Guards "took strong action against the British Office" after a demonstration and that on 29th

August three newspaper publishers in Hong Kong were sentenced
to three years each. The most interesting news was from London
where it turned out that those pictures I had seen earlier in the
Chinese papers were of the London Office of the Chinese Chargé
d'Affaires and it talked of attacks on police, guards, etc. It also
said certain limitations and restrictions had been put on Chinese
diplomats and press and commercial people. Another item showed
that on August 30th China had protested about these incidents of
August 29th and forbidden any British diplomats to leave China
and confined all their activities to their office and their respective
homes and between them as from August 30th. While this was
some illumination from the overall relations point of view, I found
some encouragement in the fact that at least my case would receive
some attention through the association of the London branch of
the Chinese news agency with the affair. Perhaps it would be in
general a help to speed my release. I was somewhat comforted
by the fact that at least something had been done by the British
government.

'Last night I found a pleasant way of spending some time,
going to sleep by imagining a perfect day. This was a snowy
Sunday in England, waking, bath, drawing curtains, seeing snow,
having delicious breakfast with lots of hot toast and bacon and
eggs and coffee, then walking to the village pub for port-and-
brandies and then back with the papers for lunch and reading,
perhaps a book and so on until dinner at the Golf Club in the
evening. I imagined this in great detail and went off to sleep doing
it. The beauty of the exercise was its creative nature.

'It is now getting colder. After a fierce storm on Friday night the
temperature has dropped and yesterday the guards came in and
asked with gestures if I had any long trousers. I pointed over my
head and said "upstairs". I am now having to wear my dressing
gown to keep warm and must ask for more clothing soon. Until
three weeks ago it was too hot to sleep.

'My current thinking is that perhaps the Foreign Ministry will
take the opportunity of my expiring visa on September 21st to
visit me and perhaps agree to expel me and so start to straighten
out some of the current London-Peking mess. But I am well aware
it could well be several months possibly running up to December
or January before anything is done but I feel that the presence of
the Chinese Office in London will make the authorities here

not anxious to keep me here indefinitely. I hope I am right. I still pray night and morning after yoga.

'Lunch today was onions and peppers with some gravy, cucumber, tomato, soup and rice and cold water. I completed yesterday Carew-Hunt's book for the second time. I spied my name *'Ger-lai'* today in the Chinese writing on the washroom wall and also picked it out in the three posters in the room. But I have no idea what these posters say.

'Wednesday, September 13th, nine forty-five, today another visit from the Red Guards who "look after" me. This time to grant my request for warmer clothes. I was taken upstairs to my bedroom and allowed to choose some shirts, jackets and my sheepskin overcoat. I also asked for some books, namely Mao's books in the lounge and was allowed to get them. I also managed to get Stuart Schram's Pelican biography of Mao from my office and this was the first time my poor three books had been supplemented in twenty-six days. I also got the red book of Mao's Quotations. This I have read with interest this evening, realising how lazy I am with my reading of Mao in normal times.

'Five volumes of Mao are sitting on the window-sill now and I estimate they will last me about a month. Some consolation! The presence of my leather jacket on the door with my grey suit and sports trousers and two pairs of shoes on the floor somehow give this little cell a more homely appearance and are rather cheering. Funny how little things that are familiar and part of everyday life bring comfort.

'My bedroom was a mess with the walls smothered with paint – and the wardrobe too. I noticed *Dr Zhivago* was still lying on my bed. In the lounge the mess was greater. Paint had been daubed on the furniture (I noticed particularly on the yellow covers of the chairs) and my Berlin picture of the Brandenburg Gate lay smashed on the floor. My long-playing records were on the floor covered in glue and books were tumbled down there too. My Ching scroll was doubled up on the sofa. The rubber plant was broken and dead. In the office paint and glue was everywhere. Chessmen were all over the floor, my radio was flung on the floor with the typewriter and many pictures of Mao had been stood up on the shelves and window-sills.

'The doors of my office had been re-sealed since my last visit on August 31st. One learned-looking Red Guard with glasses

looked carefully into the Mao books before "passing" them. I was
refused permission for any other books. I asked to be allowed to
go outside and get some air and they laughed. But when I said
I had no fresh air it was arranged a window should be unnailed
and opened tomorrow. The lack of open hostility was very striking
and a little strange. Twice the chief Red Guard tried to open the
bedroom door and the wardrobe door but I had to do it because
they were both stuck. Downstairs I asked how long I would be
kept and a Public Security man said "I don't know". The visit
was stimulating. I found a trace of happiness in seeing my familiar
clothes again and it was refreshing to go out of this tiny room
even for a few minutes. The lack of hostility was comforting
although this of course doesn't promise anything for the future!

'Having some books does ease the worry of occupying my mind
for a few weeks. Today I rose around nine, did exercises and
yoga, and had breakfast. For second day running I asked for and
got two extra pieces of dry toast and enjoyed them. As though
they were the best food on earth. Sat on the bed really enjoying
them.'

Being allowed to have Stuart Schram's biography of Mao to
read along with the four volumes of his Selected Works is yet
another instance of the illogical face-value fashion in which the
minds of people in totalitarian systems tend to work. It will be
remembered I have already cited the instances of the red swastika
on the book in East Berlin which made it anathema to the Communist East Germans, although the book largely echoed their
sentiments, and the additional sagas of the two books in my bedroom, the banned *Doctor Zhivago* and the permitted *Theory and
Practice of Communism*. As I came from the lounge accompanied
by the Red Guards I saw that the Schram book had been propped
up on a window-sill by the invaders simply because its cover
bore a portrait of Mao. Snatching at the straw without much hope,
since I had already read it and knew it was a critical and searching
analysis of Mao's character, motives and writings, I asked if I
could have it. It was fairly quickly approved by the bespectacled
Red Guard who looked in it. He could only have pretended to
read it. But because it had pictures of Mao they knew, and his
portrait was on the cover, it was probably assumed it must be all
right. There were no caricatures of him, no insulting captions, no
pictures showing him looking ridiculous, as the Chinese are accus-

tomed to see the likeness of any Western leader.

My Chinese captors would probably have been surprised had they known I was learning the quotations of Chairman Mao. They might have been more surprised to find I was also learning his poetry.

People at home wondering about my thoughts and feelings in those days of confinement might logically have expected me to hate the sight and sound of the name Mao Tse-tung and everything associated with it. He had plunged China into the chaos of the Cultural Revolution which eventually led to my confinement, even if he had not directly initiated it. And it is highly unlikely that, remote and god-like though his position seems in the Communist hierarchy, he never knew anything of it. He must therefore have at least passively put his seal of approval on the action against me. Nevertheless I still found it possible to appreciate his poetry and used it eagerly as a means of occupying my empty mind in that eight-foot square cell.

I learned 'Snow', I think his best poem, written in the thirties, from the pages of Schram's biography of the Chinese leader as I walked slowly back and forth over those eight and half paces available to me.

This is the scene in that northern land;
A hundred leagues are sealed with ice,
A thousand leagues of whirling snow.
On either side of the Great Wall
One vastness is all you see.
From end to end of the great river
The rushing torrent is frozen and lost.
The mountains dance like silver snakes,
The highlands roll like waxen elephants,
As if they sought to vie in height with the lord of heaven,
And on a sunny day
See how the white-robed beauty is adorned with rouge,
Enchantment beyond compare.

Lured by such great beauty in our landscape,
Innumerable heroes have rivalled one another to bow in homage.
But alas Ch'in Shih Huang and Han Wu Ti
Were rather lacking in culture,

T'ang T'ai Tsung and Sung T'ai Tsu
Had little taste for poetry.
And Ghenghis Khan,
The favourite son of heaven for a day
Knew only how to bend his bow to shoot great vultures.
Now they are all past and gone.
To find heroes in the grand manner
We must look rather in the present.

The September days dragged slowly by, as my diary shows, with little to brighten them.

'Saturday, September 16th, 22.00. What a way to spend Saturday night! The points I want to record are as follows: 1) yesterday was the 28th day and it was marked by the opening of one of the nailed up windows. This allowed me my first direct breath of fresh air in a month, and I stood submerged in it for a full hour drinking in the closeness of the air. The sun shone and leaves blew around the courtyard. Two birds wheeled in the sun and two green trees were visible, sounds were louder and looking back into the cell and washroom they looked black. I thanked God for the development. The other thing was that the day before on Wednesday, 13th September, I put on trousers for the first time. It seemed strange after nearly two months in shorts. I think I was much slimmer and the putting on of trousers was a strangely outstanding event.

'The weakness and helplessness of the individual alone has been brought home very forcibly to me and I have turned more to God than ever before. I pray twice every day for deliverance from this. Among things which I have decided are not so important are food and drink. In themselves they are entirely inconsequential. I have subsisted quite well on minimum food. In the last two days I have been "thinking" a walk the length and breadth of Britain. I have so far covered six days going through Exeter and Bristol, stopping at hotels and boarding houses, imagining all kinds of feasts and other experiences. It is amazing how much comfort can be obtained from thinking about drinking pints of draught Guinness, and eating hot buttered toast. The walk has become quite real.

'I have almost reconciled myself to being here for four weeks to October 1st. I think every day about release in every respect but find it difficult to imagine it: 1) because I want it so much and have thought so much of being home with my loved ones and 2) because it seems impossible in the current political climate. The Chinese hardly seem likely to give me up without gaining anything and the British are clearly intransigent. After one month of solitary confinement I suppose I am still as sane as I was before and I suppose I can hold out for a long time. But it does give me desperate moments, this terrible interminable aspect of things. I still fly up at the slightest sound outside, dreading another break in by Red Guards but there is no sign of anything reaching me. Heaven knows what is happening to the British Mission.

'Wednesday, September, 20th, ten forty-five. Today was a red letter day. With the unreadable *People's Daily*, a letter from Shirley was given to me by the guards through Lao Chiao, containing photographs of her dated 21st August. This was my first contact with the outside world since solitary confinement began thirty-three days ago. The letter itself was brief and a little depressing. It is somewhat scrappy and seemed to indicate that no details of my predicament were known to the outside world. Shirley didn't seem unduly worried and that was good. But the letter in itself was heartening and the sight of the pictures was a joy.

'The reasons for this sudden delivery were hard to arrive at. I eventually concluded that it was a sign at least that somebody somewhere had decided on some position, perhaps with a view to keeping me from suicidal depression. It was not a good sign that release was near, necessarily, but it did seem to indicate another watering down of the severity of my confinement. Perhaps they don't want to appear too harsh after my release. Whether there will be more it is impossible to guess. The letter came at an interesting time as I began to feel I would never be released.

'Hopelessness has been growing recently. Large depressions and a lot of praying. I have begun to see my imprisonment in terms of perhaps six months. I can't see how the position will be resolved. I don't know whether the British in Peking are still under restriction and have no idea of any moves to help me. Today's *People's Daily* seemed to say another Chinese news agency reporter had been arrested in Hong Kong so what the hell can happen to me? Reading in Stuart Schram's biography of Mao that Chiang Kai-shek is still, thirty years later, keeping the leader of the Sian

Incident under house arrest on Taiwan and that Westerners were put in iron shackles in the early fifties didn't help either.

'Four weeks and five days it is now in this cell. Looking back in this diary to September 8th I see my despair clearly showing and there seems nothing in view. Ten days later of course my misery still wasn't all that great. I begin to see a perspective, there just seems no hope of release even on the distant horizon at the moment. Please God help move the minds of men somewhere to bring about my release. Today I stood at the open window for an hour, as has been my practice every morning since it has been allowed open. The autumn is truly beautiful in Peking. The sun shines, the skies are clear crystal blue and there is a crisp breeze but it is warm and there are birds still in the sky. Standing at the window is quite beautiful watching the leaves blowing around the courtyard. Yesterday afternoon new loudspeakers directly outside the house opened up with a strange mixture of opera and invective. It continued today in the morning and afternoon, sounding like a new propaganda style. It was not directed towards me as far as I could see.

'Tonight I began reading the *Selected Works of Mao* and found it very interesting. His "Analysis of Classes in Chinese Society" and "Study of the Peasant Movement in Hunan" were both readable and informative and especially the section which told of parading victims in paper hats and other Cultural Revolution habits. I formed the impression some of the present movement's methods have been modelled on it.

'I am now more or less decided to write a book myself, with chapters on Mao, on the various rectification movements, on the Chung Nanhai – how I sat on my roof watching the swallows dip over the Forbidden City's roofs wishing I could see what they could – my train journey, reasons for the Cultural Revolution and other experiences and of course my confinement.

'Today I named the day the Day of Real Hope. Yesterday was the Day of Clearer Possibility, Monday was the day of Refreshing Optimism, Sunday was the Day of Inexhaustible Confidence in Deliverance, Saturday was the Day of Indomitable Will to Prevail. In my book also I want to mention the way *"Mao Chu-si"* (Chairman Mao) is said unctuously all the time, echoing and re-echoing from loudspeakers all over Peking and probably China.

'Two nights ago, I learned two of the latest quotations on the blackboards. They are: "The Socialist system will eventually replace the Capitalist system, this is an objective law independent of man's will. No matter how much the reactionaries try to hold back the wheel of history, revolution will sooner or later take place and will eventually triumph." And: "I have said that all apparently powerful reactionaries are paper tigers. The reason is that they are divorced from the people. Look! Wasn't Hitler a paper tiger? Was Hitler not overcome? U.S. Imperialism has not yet been overcome and it has the Atom Bomb. I believe it will also be overcome. It too is a paper tiger."

'Today one of the guards opened the door of my room while I was praying on my knees. Loud spitting goes on all the time. They have hung up their own blackboards today in their room with new quotations in Chinese. They have set up their office properly in the dining-room. They have beds there and two sleep while one watches me. They have a telephone which rings frequently. A big rattling tea can is carried in periodically. Three days ago I began doing advanced yoga postures which is making me quite stiff. (I have to keep covering this up with the *Peking Review* as I write because I fancy I hear one of the guards coming in to find me writing.)

'Friday, 22nd September, three p.m. Today I decided on a new attitude. After doing nothing the whole day yesterday except reflect about my career in great detail I thought that it was time to be more constructive. So on the anniversary of the ninth week in captivity (sixty-three days, one day over two months and exactly five weeks in solitary confinement) I decided that September 21st having come and gone unsuccessfully the fact had to be faced that it looked like "a long job". So I decided I should try to take a long term view of things. I cleaned my room, washed, put on a white shirt and my hard black shoes and worked out the first "twenty-three day plan". I did this simply because 15th October appears to me as a day to work towards. I decided not to think so much about quick release, but to make the next twenty-three days a period of the study of the *Selected Works* of Mao.

'I summed up the likely happenings as follows: 1. Release and deportation from China under guard, with violence. 2. Release and expulsion without violence. 3. Release and refusal of permission to leave China, possibly being ordered into the Hsin Chiao hotel or being ordered to clean up this house myself. 4. Put on mass trial and imprisoned properly. 5. Imprisoned without trial. 6. Sent to Sinkiang for years simply as a reprisal and revenge. 7. Held for long period here. Reviewing what I know of the situation Likely Happening No. 7 seems Most Likely. But I can expect Red Guard intrusion at any time, I suppose. There is not much planning I can do against it. If it is sudden and violent I am helpless. I think the worst thought of all is that something dreadful might happen in Hong Kong and I might be the object of vengeance of the utmost kind. So I'm thinking about a six month term, putting my thoughts as far forward as January. And that is how I have decided to look at things while still hoping of course that something will turn up. But it seems two months is not very long if you say it quickly. The British Government is either unwilling or unable (or both) to do anything. After October 15th I shall review the situation and make a fresh plan.

'The guards have begun to peep at me from the courtyard standing on a chair when I do my exercises now. Quite stupid really! For the third day today lorries have roared by with drums beating and gongs sounding. I believe it is because petitions of support are being presented to the Central Committee.

'Big event today! I cut my hair for the first time for two months with my nail scissors, and funnily enough, after two snips at the ends of both sides I looked much better. So the new tone is set. Please God speed my release.

'Wednesday, September 27th. Tonight I have enjoyed reading the third volume of Mao's *Works*. Tonight's enjoyment came after a bout of especially bad depression which lasted two or three days. I have been terribly low, pessimistic and defeatist. I have been unable to think of anything good and have imagined things like being kept here all my life or several years. Today it is forty days in this cell and sixty-eight days altogether. At one point today I just keeled over on my bed in despair. Very difficult to shake off depression this deep. It really does look like at least six months now and this really is a horrifying thought! I decided to try yet another "new attitude" tonight after several terribly depressing days – thinking only of future release. But really I have so little to go on for optimism. In the last few minutes I've just re-read for the first time the news agency copy of the Ministry order on me and the *People's Daily* leader of the next day which were tucked into my diary. "Grey must await further notice" they say. Well I am doing that all right!

'Tonight is quiet for the first time for several nights. Loudspeakers booming from the Tien An Men square and marching crowds going by have been a regular feature of life since last Sunday. I presume they are practising for the October 1st National Day celebration parades. Loudspeakers went on last night until after midnight...and vicious and aggressive they sounded too! The marching crowds have drums and cymbals and both boys and girls shout marching songs. I broke my watch two days ago and this didn't help my mood.

'Depression takes the form of getting up at nine a.m. and having no energy to wash and everything seems heavy and dead. Outlook seems hopeless and prayers seem lunatic. I have been doing more advanced yoga postures and am seeing some improvement now. But the Lotus posture is impossible. I worry about my dear Mother. I do hope she's all right. Heavens, home does seem remote and impossible. I pray I shall be allowed to return some day.

'Yesterday I learned two new quotations put up on blackboards – "If the United States monopoly capitalists persist in pursuing their aggressive policies of war the day is bound to come when they will be hanged by the people of the world. The same fate awaits the accomplices of the United States." (Implication: Grey is U.S. accomplice and watch out he doesn't get himself hanged!) The other one was, "The diehards always have many schemes in hand, schemes for profiting at others' expense, in double dealing and so on. But they always get the opposite of what they want. They invariably start by doing others harm and end by ruining themselves."

'My head has been itching furiously now for two or three days. That doesn't help either. The overwhelming urge to write this diary tonight came from the need to try to convey the feeling of depression of the past two days but it really is difficult to remember depression after it evaporates.

'I decided that, if it appears I am going to be here through the winter, I should ask the Foreign Ministry for a move on the grounds that it is cold and unhealthy here and I am likely to catch a disease. Today was cold and stormy and it rained very hard – the first day the sun hasn't been seen for a long time.

'Saturday, September 30th, eleven o'clock. I am sitting in my cell on the chair opposite tomorrow's breakfast and dinner. Cold meat, cheese, bread, tomato, cucumber. The reason my two meals for tomorrow are already here is that the cook says there will be too many people on the streets tomorrow for him to come to do them, tomorrow being National Day. Tonight I have read Mao's *Works* again and walked back and forth considering the latest information to reach me in the *Peking Review*. This was that another Hsinhua News Agency Correspondent and four other reporters were sentenced to three years in Hong Kong on September 13th. I feel this would have made it clear the Chinese were going to gain nothing by holding me. Release? It is imponderable. I am in a flat, reconciled mood at the moment, unable to get very depressed about what seems bound to be a very long period of imprisonment. Perhaps six months or a year even.

'Yesterday was also marked by the window incident whereby I was told to limit it to one hour and Lao Chiao was ordered to put a lock on the outside. The guards showed it me to tell me this. Today as on many others recently, singing crowds of marchers have gone by the house. There was also much loudspeaker play today outside and playing of "The East is Red" and so on. Two days ago it became cold enough to have to wear a jacket when walking back and forth. This is a complete change from the early days in here when it was sweltering.

'Tuesday, October 3rd, six thirty. "Diary of despair." I am writing this sitting propped up on my bunk wearing my dressing gown after eating a meal of boiled fish. I am feeling a little recovered after more than a day of illness – of violent diarrhoea and stomach trouble. This afternoon and evening I have been overcome with despair. Moans like "This is hell on earth" and "a living death" have escaped my lips. It seems I will never get out of this terrible, awful prison. I feel helpless and desperate and at times I feel as though I am on the verge of going crazy. The illness began about three thirty yesterday. Then I lay on my bunk for a time. I had almost nothing of my dinner except the soup and one slice of dry toast and it stood all night on the chair. I just fell on the bunk and dashed back and forth to the lavatory throughout the evening. I went to bed in my dressing gown with an extra blanket and got up during the night. (Frantically hid my diary and pen at this point because I thought I heard a guard coming but it was a false alarm.) Today I haven't walked at all and the smallness of the cell became almost unbearable in the afternoon. I have remained on my bed reading and thinking and the time has gone very slowly.

'O God what is to become of me? Today also I have found it particularly difficult to keep my pledge not to be annoyed by the constant hawking and spitting of the guards. The noise they make outside is quite disgusting, today particularly so. It is a matter of fighting back the revulsion. In addition to the sickness I also have a stiff neck to make matters worse. The window was left open all day by the guards perhaps as a concession to my illness.

'The slogans in the cell hit me afresh last night, possibly during the period of an "overheated brain". At my feet "Long Live Chairman Mao". At my side "Those who oppose China will come to no good end". To the left "Down with British Imperialism", and "Long Live Mao Tse-tung" in English under his portrait. The posters above my head and the slogans "Down with A. Grey" and "Down with British Imperialism" on the back walls. How disgusting and trite and stupid!

'On October 1st, National Day was not too interesting. The noise of marching columns began very early and about ten a.m. an excited screaming burst out as the loudspeakers proclaimed that Mao was on the gate. Lin Piao's sing-song voice droned on for about half an hour then lots of "Sailing the Seas depends on the Helmsman" as the crowds marched by. In the evening I watched the fireworks from my window (remembering how I had idly thought back in August whether I should be here for them. I wondered whether I should be here for next year's or for May Day).

'The papers on October 1st contained pictures of an H-bomb explosion with idiots waving red booklets at the explosion. Mao looked well in the papers on both days. Today I began volume four of Mao's *Works* and reckon on finishing them within a week now. They are fascinating historically but sometimes a bit of a grind to get through. O Heaven please smile down on me and hasten my release. Yesterday and today I did no yoga exercises for the first time because of my illness and missed it very much. Yoga has become very important to me.'

CHAPTER FOURTEEN

Struggle

There is a third story of mindless violence and humiliation to tell here at this point. To add to the catalogue of terrorisation meted out to the British diplomats and myself there is the saddening account of what the Chinese did to one of their own people, Wang Chung-mao.

Wang Chung-mao was my driver. I knew him as Lao Wang or 'Old' Wang. This is a term of respect used in China for an older person. Only when I arrived home in England in the autumn of 1969 did I discover what had happened to him. It is an appalling story, appalling not least because of the pointlessness of the action taken by a mob against him. This resulted, I believe, in his losing his mind, at least temporarily.

Lao Wang had worked for Reuters in Peking for nearly ten years, driving the car for successive Reuter correspondents there. He did his job efficiently and willingly, was paid wages on the exact scales laid down by the Peking authorities dealing with Chinese employed by foreigners and was never asked to do anything improper beyond his duties. He was, as far as anybody connected with Reuters knew, perfectly loyal to his own country, his government and its political institutions. But despite all this in mid-September he was dragged before a crowd of 15,000 Red Guards and according to their own account 'was so frightened that the sweat stood out in beads as big as beans'. I was referred to in the account as 'the big spy Grey'.

Lao Wang, a shy quiet man who spoke not one word of English or any other language except his own was forced to stand bowed before the yelling 15,000 while other Chinese who worked in my house produced a statement 'to unmask the towering crimes of the slave to foreigners who has sold out his motherland'.

An account of the action against him and an 'indictment' of his behaviour going back to his youth was printed in October 1967

in a Red Guard newspaper published in Peking. I shall reproduce some of it here since it is a microcosm of the scarifying
defamations that became part and parcel of the Cultural Revolution at all levels. Lists of crimes of the kind of which Wang was
accused were common coinage on Peking's wall posters concerning high and humble figures alike in the party and government.
Distortion, exaggeration and completely fictitious fabrication are
methods employed in this report – the only one about which I
have some personal knowledge of the facts. Usually there is a
basis of truth since those writing the indictment search any
available files and question acquaintances of the victim. The
most ludicrous snippets of gossip are turned into mortal sins –
in the same way as I was accused of 'drinking alcohol', 'despising'
my paper tiger effigy and 'sneaking around' my own house.

Such things are not uncommon in Communist countries. Each
time anybody claimed by the West Germans to be a prominent
East German flees to the West across the Berlin Wall the Communist press in East Germany produces reports showing that he
had been an inveterate life-long criminal they are well rid of.
Moscow news media often do the same when defectors flee
Westwards. But Chinese-style character-blackening is more
thorough and detailed than any I've previously encountered.

The 'struggle meeting' is a method of intimidation and
persuasion used against dissidents. It is peculiar to Chinese Communism and is part of the very effective process of thought
reform – sometimes referred to as brainwashing – evolved by the
Chinese Communists during the long years of striving for power
in the civil war, and refined since. The process of 'struggle' –
the term is a kind of shorthand form for the idea of struggling
against somebody until his resistance is overcome – involves vary-
ing degrees of physical violence, humiliation, recitation of 'crimes'
and shortcomings, often followed by close confinement. In the
fuller process of thought reform intensive group indoctrination,
interrogation, criticism and self-criticism and confessions follow
and is possibly accompanied by humiliating or harsh, pointless
physical labour. The prospect of return to normal life is held out
only after admission of all 'crimes' and a reformation of one's
thinking and style of life to comply with that of the régime and
one's accusers.

The struggle meeting is usually the opening of the proceedings but can be continued intermittently, perhaps like electric shock treatment. Mao Tse-tung himself, talking about the subject of thought reform has said: 'The first method is to give the patients a powerful stimulus, yell at them, "You're sick" so that the patients will have a fright and break out in overall sweat; then they can be carefully treated.' The two accounts of struggle techniques in this book involving me and Lao Wang confirm adequately that Mao's reference to an 'overall sweat' is an integral part of the proceedings!

The Red Guard action against me on August 18th took the form of a 'struggle meeting' and solitary confinement followed. But it stopped short of enforced physical labour or any active attempt to indoctrinate me or reform my thinking. Perhaps the constant propping of blackboards bearing Mao's quotations before my eyes might be interpreted as an effort to intimidate me mentally and alter my thinking but it was a passive rather than an active attempt.

I found a parallel with my experience in that of Ma Sit-son, internationally-known violinist and composer and the most prominent Chinese to have fled from Mao's China to the United States. He was president of the Central Music Academy and there a mob accusing him of bourgeois habits poured a bucket of paste over him, stuck wall posters on his body and put on a tall dunce's cap labelled 'Cow Demon'. A cardboard plaque hung on him said 'Ma Sit-son agent of the bourgeois opposition'. He was paraded through crowds to a stage, was punched and spat on en route and lined up to bow his head with others to hear an account of his crimes. Later he was imprisoned in a room used previously to store pianos. There was only just enough space for a bed. On the walls were signs saying 'Down with vampires', 'If you are not honest we will crush your dog's head'. He had to study Mao's *Selected Works* as I was able to do – I didn't *have* to – and he was made to do humiliating and pointless physical labour, cleaning latrines and piling up heaps of stones, without reason. But the parallel between his experience and mine is striking enough to show that the treatment I received was similar in part to that handed out to Chinese intellectuals who had committed the crime of appearing to think for themselves.

It was nearly three months after I had last seen my driver Lao

Wang that I got any word of him. He had gone off on his annual holiday at the end of July shortly after my house arrest began. One day in October as I sat in my eight-foot square cell a typewritten note was brought to me. It purported to be written on the instruction of Lao Wang himself. It said he was resigning as from the end of September without giving a reason and I should give two months wages to the cook to take to him. I was allowed to have money drawn from the bank to pay his two months outstanding wages and the next day I asked one of the Chinese who brought my food how Lao Wang was. By a mixture of sign language and the odd word of English he indicated that Wang was in hospital, that he did not recognise anybody but stared dumbly ahead with his mouth hanging open all day and would drive no more.

I imagined from this that Lao Wang had become ill. It did not occur to me that he had fallen a victim of the Red Guards too. To 'struggle' the poor, defenceless man was such a pointless thing to do that it did not cross my mind. But when I emerged from my two years of solitary confinement I was able to read the Red Guard newspaper report of what happened to him.

The newspaper called *Eastern City Storm*, published on October 19th, 1967 by the Peking Municipal Revolutionary Workers' Congress, carried an account of Lao Wang's degradation which had taken place about a month before on the afternoon of September 15th. The report was carried under a headline which read: 'Pluck out the Counter-Revolutionary Slave to Foreigners and Show him to the Masses.'

It said that at the Peihai Sports Stadium the Peking Proletarian Revolutionaries' Anti-Imperialist, Anti-Revisionist Liaison Station held a rally to struggle the counter-revolutionary foreign informer Wang Chung-mao. The meeting was attended by more than 15,000 proletarian revolutionaries from all units. 'Raising high the flag of Mao Tse-tung's thought and with Mao Tse-tung's thought as their armament they used a large number of irrefutable facts to unmask the crimes of the British Imperialist running dog,' the report said. Lao Wang was insignificant politically. As insignificant as any man anywhere doing a rather dull job driving a car, wanting a quiet life and wanting to keep out of trouble. But the report, far from expressing the slightest shame or regret that 15,000 people set on a defenceless man and terrified him, treated the act as laudable and triumphant and one which would bring added prestige to China and Mao Tse-tung, and cause politicians to tremble in Washington and Moscow!

It said: 'In their attitude towards counter-revolutionary foreign informer scum Wang Chung-mao, they showed their unanimous hatred and anger and their fearless revolutionary fervour. Like the blade of a knife, the rally struck time and time again at counter-revolutionary foreign informer Wang Chung-mao, who was so frightened that the sweat stood out in beads as big as beans. Representatives of the Peking Aeronautical Red Flag and Light Industry Red Eagle said in their statements "Will anyone say that this kind of scum of the Chinese people ought not to be struggled? Of course he should be struggled! That will boost the strength of proletarian revolutionaries, extinguish the foul breath of the enemies and strike a blow at counter-revolutionaries. In a word, it will increase the prestige of Mao's thought and make imperialism and all reactionaries tremble before them. Let American imperialism and Soviet revisionism take refuge in their day-dreams!" '

The report revealed that the other Chinese working in my house had been called upon to testify against the driver. It said: 'Representatives of Chinese workers in the employment of the British Reuters Agency produced many facts in their statements to unmask the towering crimes of the slave to foreigners, Wang Chung-mao, who has sold out his motherland.'

Other Red Guard representatives made similar statements and after a leader of the Workers' Congress had made a concluding speech 'at five o'clock in the afternoon the rally came to a triumphal end to the strains of the Great Helmsman'.

Lao Wang's 'crimes' were listed in great detail. Referred to constantly as 'scum of the Chinese people and counter-revolutionary foreign informer' he was said to have committed unforgivable crimes against the people and the state. The indict-ment stretched back to his youth and since he had lived, like many Chinese of his age, through the period of Japanese occupa-tion and the era of Chiang Kai-shek's rule – which the United States supported – he was castigated for this. Eating and drinking were listed among his transgressions too!

The Red Guard record shows: 'During the period when he was serving the interests of Japan, America and Chiang Kai-shek he was full of deceit and practised all manner of foul things and his way of life was extremely decadent – he ate, drank, wenched and gambled and even smoked opium; he lived a foul life. After Liberation, in order to maintain his bourgeois style of living he had on two occasions sold on the sly petrol belonging to the State and was sacked for his pains. But his base nature did not change. He continued to behave like the riff-raff of society. He used false names to swindle people and indulged in sexual frolics. This was the shameless cur who after Liberation concealed his filthy history, changed his appearance and, harbouring unspeakable designs, wormed his way into foreign affairs articles...'

Wang was employed as a driver and often I would ask him to drive me through the streets of Peking so that I might see what was going on. All foreign correspondents did this each day. Often I would stop if there appeared to be interesting activity and I would sometimes photograph the lurid cartoons insulting the head of state, President Liu Shao-chi. My driver never took any part in this. On one occasion as we drove by a slogan-screaming procession I repeated some of the chants to him in my awful Chinese and asked him if I had heard them correctly. Once back at the office he wrote a note in Chinese and carefully asked my interpreter to read it to me. In it he asked me not to draw his attention to what was happening in the streets since it interfered with his driving concentration. I apologised and told him he was quite right. This was clearly the action of a man who wished to make it quite plain that his job was to drive and nothing else. An act of self-protection against any possible suggestion that he was involved in what I wrote or did. Wang spoke only Chinese and I had to give him precise instructions through my interpreter or with a few vital words of Chinese I had learned. This did not prevent his accusers from alleging he bought and translated pamphlets and newspapers for me.

Again the tarnished record: 'The slave to foreigners Wang Chung-mao also collaborated during the Cultural Revolution period with the British journalist spy Grey to purloin intelligence about our Cultural Revolution. He used to drive the British reactionary journalist around in a small car and go everywhere in Peking, active and busy in all sorts of espionage tricks. On one occasion he took Grey to the Peihai Round City to take stealthy photographs of all posters about certain important internal questions. On another occasion he photographed cartoons criticising Liu Shao-chi, thus supplying imperialists and reactionaries with a large amount of material for attacks against our Cultural Revolution.

'Every day Wang Chung-mao used to take out reactionary journalist Grey in his car. The traitor used to observe important points about the social situation, and when important rallies and meetings were held in the streets they became even more active. At such times Wang Chung-mao would drive the vehicle slowly and cut into the ranks of the demonstrators to give Grey a chance to take photographs and make tape-recordings within the car. Furthermore Wang Chung-mao used to buy leaflets put out by mass organisations, also criticism material and all sorts of Red Guard newspapers, and this slave to imperialism was even shameless enough to translate the contents of the newspapers for Grey.'

The 'struggle' meeting descended to depths of incredible farce with the saga of a green antique vase that stood in the lounge of my house. It had been bought several years before by a previous Reuter correspondent, Clare McDermott. The Communist authorities in Peking have never prevented foreign diplomats and correspondents buying traditional Chinese paintings, pottery or furnishings, and most Westerners who go to Peking, even today, return home with some beautiful examples of the fine work of Chinese artists and craftsmen of the past. It provides foreign currency for China if nothing else. But the Peking customs authorities naturally enough demand to see all things that are to be exported and very occasionally, for reasons best known to themselves, refuse to approve certain items. Clare McDermott was refused a permit to take out his antique vase and each successive correspondent at the end of his tour of duty took the vase along to the customs to see if there had been a change of heart and to see if they could take it out for Clare.

On my arrival I decided to have a light fitting attached to the vase to turn it into a table lamp. With two years of my expected stay ahead of me in Peking the question of whether I should try to take it out with me had not arisen. After finding a shop that could convert the vase into a lamp I sent it in the car driven by Lao Wang. This resulted in an accusation by the Red Guards that he had tried to 'steal national treasure'.

The 15,000 were told: 'Inside Reuters house there is

a green-coloured antique vase decorated with the eight trigrams. The State put it there for the purpose of decoration and under the import-export regulations of our country it is forbidden to export it. However, successive British journalists with Reuter have all tried by every means to steal it, but they have in every case been discovered by the departments concerned and have failed in their objective. The treacherous cur Wang Chung-mao thought it was a good opportunity to ingratiate himself with British journalist Grey. He personally took off the valuable vase to have it made into a table lamp in preparation for its illegal export. Unfortunately it was just at this time that Grey had his freedom of movement limited by our Government and so this piece of craven-heartedness on the part of Wang Chung-mao came to nothing. But this criminal trick to steal national treasure is enough to show that Wang Chung-mao is an out-and-out betrayer of his country's interests, and thorough counter-revolutionary no better than dog's dung.'

Before my house arrest began Lao Wang drove me to the China Travel Service office to buy my air ticket and to the Public Security Bureau to pick up my visa. This became the basis of a charge that he had 'tried to help the British spy Grey to escape'.

The report said: 'At the time when British imperialism was stirring up an anti-China wave and the British authorities in Hong Kong were carrying out persecution of the working personnel of the New China News Agency in Hong Kong, the Chinese staff in Reuters office took just and necessary action and struggled the British spy journalist Grey, and it was at this time that our Government limited the freedom of movement of the reactionary journalist. Just at this juncture the counter-revolutionary foreign informer Wang Chung-mao tried by every means to help Grey to escape. He resorted to all kinds of deceitful methods to buy an air ticket for Grey and went through the exit formalities at the Foreign Ministry. But all this was in vain, for despite his tricks in going through the formalities for Grey's escape, he in fact did not escape the fist of the Chinese people but was caught by our Government before he could get out.'

A further allegation that he had driven a former correspondent home when he was the worse for drink caused the rally of 15,000 to conclude that this was an act worthy of the *death penalty*.

'He was extremely craven and obsequious in the presence of imperialist foreigners and lost much face for the Chinese people. Wang Chung-mao waited loyally and shamelessly upon all those British journalists who employed him, he revealed a slavish disposition which was quite nauseating. Once a British imperialist was drunk outside. He was rolling around crazed with drink like a pig and that slave Wang Chung-mao, without the slightest sense of shame, brought him home. This sort of craven behaviour caused great loss of dignity to the Chinese People's Republic and is a crime worthy of death. Wang Chung-mao's slavish nature and fatherly concern for foreigners was something which took no heed for national dignity. Money from the sale of Reuters newspapers and magazines could also find its way back to his wallet, on each occasion some thirty or forty dollars. And again every time that Wang Chung-mao co-operated with foreigners and went out and successfully collected intelligence the journalists would take from a drawer a big bunch of notes and give them to him, every time at least forty or fifty dollars. Consequently Wang Chung-mao's way of life was naturally extremely lavish.'

Lao Wang was never paid anything except his regulation wages and allowances by me and overtime if he worked beyond the stipulated hours.

Then one final enormity that incensed the 15,000 was recounted before they were satisfied that a great new victory for Mao Tse-tung's thought had been achieved.

'Foreigners spent so much money on buying him over that he did not disappoint their hopes and was very accommodating to these imperialists. Once a journalist was just having a midday nap and the wash-amah was in the yard beating the carpet. Wang Chung-mao angrily scolded the wash-amah saying "Haven't you finished beating it yet?" He was afraid of disturbing his foreign boss's beautiful dreams . . .'

The evidence at an end the rally report concluded: 'Above are just part of the crimes of counter-revolutionary foreign informer Wang Chung-mao. As of today he has already been plucked out and shown to the masses by revolutionary rebels and this is another great victory for Mao Tse-tung's thought.'

The gate to my courtyard in June 1967. David Oancia, correspondent of the *Toronto Globe and Mail*, stands beneath a straw effigy of a paper tiger with a top hat strung up on the curved roof of the gateway. The daubed slogans say, 'Down with the British Imperialist rotten eggs. U.S. Imperialists and British Imperialists are all paper tigers. Don't be crazy, those tired dogs – the British Imperialists. Pay back our debt of blood, you British Imperialists. We will back our countrymen in Hong Kong to the Hilt!'

Children gleefully joined in rocking the car of Canadian correspondent David Oancia when it was surrounded, with him inside it, outside my house during a demonstration. Showers of stones flung by the demonstrators prevented me from getting further photographs from the roof after this one, taken with a zoom lens.

Crowds waving red books of Mao's quotations, his portrait and anti-British slogans at the gates of the British Mission in Peking during the Hong Kong crisis of May 1967.

The gutted shell of the main hall of the British Mission after the Red Guard sacking.

The ill-fated Ming Ming helping me with my chess game a few days before the Red Guard invasion.

The courtyard of my house photographed in October 1969. I was 'jet-planed' on the top step outside the door. The cat was hanged from the balcony above. The ground-floor windows partly obscured by the tree were those of my dining-room which the guards occupied. The window under the balcony was the window of the twelve-foot square room where I spent almost two years.

The eight-foot square room. A window is still partly painted black. On the left is the door to the washroom. To take a photograph in such a small room it was necessary to stand on a table.

My bed in the twelve-foot square room. At its foot was the ever-open door through which the guards watched over me. Behind the curtains, the window, nailed up in May 1968 although it faced a high blank wall. The slogan-covered walls were whitewashed shortly before my release.

The staircase. The whitewashed patches show where slogans were painted out by government workmen shortly before my release.

Slogans and paint on the furniture of my upstairs lounge which survived two launderings.

CHAPTER FIFTEEN

Superstition

Meanwhile, back in the eight-foot square room that was once driver Wang's, 'the big spy Grey' celebrated his fiftieth day in solitary confinement – with the mother and father of all depressions!

The diary tells the tale: 'Today is the fiftieth day of solitary confinement (No celebration was held at the request of the prisoner!). The high point of the day was perhaps the worst-yet depression brought on by the delivery of a bill for three months rent for the house up to December. I declined to pay it immediately and afterwards wondered whether this was wise. Then I was hit by the realisation that it seemed to mean another three months here at least. When the bill was apparently brought to the gate two days ago it was held by the guards I think and there was a lot of telephoning in my dining-room and I thought I even heard the name of the Public Security Minister himself, Hsieh Fu-chih, mentioned. So I had the feeling the delivery to me today of the bill represented a decision making clear I was to be held for at least three more months in this cell and probably more.

'I keeled over on my bunk in absolute despair with all strength gone at one point. I couldn't even find it in me to walk. I have begun to force mutters of "You fucking bastards" out of myself to relieve my feelings. But today even when I managed to start walking again the despair and dispiritedness overwhelmed me and I was reduced to begging for help from God, standing with my head hung backwards and my eyes closed feeling absolutely lost, miserable and hopeless. I tried to pull myself together and be more "positive" and somehow fortunately managed it. This evening I managed to finish reading the fourth volume of the *Selected Works of Mao* ...

'Yesterday was also remarkable because fortune smiled on me

in a small way. For several days the refill of the broken-down little biro with which I write this diary has been in danger of running dry. But Providence miraculously presented me with a replacement yesterday. After writing some figures regarding money on a scrap of paper in the cell, one of the Chinese domestic staff left his biro behind for a couple of minutes. Unable to believe my good fortune I whipped out the refill, which was new and fitted my splintered pen exactly and replaced it with my almost empty one. When he came back he didn't notice the switch and I now have a completely new refill. I was elated all day yesterday at my good fortune and successful quick thinking – not always my strong point. Looking back I see that the last time I wrote was on the day I was ill. The next day I resumed walking back and forth, it was such a welcome relief. Just walking up and down is very important. It was also like welcoming an old friend to start doing Yoga exercises again.

'My thinking of release is becoming really reconciled now to the long term. It seems not impossible that I shall be held for a year or even more. Six months seems almost certain. It is only two and something months to Christmas and I find it impossible to imagine release before then. And very far into next year... My prayers are more fervent than ever these days. I do worry about my mother and hope she will be all right. I have been unable to convey the despair I feel today because I am tired now. But it was terrible. Tonight I resolved to take the next seven days "Like a Man" (trying to shake myself into resistance).

'Two days ago I asked the cook for milk, cheese, butter and fruit and he said rudely that the Red Guards had written down what I shouldn't have and all these things were mentioned.'

The following diary entries show how the empty, unstimulated mind will play with figures to make lucky numbers and combinations of numbers. In the little eight-foot square cell I always knew exactly how many days I had been in it. My only job of real importance then and for every one of the 806 days was each morning to add one number to yesterday's date and keep the figure in my mind. In fact on not one of the days of those twenty-six months did I fail to know what the date was the instant I required it in my thinking. But the way in which I manipulated figures to help me have grounds for optimism perhaps harks back to the way this was done originally in ancient times – and not so ancient times – by simple minds. Also silly superstitions took a strong hold.

I would think things like: 'If the guard going out of the front door of the house lets the wire frame mosquito door slam with a crash everything will be all right. If it closes quietly you are going to be here for a long time. If you get your Yoga mat folded up before you hear the footsteps of the cook bringing supper hit that creak at the bottom of the basement staircase you are going to be released within a month, if not you're in trouble; so hurry.'

There are other accounts of minds under stress taking this kind of superstition seriously. Much later I read an account by China's last Emperor, Aisin-Gioro Pu Yi, of his life as head of state of the Japanese puppet state of Manchukuo in the thirties when he was a virtual prisoner in his own palace.

Pu Yi wrote that when he thought the Japanese were going to murder him he would consult oracles. 'Avoiding calamity and bringing on good fortune became the guiding thought behind my every action. I ended up by asking myself what place, what garment or what food was propitious and what was unlucky. There were no fixed criteria by which to answer these questions. If I was walking along a path and I saw a brick in front of me I would make a ruling: "If I pass it on the left it is lucky and if I pass it on the right it is unlucky." Then I would pass it on the left. I could cite numerous other examples like whether to cross a threshold with one's right leg or one's left foot first and whether to eat something white before something green or vice versa. Wang Jung (his wife) was as engrossed in this as I was and she made a rule that whenever she encountered anything un-lucky she would blink or spit. This became such a habit with her that she would blink and spit incessantly.'

I read these words in the final months of my imprisonment when I was allowed access to some of my own books and was struck by the similarity of the reactions of minds under pressure. I found I had long before adopted quite independently, exactly the same quirk as the former Chinese emperor. As I walked each night I found that I felt it imperative on the last stretch of the hour or so's walk to cross the crack of the threshold of the door to the washroom with my right foot first. I would go on, back and forth, the spot where my right foot fell changing slightly each time after the turn at either end, so that I should not stop after crossing the line with my left foot. I continued this practice almost subconsciously throughout the entire twenty-six months. Often it meant I continued to walk for some time after I wanted to stop in order to get it right and not provoke an unnamed and unthought-of fate.

Even while I thought these neurotic thoughts I knew them to be ridiculous but nevertheless found it impossible to avoid them altogether.

From the shorthand outlines written in the gloomy October days of 1967 I have found that I was doing all kinds of mental juggling with the number thirteen to convince myself that it meant something good for me. I had lightly adopted thirteen as my lucky number when quite young, in my early teens, I think. I knew it was a notoriously unlucky number and I think because I was an obstinate and recalcitrant youth that was why I made it mine, probably to show with a fit of bravado that I didn't believe in anything so stupid as superstition. Anyway it stuck and the memory of it as my lucky number returned to me in those empty-minded days and I took it over with all the enthusiasm of the lifelong horoscope-consulter.

The diary gives me away: 'Wednesday, October 11th, ten thirty. Today hasn't been remarkable in itself but only as part of a wave of optimism which I have been sustaining since I wrote the last entry on October 7th. The big event since then was the arrival on Monday of a really good letter from Shirley. This was a six-page letter written on 25th August and contained the first real details of events unlike the previous two communications which were devoid of anything really interesting. The letter (which arrived on the fifty-second day which is divisible by thirteen) gave me an enormous boost in morale. It said how much Shirley missed me and told me lots of little details about her life and brought me closer to her than for many weeks. I feel the letter was a sign that the worst is over, that the turning point has been reached. I was elated by the letter and felt splendid for a time. The mood brought on by the letter plus the determination to be more positive this week has resulted in four better days.

'I am telling myself now that there are several good days to come. They are Friday, October 13th (thirteen being my lucky number) and October 15 which is the end of my twenty-three day plan plus the fact that the three months anniversary comes

on the 21st of October and the 22nd is thirteen days on from
October 9th when I got the letter (I have noticed that multiples
of thirteen days have been "good" days. August 31st, the thirteenth
day of solitary was the first (peaceful) visit of the Red Guards to
get my cheque book from upstairs, September 13th was their
second visit so I could get some trousers and Mao's *Selected
Works*, on September 26th nothing happened but since nothing
bad happened it was a good day (that's straining the theory a bit
but it just stands up, I think) and October 9th was the letter.
So with the four above-mentioned days to come things are
promising!

'I am becoming a little restless now for the first time and also
attribute this to the possibility of something happening. I speculate
that possibly there might now have been time for some Sino-
British negotiations. But then I shall probably be looking back
to these outlines in a month's time and smiling to myself at my
optimism! !

'I still pray hard three times a day and hope God will help me.
Heavens above only knows how long it will be. I hope my
prediction about looking back at this in a month's time is wrong.
In Shirley's letter there was mention of a report in *The Times*
but she did not say what it said so I still don't know what the
world knows about me. It seems letters still arrive in order but
about six weeks late.'

On the night of Friday, October 13th, 1967, with some two
long years of solitary still before me I wrote of my optimism.

'I allowed myself to believe today that release would take
place some time within one month: that is on or before November
12th. This is a kind of prediction within the larger framework of
a more certain belief that the whole period can't possibly last
more than 160 days – beyond December 28th. This is based on
the "evidence" of the arrival of Shirley's letter on the 9th making
it "clear" that the halfway stage had passed on at the most eighty
days. I sustained my optimism with the view that Britain holds
the cards with two big New China News Agency offices in Hong
Kong and London and that this must in the end prevail. Today
it is twelve weeks and I calculate now enough time has passed to
"save face" and to allow some kind of negotiations to take place.
Eight weeks are marked on my wall in little groups of seven nail
marks. I hope to God release is near. If all these predictions and

expectations are wrong it will be clear I have no future as a fortune teller! For some reason I imagine myself arriving in London on a wet November night with rain blowing in the wind.'

The meaningless days dragged on through the dreary month of October. The emptiness is impossible to record. It is perhaps only possible to indicate the things with which I tried to fill the desolation of those days.

'Tuesday, October 17th, nine thirty. Tonight the bulb in the washroom went out. I don't know why I write this apart from the fact that it is a fact. This morning I asked for extra toast and enjoyed five whole dry slices – what luxury! Today I cleaned out this cell as best I could. It's still fairly filthy. The guard told me to close the wire insect screens of the window during the short time it was allowed open today so I could not breathe the fresh air directly.

'These are many disconnected facts which I am recording I know but I am coming to regard this diary as a historical document. But today I am able to mark up ten days of consecutive optimism. Since that terrible depression of October 7th I have managed to keep my spirits up. At present I am keeping them that way without too much difficulty with my eyes fixed firmly on the week-end. The week-end contains a remarkable series of "lucky days". October 20th is the anniversary of the thirteenth week, the 21st is the three months anniversary and the 22nd is the multiple of thirteen on which good things have happened.

'What hope really is there of release? I think the fact is that I am becoming really adjusted to this horror now. No doubt many sour depressions lie ahead but the past ten days have shown how I can adjust. I do think each day now that perhaps something will happen today. But of course it doesn't happen.

'But being depressed makes things so much harder to bear. Today is the sixtieth day. I reported this to myself aloud several times this morning, as I paced slowly back and forth because it sounded so incredible. Sixty days in this cell, eighty-eight days altogether. My God will it ever end? I pray now three times a day and hope fervently for deliverance.

'The moon tonight is full and bright through the darkened washroom window. As I write this one of the guards has just spat water noisily three times into the courtyard after swooshing it back and forth to clean his mouth. The noise was so great I stopped writing because of the anger it caused me. The guards have gone back to twelve-hour shifts now. Most of them spend their time writing new slogans on their little blackboards in Chinese, writing the characters in a self-conscious, almost child-like way.

'As I sat hunched on my bunk eating my midday food from the tray on the seat of the chair I looked up to see a crowd of Chinese faces peering in through the unpainted panes at the top of the washroom window. They grinned, jeered and clapped derisively when they saw that I had seen them. Good night diary!'

CHAPTER SIXTEEN

Doctor

Wherever there is a prison there will be a grapevine. Perhaps without being too impertinent I can paraphrase Mao Tse-tung who has been accustomed to say about other things 'this is an objective law independent of Man's will'. Or so it seems to me. I believed during my early confinement that nothing filtered through to the outside world about my conditions of life and the treatment I received. But on release I discovered that some scraps of information did reach the British in Peking. It was known for instance during those first wretched months that I was being fed a 'Chinese peasant diet', that there had been a 'bloody incident' involving my cat and that I was still 'all right'.

How did this happen from what seemed an impregnable one-man prison in a strictly-disciplined Communist country? Without indicating exactly what route these snippets of information took, I think it is worth remembering that I was guarded day and night by groups of at least nine Public Security Bureau men. They were part of a large force which also stood guard in the Wai Chiao Ta Lo, the diplomatic housing compound. Many Chinese cooks and domestic staff worked in the compound for Westerners and Communists, for Asians, Europeans and Africans. Chinese domestic staff worked in the house in which I was held prisoner. None of the Chinese involved would have dreamed of compromising themselves by passing on information deliberately. But probably all human beings are gossips of one kind or another. Some Chinese working for diplomats of countries friendlier with China than those of Western Europe might have inadvertently retailed gossip from Public Security Bureau friends which found its way to British ears.

Or perhaps it happened some other way.

Or perhaps the leakage was officially inspired. Somebody may have thought it would wring the heart of British officialdom and make it bow to China's demands over the imprisoned Chinese in Hong Kong. There is no real way of knowing, and the Peking grapevine, meagre though its fruits were, remains as mysterious as its more comprehensive counterparts clinging round formalised prison walls in Britain, the United States and elsewhere. But by whatever route it travelled, the gossip did go. It eventually became known also that I was receiving 'better food'. And it became known that I had been moved to a 'bigger room'. From this it was deduced that I had been held for a time in a very small room. What was not known was that my improved food, and I believe my eventual emergence from the eight-foot square cell to a room four square feet larger, probably resulted from my second illness. I don't believe it resulted from any compassionate instinct on the part of my captors but simply from the realisation that if they were to keep a hostage they had to keep a viable one and that a hostage constantly being ill and possibly worse was not going to be much value as a lever on the British.

Again I return to my diary written at eleven p.m. on the night of Thursday, October 19th.

'Not long ago the guards "gave me my medicine". I had a visit from a doctor tonight after a second and more severe bout of stomach trouble. It began yesterday morning and got worse during the day. The night in which I didn't sleep at all was terrible. I slept only a few minutes after it got light. During the night I saw a star through the courtyard window – the first time I had seen a star for two months – and perhaps ridiculously I wished very hard on it for release and recovery. The night was the longest I have ever known. The doctor eventually came tonight with a very tall English-speaking Public Security Bureau cadre, who wore bifocal spectacles, a droopy moustache and spoke with a strong American accent. The doctor was a harassed little man who peered over his spectacles in what appeared to be a manner common to doctors the world over. He let his gaze flicker only briefly around the cell, hardly looking at the dirt and the daubed paint slogans everywhere. I formed the impression he was used to behaving in a way necessary for survival. (Doctors at the Peking Medical College Hospital were among the first accused of bourgeois tendencies in the Cultural Revolution and were seen scrubbing floors and lavatories.) I wondered whether the doctor had undergone a similar experience himself. I sensed a feeling of compassion in him although this may have been the mistaken idea all patients have of doctors. He examined me without a word, speaking only to the interpreter who instructed me how to sit, etc. The fact that at last here was somebody not being hostile, only neutral, towards me was somehow comforting. I am reminded anew of the frailty of the individual alone.

'I felt ridiculously grateful to him and as he prepared to leave I summoned up the only Chinese words I can pronounce with any proficiency. '*Hsieh-Hsieh,*' (Thank you) I said and I thought there was the barest trace of a smile as he looked quickly at me and hurried out after the guards.

'He wore a white coat, carried a worn shoulder satchel with a red cross on it, and timed my pulse with a battered wrist watch that looked like the kind that at home would have been given to the children to play with because it was worn out.

'About ninety minutes after the doctor left the guards came crowding into the cell. I have begun giving them names and a rather slim, young, girlish-looking one I have named "Charles" because he reminds me of a boy in my class at school, shook out two green pills from a packet and one little yellow one and poured some yellow liquid into a glass of cold water I was holding as they entered. I wondered whether I should throw them away since I am in such a hostile environment but I didn't really feel well enough to care. Neither tasted bad. Then "Charles" and the other two guards went off giggling like girls at the idea of young "Charles" doctoring the foreigner.

'I didn't shave or wash today. Became very, very depressed, the worst for a long time and felt I couldn't expect release in a year. I managed with an effort to pull out of this depression in the evening and had an hour's sleep on the bunk.'

Two days later on Saturday October 21st, I celebrated exactly three months of house arrest.

'July 21st seems years ago now,' I wrote. 'Today has seen my gradual recovery from my illness which has lasted four days. I have been allowed to have a large vacuum flask of hot water in my cell since my illness and can now drink it hot instead of cold all the time. Today in the afternoon I again felt nervy and edgy and thought again about the possibility of having some kind of nervous breakdown with the strain. But prayer helped me overcome this. I thought about religion in some depth today and decided after several hours that I believed in God only because I want to. From this all else follows in my case. Trying to find a rational explanation for belief is impossible. I have eaten very little in the past four days but have no hunger. Yesterday it seemed I would never again enjoy eating anything, but I ate my humble meal tonight with more enthusiasm.

'In a very strong prayer today I promised God I would prevail. This followed immediately after my deep depression and nervousness and made me feel better. The possibility of a year in this cell is becoming very real now and I am not saying this simply because I hope that it won't then follow. Although of course I hope it won't follow. After all I have done a quarter of a year alone already.

'This afternoon I was struck terribly strongly with sheer inability to comprehend the situation. Why am I here? What purpose is it serving? How long shall I be here? Where in the world is the end of it going to be?'

CHAPTER SEVENTEEN

Plan

Looking back on the time spent in that tiny room I see myself on successive days wheeling and plunging to the depths of depression and back again to bearable levels of optimism. Up one moment down the next. Clutching at the smallest signs for grounds to hope. Six toilet rolls bought and placed on the shelf in the washroom. They represent a long time in their potential. Despair. Some days later, four of the toilet rolls have been removed, possibly to another part of the house and only two remain. They represent a reduced span of time. Rising spirits.

Groping for 'new attitudes' to overcome the lassitude, the all-engulfing depression of being alone and the victim of unreasoning, mindless hostility. The guards see me standing at the window enjoying breathing the fresh air direct into my lungs. So they order that the wire insect screens shall never be opened although the window shall be open an hour each morning. It isn't an instruction from above. It is simply the guard commander of the moment exercising the tiniest shred of authority which is allowed him under his iron-clad system of discipline. This is his contribution to the class war, to the 'hurting' of the reactionary newsman Grey. Don't let the window be open a minute longer than an hour each morning. Cut off the fresh air as if with a knife. Put a lock on the outside and instruct the boilerman to fasten it carefully at eleven thirty a.m. locking the prisoner securely back into the room with his own breath. Stare at the prisoner. Spit and hawk more noisily and more frequently than you would bother to do outside for this is the house and home of a bourgeois – what a dirty word – element and they live delicate refined lives so it will upset the prisoner very likely.

To counteract the closeness of the walls, the closeness of the guards and their hostility, to counteract the innate aggression in every moment of the day I needed a plan. I needed something to aim towards and something to strive for. I needed a purpose in my purposeless existence. I needed something tangible and continuing to which I could refer. However small and insignificant the aim or target, I needed it.

I have always had the greatest suspicion of political slogans or slogans of any kind. They have always represented over-simplifications which I have regarded as dangerous in a complex world. I have always had a suspicion of defining a life philosophy in a few words, or committing myself to a belief in the cut and dried terms of a few sentences. Life is fluid and flexible and that is how I have always wanted to hold myself. I have always shied away from exact plans for myself, preferring to 'play things by ear' and I have always had the greatest contempt for the concentration of ideas into a single phrase as in the jargon of television advertising. But perhaps because of life's complexities, which sometimes become overpowering, we seek shelter behind the over-simplified slogans of the politicians and the punchy phrases of the advertising copywriters. Whatever the reason, I found myself descending into this kind of sloganised thinking in times of stress throughout my two years alone.

Many friends – and strangers too for that matter – have said to me since my release that they couldn't understand how anybody could stand such a term of solitary confinement. My reply has always been that anybody faced with no alternative would find their own way. Perhaps that is the real justification for setting down now what might appear to be ludicrous details of my thoughts.

The idea of a 'twenty-three day plan' – a completely arbitrary period of time chosen without any reason – first presented itself to me in September when I vaguely decided to make it a period of studying the four volumes of the *Selected Works* of Mao that I had been allowed. The basic idea of course derives from the Communist practice of evolving Five Year plans – or longer or shorter periods – for the all-round development of the economy of the state. This idea of an all-embracing outline for life appealed to me as a discipline in my strangely isolated position. And on October 24th I drew up what I called a Creed and a seven-point plan to follow over the coming twenty-three days.

The title of the plan in the worst tradition of political sloganists was 'Determination not Dejection'.

This was the plan taken from the shorthand note in my diary for October 24th.

Creed: I know that I shall prevail and one day get out of here. Every day that passes is one day nearer release. Dejection can only do harm not good. Therefore it must be resolutely repulsed by determination to remain optimistic and calm. The Chinese authorities have nothing to gain by keeping you here and they know this. Days and weeks seem long but Governments work slowly to save their faces. Be patient and try to keep busy and think only of preparing yourself for the future.

The plan is divided into seven different parts.

1. Determination not Dejection Creed is to be referred to regularly and certainly whenever depression comes.
2. Seek permission to go upstairs to get: as many books as possible, chess set, stomach tablets and other medicaments, wool shirts and suits and towels, English coffee and marmalade from store cupboard.
3. If 2 unsuccessful try to buy books from Foreign Languages Press book shop through Chinese staff.
4. Plan the book to be written later, both chapter-wise and by jotting down thoughts.
5. Study Yoga more closely, practise it an extra hour a day, read about advanced postures again and generally tighten up approach.
6. If upstairs books and bookshop books unobtainable re-read Mao's most important works.
7. Innovate where possible, introducing new thoughts or activities. Try to be busy and not be extremely lazy for days on end.

This plan expires on November 17th.

Eventually I made a 'Plan' on the first day of each month and found this gave some meaning, however small, to the passage of time. But my diary entry of two days after the formation of that first detailed plan showed how difficult it was to hold on to the resolution.

'Thursday, October 26th, seven thirty. Will they never let me out of here? This plaintive question has escaped my lips several times today – a day of bad depression. It became acute this afternoon while I was walking and led me to drop to my knees in prayer at my bunkside. I read for the first time my "Creed" of Determination not Dejection. But it was not all-powerful. Today there have been five or more guards on at one time which I don't understand. It has been a very hard day of very big depression. I have just finished a meal of liver, carrots, soup and vegetables. This morning I had another stomach upset but I am hoping it will not be severe.

'Yesterday I launched my new "Plan" but up to the moment I have had no reaction from a request put to the guards through Lao Chiao to go upstairs to get books, etc. I have been reading Yoga and doing my exercises for two days. On Sunday, October 22nd, I got a postcard from Shirley in which she said "Damn, damn, damn that you are there". The next day I received a letter from her telling me nothing important but giving details about her taking driving lessons. It was the third letter from Shirley.

'I am still reading Carew-Hunt's book for the third time and finding it interesting. Today I was allowed to make out cheques for the wages and for the rent and car licence and electricity. I had a long tussle with myself about whether or not to pay the rent and still feel a little weak for not holding it. But it wouldn't get me out of here, I don't suppose. There has been no sign for me to grab or cling to and my morale today appeared to be getting rather low. I pray tremendously hard but sometimes feel there is no God. I try to fight this. It has become so cold now that this morning I had to put on a sweater over my cardigan and then a jacket on and walk about with the collar turned up. Winter is going to be hell in this cell. The staff today asked me for forty yuan for their winter uniforms. Oh God how long will this hell on earth go on? I do so long for some encouragement. I am very low in spirits.'

CHAPTER EIGHTEEN

Apple

'I have just eaten, with delirious enjoyment, an apple. I smelled it like an idiot, caressed it, washed it, polished it and almost made love to it. And then cut it in half and ate it and have just been asking my stomach out loud what it thought of that after seventy-one days, eh?'

This ecstatic diary entry was written at precisely seven p.m. on Saturday October 28th. During my occupation of the eight-foot square cell I had often scratched my head. Not in puzzlement but because it itched, often furiously and for prolonged periods. A mere trifle in the normal course of events but I came to feel it keenly as part of the generally jaded condition produced by lack of air and exercise, low-grade food and frequent depression. I had lost weight considerably and when I washed my hair which had grown long and unkempt over three months I had to haul horrifyingly large clumps of it out of the plughole before the water would run away. In depressed moments I saw myself emerging, if ever, as some kind of latter-day Ben Gunn, emaciated, with grey, stringy hair, or worse, hairless, and cackling insanely. This perhaps sounds lighthearted now but at the time the fear was a real one. As the months stretched out my basic aim became to emerge as normal in mind and body as possible. It was to this end that I pursued my Yoga exercises so purposefully and also tried to exercise my mind and body in other ways.

From time to time when the cook brought in food on a tray I had pointed to my hair and teeth in the ridiculous mixture of dumb show and pidgin English necessary to communicate with him. I would try to indicate the dangers of teeth and hair falling out without proper food. But always he pointed to the daubed slogans on my walls and said in a mixture of Chinese and English, 'They say not have'.

I don't know what the protein, calorie and carbohydrate content of my diet was. It was probably adequate in a sense. If it was a genuine 'Chinese peasant diet' I suppose it should be remembered that eighty per cent of the largest nation on earth work fairly hard on it. But for the first seventy-one days in the small room I was denied butter, milk, cheese and fruit to which I had always been accustomed. Hence the ecstatic diary entry above when the embargo was lifted. The account of that simple meal continued:

'The shattering arrival of a big yellow autumn apple and a small square of butter came on my dinner tray this evening. Sao Kao explained that people who wrote slogans had said Yes. The thrill of eating an apple was unimaginable. The smell was delicious and I couldn't take it away from my nose. It tasted splendid. I ate it in a semi-daze. The butter on the normally dry toasted bread was good too although not so strong in impact as the apple. The piece of butter was very small but to eat toast with it on again was tremendous. These two things I have found have made me almost happy. My mood which this afternoon was very pessimistic and bad has changed to an almost elated one. I believe these small quantitive changes are clearing the way for eventual release.'

On the morning of the day that I was allowed my apple there had been unusual activity at the house. From the cell I could look into the courtyard, but the gateway itself was not in my field of vision. Every time the gate opened or the bell rang I sprang to the window to see if it heralded a sign of hope. Since the night of the Red Guard invasion there had only been the two visits of my Red Guard and Revolutionary Rebel 'supervisors' to take me upstairs to get a cheque book on one occasion and to get warmer clothes on the second. But on the Day of the Apple the Fat Cadre who had been present on the night of the invasion was suddenly admitted at eight thirty a.m., waddling quickly across the courtyard after three long rings on the bell. In the next hour there were three similar three-long rings and a conference followed into which Lao Chiao, the boilerman, and Sao Kao, the cook, were drawn. The Fat Cadre stayed all morning but nothing happened. I noted in my diary: 'Strange. I thought the repeated ringing of the bell made it sound like a rehearsal for something. The activity was somewhat exciting. Perhaps consular access is to be allowed to break this damned isolation.'

The day after the Day of the Apple I was allowed meat at

midday for the first time in seventy-two days, an apple at break-fast, a pear at lunch and an apple at dinner. It was the 100th day of house arrest and I wrote in my diary: 'I have hope in the wake of fruit and butter after the misery of recent days.'

Another example of my desire to see symbolic encouragement in the smallest thing appeared in my diary of Saturday, October 28th.

'The wind is howling outside very strongly as I write. For a long time I have watched fascinated and with great excitement as a long strip of one of the posters that the Red Guards pasted over the top of the outside of the black-painted window gradually tore itself free. The wind is a freeing force, I said to myself over and over again. Sometimes the glue seemed to be holding it fast then a strong gust would rip the strip further. It lashed against the window as it became longer and, to me, stronger. Just when it seemed the pause between the gusts was growing longer, that perhaps the wind was dying down, a great flurry seized the strip of paper, ripped it free and sent it whirling away over the courtyard wall into the street and out of sight. I had been desperately anxious that it should tear itself free and was delighted to see it disappear over the wall. It helped me believe that someday too I will be able to tear myself free of this little cell.'

On Tuesday, October 31st my hopes skyrocketed suddenly when the bell rang the ritualistic three times again and the now-familiar faces of the Red Guards and Revolutionary Rebels of the Photo Machine Factory came into view in the courtyard.

The fluctuation of my hopes during that day are recorded in the entry for that day.

'Tuesday, October 31, 22.00. Well, well, well. Today another visit from the Red Guards – my "proletarian friends". Clearly the object of the Saturday three-bell rehearsal, they came around eleven a.m. and threw me into a dither of excitement. They did not come to my cell immediately but after a while went upstairs and clumped around then came to me, came in and peered all around the cell, into corners and behind the door. Then, making my pulse rate rise, they went outside and broke the paper seals across the outside door of the cell.

'My heart beat faster and I sat and prayed on my bed and thought about being allowed back upstairs, having a bath, read-ing and writing and living again. I thought seventy-four days is not too bad after all. But alas! I was a bloody pathetic fool. Not only was I not allowed back upstairs but was told by Lao Chiao that he could bring nothing down for me. I finally concluded that the house was "unsealed" simply because the heating had to be turned on today and the radiators upstairs ended. What I saw after my first disappointment as at least a small concession, was in fact no concession at all and was not even the slightest help to me. On the contrary it was evidence of a long term stay. I believed it to be a concession for about an hour. When realisation dawned I was in despair even deeper than before. After lunch when I found I could have nothing from upstairs it was worse. But somehow it has strengthened my resolve by making absolutely clear that I am again settling down to a long term. Christmas is eight weeks away less one day.

'Today's events were very frustrating but the whole thing about seals and the "control" by the Red Guards is worth noting in the "book" if it ever gets written. I recognised several of the same faces from the two previous times but they wore capes and winter jackets and it was difficult. They stared at me through the window as they trooped out afterwards. Not a word was spoken this time.

'It looks as if the breaking of the seals means that the direct "supervision of the masses" is at an end. That is probably why my proletarian visitors had such long faces. They didn't like even that pseudo-control over "the foreign devil" coming to an end I think.

'What a bloody visit! I remember praying over and over again "Please God it looks good, please make it absolutely good". I cursed myself for being such a fool afterwards. Food has improved and is now good and eatable. Yesterday Sao Kao asked for more money for the rent since there was a fine for paying it late. This served to emphasise my abject dependence on them here and sent me plunging into another fit of misery when I had given him twenty extra Yuan. I dropped my plan to try to get books bought today because of the excitement. So ends the month of October 1967. Goodbye October you were one of the worst months of my life! '

CHAPTER NINETEEN

Yoga

'Nothing but good can befall you. Peace, happiness and content-
ment lie ahead. Prepare yourself for happier climes with a calm,
untroubled mind free from worry or fear. You have a good future,
your fate is in God's hands. God will deliver you. Something good
is coming.'

Alone, apprehensive, jumping at every sound in that confined
space I was in great need of reassurance, something to hold on
to. The only source it could come from was myself. So I gave it
to myself in the words of that odd little paragraph written above.
It looks strange now in print. The words are as familiar and second
nature to me as the Lord's Prayer or the National Anthem. At
least once each day for the entire two years, sometimes two and
three times a day, I repeated the words softly to myself at the
beginning of each session of Yoga exercises. In Yoga terminology
they constitute a mantra.

I have always had a healthy scepticism about what are popularly
called religious cranks, Yoga cranks, vegetarian cranks or cranks
of any other variety. It seems to me now, at this long distance
from China, that practically anything I write about my experience
in isolation is going to seem more than a little cranky. There were
times during my confinement when I wondered whether I wasn't
becoming at least a little eccentric. It has been said that we only
exist as our personalities are reflected in others and since there
was nobody to reflect whatever I was becoming, nothing to
measure myself against, it was often very difficult to know
with any certainty whether I was really winning the battle to remain entirely sane. During the early days after my release I found
myself sneaking a look at my friends to see if they were regarding
me oddly.

But if I have a guardian angel then I am sure she was right
behind me in Hong Kong on my last afternoon before going into

China. As I strolled idly in the street she came right up behind me. Then gently, but with firm insistence she propelled me into a bookshop. She probably tut-tutted and raised her eyes heavenwards in slight exasperation when I selected and bought John Le Carré's *Deadly Affair*, then again gently nudged me in the direction of a book entitled *True Yoga* by William Zorn. Only when I had bought it did she melt away, her essential work done.

If I had to single out one factor above all others which enabled me to endure the isolation I would say that it was Yoga. Its benefit was twofold. It helped me to adjust mentally to the isolation and confinement and helped me to keep myself in as good a physical condition as the circumstances allowed.

The two sometimes terrifying problems of solitary confinement are what to do with your body and what to do with your mind. Yoga provides activity on both planes. I knew nothing of this ancient Indian teaching before I went to China. I didn't have time to read the book I had bought in Hong Kong until I was put under house arrest in July. I had bought it in Hong Kong with the idea in mind that Peking was a pretty dull place socially and I thought that, with plenty of spare time, I should have an opportunity to look into Yoga. That Peking was dull socially proved to be true but the task of trying to understand the Cultural Revolution seemed to leave little time for anything else.

Perhaps my guardian angel appeared again briefly on the evening of August 18th before the Red Guards raided me, to ensure that the Yoga book was in my bedroom and not in a room that was to be immediately sealed off. Thus I was able to take it with me to the downstairs 'cell'. The word Yoga itself is a derivation of the Sanskrit word *Yuj*, meaning 'to join' or 'to yoke together' and it means union – the union of an individual soul with total reality or the divine source of life. To achieve and feel this union should be the aim of the Yoga student and when he has achieved it he becomes, in the terminology of the teaching, a Yogi.

Yoga is traceable back to about 1,500 B.C. and is basically a system for improvement of the body and mind. It has several basic branches. I concentrated on Physical Yoga in which different postures are assumed to exercise muscles, joints and internal organs so as to bring the body to a peak of normal efficiency at its normal weight. It would not be possible to train to win the 100 metres in the Olympic Games on Yoga exercises since they are designed simply to maintain an efficient, fit bodily condition. Physical Yoga prepares the mind for Mental Yoga, in which the aim is to make the mind calm and still in order to discover its true nature and release its full potential.

In the course of his brief but lucid description of Mental Yoga, Yogi William Zorn says: 'There are several methods by which we can become master of our thoughts. Undesirable thoughts can be suppressed by constant pondering over opposites. Hate is suppressed by thoughts of love, unhappy thoughts by thinking about happiness, selfish desires by non-attachment. The mind becomes calm by cultivating attitudes of friendliness, sympathy, gladness and indifference respectively towards happiness, misery, good and bad.'

Exercises in concentration to control the mind helped me in those days. With closed eyes, sitting on my bunk, I would summon the image of a rose in front of me and I would remember Mr Zorn's exhortation. 'As soon as the image disappears, bring it back. Do not allow the mind to go its own way.'

When my contempt and disgust for my guards and persecutors reached its depths I tried to follow another of his instructions, 'Discover all the good of an object, an occurrence or a person. Count your blessings. Think how wonderful it is to be able to see, hear, touch, taste, smell, to have loved ones, friends and so on.'

Back in the fast-moving, frantically competitive scramble of modern life again these simple teachings perhaps sound naïve. I don't pretend that the teachings enabled me to think only noble thoughts all the time. But I did make a conscious effort to balance good and bad and at all times I was able to congratulate myself that nothing irrevocable had yet happened. I was still in one piece, still of sound mind, still hopeful of release, hadn't been sentenced to twenty years or to death. It is what might be quickly and lightly called 'looking on the bright side', but it became an essential exercise to do in detail to counteract the depression of isolation, the feeling of persecution and the debilitating despair of self-pity. In time I learned not to let myself fall into the habit of self-pity since it was self-destructive.

Often with closed eyes I would focus my mind, according to Yoga teaching, on the space between my eyebrows. And holding it there I would imagine in detail the seascape from the clifftop at Sheringham in North Norfolk – where I had worked for a year as a local reporter – with the afternoon sun glinting on the waves. I would think in great detail of the stonework along the promenade, the colour of the breakwaters and the tints of the sky. Or I would paint a mental image of the quiet, empty playing field of my school, or the still woodland of a Norwich park. This gave me comfort and a feeling of calm.

The mantra or affirmation given at the beginning of this chapter, which came to be a part of my daily life, was more complex than other, shorter ones which I also found effective in my battle to fight off the oppressiveness of the tiny space which sometimes brought me close to unreasoning panic. Yoga also teaches the importance and beauty of breathing and often I would sit on the folded blanket on the stone tiles quietly concentrating on my breathing. On each inward breath I repeated to myself the one-word mantra 'Health' matching it to the length of my breath and half-uttering it in a long-drawn, sibilant whisper. Then on the outward breath I would match the word 'Calm' to the length of the exhalation. Repeated again and again this has an almost hyp-notically calming influence on the mind.

I did not learn to stop my heart beat and I did not sit on a bed of nails. These tend to be popular misconceptions about the essentials of Yoga. Mention Yoga to most people unfamiliar with it and they will say with a laugh 'Oh, that's where you sit and con-template your navel isn't it?'

I suppose I ought to say for the record that I did not spend a single second 'contemplating my navel'. Also I don't think I got anywhere near to becoming a true Yogi. I did not go in for con-templation in the sense of long, deeply-concentrated mind-fixing. I adapted Yoga as I needed it. I got most satisfaction from the physical postures. They are deceptive. They should be done gently, without undue exertion and are performed by quietly assuming positions, not normally necessary in routine daily activity, which bend and stretch and tone the muscles, joints and organs. But on those hot August days in that little cell, stripped to the waist, I sweated profusely during the quiet exertions. Invariably when I did the postures with concentration and care I got up from my folded blanket feeling calmer and more relaxed than when I started. In the early days, as I adjusted to the traumatic change in my life from comparative freedom to close confinement, I did three sessions a day, morning, noon and night, each session often lasting between half an hour and an hour. It occupied me, it calmed me, it helped me affirm that I existed positively, it kept me comparatively fit. I adapted and watered down the strict Yoga disciplines for one reason. I was worried about my mind and didn't want to focus too much of my attention on it by deep contemplation of it. Perhaps a real Yogi would be ashamed of me, telling me I could only find peace within myself. Perhaps he would be right too. But nevertheless, I didn't like to take the risk. I thought I would temper the ancient Indian teachings with what I suppose can best be described as the equally ancient British penchant for 'muddling through somehow'. In between my sessions of calm breathing, mantra chanting and pleasant-image summoning, I would let my mind freewheel idly around and try to forget that it existed as a mind at all.

The book I had with me in the cell contained 100 illustrations of the Yoga postures or asanas, clear photographs of how to assume them precisely and without strain. Yoga postures are based on ancient scriptures in which Lord Shiva was said to have assumed 84,000 different postures thus creating all the living species in the universe. Some eighty-four of these were found to be useful to mankind, but easier variations were developed through the ages because many were very difficult for the human body. This is why the eighteen basic postures go under names like Fish, Cobra, Eagle, Tree or Locust, since the postures simulate the form of the animal, bird or tree. Among the advanced postures there are names like Tortoise, Peacock and Lotus.

One of my favourite elementary postures, the Thunderbolt or Vajrasana is assumed simply by kneeling and sitting comfortably on the backs of the heels, the length of the shins touching the floor from knee to ankle. Sitting up straight with the palms of my hands lying flat on my thighs and with eyes closed and concentration fixed between my eyebrows, I would achieve a feeling of controlled relaxation. I would often sit for long minutes in this way and such was the sense of well-being it promoted that I often told myself, quite ridiculously I suppose, 'While you are in this posture the decision to release you will sometime be taken by someone, somewhere'. Perhaps my favourite posture of all was the Tip-toe posture or Padangusthasana. This is assumed by squatting on the haunches then raising one foot and placing it on top of the other thigh and balancing on the toes of one foot with the hands held together in front of the chest in an attitude of prayer. At first I found this quite impossible and as soon as I tried to bring my hands together in front of my chest I would tumble wildly off balance. Time and again I could achieve nothing in the way of balance but after much sweating and falling I began to increase the number of seconds I could count before keeling over. And eventually I competed one leg against the other, counting each time to see on which leg I could balance longer. Perhaps the posture is easier than it looks, but because it seems to be difficult it gave me more satisfaction to master it.

One posture I never mastered, or came anywhere near assuming fully, was the Lotus. This involves sitting cross-legged on the floor then tucking the feet up on top of each opposite thigh, rather in the way one would fold one's arms. I tried to increase the effort and inch towards perfection each day but I suspect my slightly bandy legs made it physically impossible to get my feet up on opposite thighs. Again, no doubt, the true Yogi would tell me perseverance would have made it possible. But I took comfort in the explanation that it wasn't essential to master all postures to succeed in Yoga. Yoga for me was not without its sense of fun. My grunting, unsuccessful efforts with some of the more difficult postures often made me smile or laugh at my own ineptitude. I did my regular Yoga sessions on a folded blanket – one on which the Red Guards had daubed black paint slogans in Chinese saying 'Down with Grey'. The slogans remained stained into the blanket throughout the two years despite a laundering.

In addition to these sessions I did Yogic breathing to calm my mind as I paced back and forth in the confined space. There are several forms of Yogic breathing but the one I adopted for my use was Kumbhaka or Rhythmic Breathing. It can be practised sitting still, or while swimming or walking. I would breathe in deeply to a count of two paces, hold my breath for a count of eight paces then gradually exhale over the next four paces. Repeated over and over the gentle rhythm does calm the mind. This is one of the methods by which the Yoga student gradually moves towards total control of his mind.

Later when I was allowed outside to walk up and down my courtyard for short spells under the gaze of two guards, I often counteracted the discomfort of their baleful stares by fixing my mind only on the gentle soothing 2-8-4 rhythm of my breathing.

There are other branches of Yoga; the Yoga of Devotion in which the student applies himself assiduously to the religion of his choice; the Yoga of Action which concerns itself with development of moral standards in everyday life by the practice of such attitudes as moderation, kindness and positiveness; and the Yoga of Knowledge in which truth is sought through the study of the religious and philosophical teachings of the early Aryans.

Mr Zorn's book is a simple introduction to Yoga, a mere eighty-four pages, so I was not able to study deeply the philosophical basis of the teaching. But in the odd telling phrase he indicated the roots of the belief that the individual 'I' (or Atman) is part of, and the same as, total reality or the divine source of life (Brahman) 'just as there is no absolute difference between the space enclosed in a pot and the space outside it, with which it will merge again when the pot disintegrates'.

His final paragraph on meditation made me at least aware of how the Yogi might detach himself from worldly values, even if I was never able to achieve this entirely myself. In short I believe I was able to gain much from this ancient set of teachings without embracing them as totally as the Indian fakir on his nail-bed.

Penned constantly in the eight-foot square room I found considerable comfort in the simplicity of Mr Zorn's words on meditation: 'As the sun shines on the ocean, it causes vapour to rise. From this vapour clouds are formed, and these clouds drift over the earth. Sooner or later these clouds become either dew or rain drops. From this dew and rain, small streams are formed and these in turn form great rivers and in this way every single dewdrop finds its way back to the source, the ocean. Although the tiny dewdrop may seem separate and insignificant, the attraction of the ocean will draw it back to its source, no matter how far the distance and how great the obstacles may appear. If the dewdrop would regard itself as just a dewdrop it would feel very small indeed. It would feel ever so much stronger and happier if it knew it was part of the mighty ocean, yea that it was the ocean itself, that its destiny was guided and that nothing can prevent its final triumph when at last it slips into the shining sea.'

CHAPTER TWENTY

Removal

The time I spent in that tiny, eight-foot square room in Peking has an especially horrific quality of its own in my memory.

In comparison with the overall total of twenty-six months it was short – some two and a half months or seventy-seven days. The mind-numbing emptiness of each hour, the ever-present feeling of latent aggression against me personally in every minute of the day because I was always held fast in the confined space; the black sticky paint covering most of the window panes that came off on the fingers if touched; eating from the seat of a rough wooden chair; the closed and nailed up windows over which I had no control; the dirty-yellow patterned stone tiles of the floor, the dull glow of the single bulb at night, and the ants; the pink paper posters and the daubed slogans in black and blue paint, the nail scratches on the wall representing each of the slow-passing days, the large colour portrait of Mao with its hint of an enigmatic smile on the otherwise expressionless Asiatic face.

Sometimes as the sun went down behind the Western hills some streaks of light would fall on the sallow face and in the glint of the sun's rays it was not difficult to imagine a sardonic, contemptuous grin flitting across it. But strangely enough, I never had any urge to tear the portrait down. I got satisfaction from telling myself that its presence did not affect me even slightly. I knew that it was put there as an act of mental aggression. The planting of a foreign idol as my constant companion was an act that they could reasonably expect would annoy me. It was because I instinctively realised this that the presence of the large, three-foot square portrait never really bothered me.

I knew that if I ever touched it in the sight of the guards, tore it, or put a moustache or a monocle on it, I should be laying myself open to the possibility of being accused of the greatest crime in Cultural Revolution China – insulting Chairman Mao. As part of my effort to show myself completely unaffected by its presence, instead of tearing it down I went out of my way to keep it up. I pointed out with sign-language one day to Lao Chiao that the corner of it was peeling away from the wall because the glue had dried out and it might all eventually fall down. Ought it not to be put back properly? He duly came back and secured it at all four corners with drawing-pins, after consulting with the guards. They came to watch, looked at me expressionlessly and I looked back expressionlessly.

During my time in the small room I was never once allowed to step outside the house into the fresh air and I often seethed with anger at this deliberately unreasonable restriction. I can still remember clearly seething with anger too, at the sight of the midday meal. Sometimes the main dish was just a mess of chopped egg-plant on a plate and I would convey this to my mouth, by means of the provided chopsticks, with great distaste. There was raw cabbage, half a hard-boiled egg and cucumber on a smaller dish, and a very small bowl of thin, tasteless soup to go with it – and a couple of slices of dry bread. Or perhaps the main plate would hold simply an unadorned dollop of mashed potatoes or on another day a stodge of chopped onions with some brown gravy-like sauce over and around it.

The presentation of these meals to me by a cook who was accustomed to preparing delicious, traditional Chinese dishes for formal dinner parties in the dining-room now occupied by the Public Security Bureau guards was another calculated act of humiliation for the bourgeois newsman Grey that they knew would make an impact beyond the actual low-grade quality of the food.

At the onset of the Cultural Revolution the prime targets were intellectuals who were contemptuously dubbed the 'Black Gang'. Teachers were daubed symbolically with black ink by students, other intellectuals were covered in black paint during struggle meetings, as I was, 'black dens' were set up in small rooms in schools and intellectuals were herded into them. Some of the teachers and university professors are known to have leapt to their deaths from windows, preferring suicide to the continual humiliation.

Perhaps I was fortunate in that the humiliating treatment forced on me was never visible to anybody for whom I had respect. I didn't have to face the problem of what other people thought. I was able to nurse myself along, trying to keep my own self-respect intact behind a shell of outward indifference. I never in those seventy-seven days thought of suicide. But the experience made it easy for me to understand the sometimes suicidal actions of those unfortunate Chinese intellectuals who came under pressure. Later, as the long weary months alone dragged by, I occasionally became prey to the irrational fear that I would perhaps take my life unwittingly in my sleep. I will explain this in a later chapter. But the time in that tiny room did end, and although I got only four extra square feet when it did, I was glad to have survived it without apparent damage to myself.

On November 1st my diary shows that I was grappling with the problem of adjusting to the disappointment of the previous day when the Red Guards had broken the paper seals in the house but nothing had happened to me. I coined another slogan, gave myself another point in time to work towards. 'Tonight I decided today would be the first day of a Calm to Christmas campaign,' I wrote. 'I have succeeded in keeping a calm mind all day and feel I have grasped at last the essentials of Yoga.' The 'Calm to Christmas' slogan was much more successful than previous ones and I did find myself repeating it to myself and holding on fairly firmly to a steady state of mind during the succeeding weeks.

I recorded a dream because I wondered if in my isolated state I was developing the ability to prophesy in my sleep. I wrote: 'During the night I had an odd dream about being held in a house in England, escaping for a few hours to have a meal with some friends – British diplomats from Peking – then returning to captivity voluntarily to find my two guards, British policemen, had noticed my absence and said it would be the last chance I would get for another year. I asked if they really thought I would be held for a year and one said "For eight months anyway". I thought this worth recording just in case it is a prophetic dream. I sincerely hope it isn't.'

As it turned out it was not at all prophetic – but not in the way I expected. I had hoped release would come much sooner than one year. In fact it was still practically two years away.

Then on the morning of Thursday, November 2nd, there was some unusual activity in the washroom as I sat in the eight-foot cell with the door closed. I immediately began writing a diary thinking that if it was an important development I should record it as it happened. I also wanted to set down the conditions in which I had been living since I fancied perhaps things were about to be restored to normal.

'Thursday, November 2nd, 09.30. This unusually early diary is being written as Lao Chiao and Mrs Hou are cleaning the washroom next door. It is a good point to record the "state of affairs". The windows in there and here were covered so thickly with black paint that they are still wet after eleven weeks. The bath was sloshed with paint as were the lavatory seat and bowl, the mirror, window-sills and doors. Paint ran down the wall from the slogans on either side. It was extremely dirty and unhygienic. Wood was nailed across outside the windows and they were also nailed up. Posters and paint were also stuck up on the walls and under the towel rack. I was allowed to clean off the mirror but nothing else. I had no intention of cleaning the bath and didn't ask. The clean-up appears to be the direct effect of the visit of the Red Guards. I wonder what else will follow, if anything. I feel this is a sign of a sort of admission that it is inadvisable to carry on this treatment, or at least the extreme severity of it.'

But my hopes were not justified. I wrote later in the day: 'Part II 23.15 same day. The clean-up covered the bath, lavatory and sink. The slogans remain. There was quite a pathetic touch. Two daubs of paint across one wall which meant nothing but were just messy blobs, made as the slogan-painting brush was dragged across into another slogan, were left intact, obviously on instructions, as if they were sacred writings. Posters also remained. The bath can't be got clean. I tried to get books today but no luck. The paper arrived in mid-afternoon. No mail, and I was ruefully saying to myself it wasn't my day, when the bell rang and after a while it turned out to be a cable from Shirley. This was the first cable of the whole fifteen weeks. And it was clearly a decision of the Foreign Ministry Information Department to allow it in. The four words in the cable saying that she cared were comforting. At least somebody cares. Not anything fantastic in itself but another small pointer perhaps. I was thrilled.'

And the next day was the last in that cell.

'Friday, November 3rd, 23.45. (Sitting on the loo with the lid down). Today I was moved. Into the former translators' office.

Without warning after lunch I was asked to sit in the washroom while office equipment was moved into it from the office and eventually into my little cell. All three staff moved one single bed down from upstairs and prepared the room. The "cell" was filled with furniture, filing cabinets, etc., and locked. I don't know why it happened. It appears to be a result of the Red Guards' visit and I trace everything including fruit and meat at all meal-times back to the Saturday visit of the Fat Cadre a week ago. Anyway I have a new bed, and I am somewhat unsettled. I have just done an hour's unsatisfactory Yoga in the dark and have not yet found a new pattern. Walking tonight was strange, going right up to the open door of the office and coming face to face with the guards acrosss the passage in the dining-room. In general I find the change encouraging. I had asked God in my prayer this morning for a sign of encouragement and I think this was one. I was almost totally indifferent at first to the change but some two or three hours afterwards I feel tremendously relieved to be out of that small cell after exactly eleven weeks. I thank God. I'll write more about this tomorrow. My impressions are still a little con-fused.

'Saturday, November 4th, 22.00. (My second diary sitting on the loo with the lid down because I don't feel the room so near the guards is secure enough to write in.) I am now more settled in the new environment. Today has been a pattern setter. The morn-ing was dramatic. I was doing my Yoga when the guard I've come to call "Loud Lout" flung open the door in his typical quiet way. I got up angrily from my postures and closed it. He threw it open again and I charged back and closed it again saying "Not until I am dressed". Miraculously it stayed closed until ten o'clock. I completed a rather scrappy set of exercises during which I couldn't quite calm down. After that it was my first breakfast at a table for eleven weeks. I walked and stood at the window and did Yogic breathing until lunch and put my clothes in drawers of the typing desk after lining them with newspapers. The door remained closed during breakfast for half an hour and during lunch for an hour. The afternoon was spent walking and thinking and I decided to do a regular Yoga session at five thirty in the washroom. This was more successful and I spent fifty minutes at it. After praying at the bedside came dinner at six and afterwards more lolling on the bed, walking, Yogic breathing and time-wasting. I have read nothing since finishing Carew-Hunt's book. Somehow the day has seemed longer than most.

'The room has three great, crudely-daubed slogans against me personally – "Down with *Ger-lai*" in Chinese – and two against British Imperialism. Two signboards on which quotations are chalked have been set up facing my bed. The window has been open all day. On the wall behind my bed in English it says "Down with all reactionarys" (sic). My walk is ten paces now so is two paces longer. My mood continues to be completely calm and detached. I am very proud of my new control. The one encouraging event of the day was that my cheque book was given back into my control by Sao Kao, but no pen. This was very small but was a gesture that was sufficient to keep up the tempo of little improvements away from humiliation. The cheque book not being in my control was a deliberate humiliation. I slept very badly in my new, comfortable bed and was awake at seven and didn't sleep again. My bigger view of life (the courtyard) from the window didn't produce anything startling. The larger size of the room is pleasing but the overall impact of the change is not great. The washroom as I write seems small and the "cell" now closed up does look terribly small. I am happy at the continuation of this "concession" trend. Today Lao Chiao and Mrs Hou were cleaning and banging upstairs. I saw Mrs Hou go out with the torn upstairs door seals in a dustpan having swept them up. They were clumping around in the bathroom and all over the upper house but I have no idea of the importance of this, if anything. It could well be that the concessions and developments have finished now for a long spell. But of course I am hoping, as ever, for the best. Today was another multiple of thirteen and the cheque book being handed back saved it from being barren. I have put a towel over the mirror because it is too depressing seeing myself walking up and down. I look pale, thin and sickly and this isn't good for morale to see all the time.'

Part 3

CHAPTER TWENTY-ONE

Hard Luck

This chapter is a hard luck story. It is sometimes said that a good journalist is one who is always in the right place at the right time. Looking back it is clear to me that Peking was the wrong place to be and July-August 1967 was the wrong time to be there. But perhaps I can comfort myself with the thought that at least I was trying – although unsuccessfully – not to be there when trouble arrived.

The hard luck element became clear when I began, after my arrival home, to piece together the background to the events of that wild summer in Peking.

It seems that, unfortunately for the British in Peking, violence, chaos and confusion reached a climax on three separate fronts at roughly the same time. The domestic Cultural Revolution reached a height of turmoil in China generally and in a kind of chain reaction the Hong Kong trouble escalated similarly and, most important of all, the strife and confusion within the precincts of the Wai Chiao Pu – the Foreign Ministry – in Legation Street led for a few frenzied days to a kind of epileptic spasm in its dealings with foreigners.

At the precise moment when I was put under house arrest on July 21st the resistance to Mao reached its peak with the kidnapping in Wuhan of his Public Security Minister Hsieh Fu-chih – the equivalent in Mao's China to Beria in Stalin's Russia. There were wall poster reports of Mao moving gunboats, troops and aircraft against the dissident army commanders in Wuhan who staged the kidnapping of the Minister when he went there with Wang Li, another top leader, to try to pour oil on the troubled waters of factional in-fighting.

This event, which has come to be known as the Wuhan Incident, and the proliferating wall poster reports of increasing violence throughout China must have induced a state of near panic in the Maoist leadership in Peking which was felt in all government departments, not least in the already-strained Foreign Ministry. It might well have prompted the Ministry's officials to extend their campaign against foreign correspondents, who were filing embarrassing reports to the outside world, beyond vague threats of spy charges for reading wall posters to a clear reprisal of house arrest against one of them.

About this time the small Western press corps in Peking was practically decimated. David Oancia of the *Toronto Globe and Mail* and Harald Munthe-Kaas the Norwegian correspondent both left China, one temporarily and the other permanently, after being manhandled and humiliated in the street and having their car smashed by Red Guards. Hans Bargmann of D.P.A. was on home leave during that summer and when the residence visa and accreditation card of the Agence France Presse correspondent, Jean Vincent, expired around that time, the Foreign Ministry Information Department declined immediately to renew it, leaving him ill-at-ease, and technically putting the last Western press representative out of action.

The direct cause of my house arrest was the sentencing of a number of Communist journalists in Hong Kong to prison terms for offences connected with rioting in the colony. The increasing violence and disorder of the Communist-inspired confrontation campaign had led the Hong Kong authorities to introduce uncompromising emergency laws and tough anti-riot measures to control the situation.

But one basic question which I touched on briefly in Chapter Three may seem puzzling. Why does China, the most stridently anti-imperialist nation on earth not take back the tiny colony on her doorstep from the waning British imperialists? It is a standing joke in Hong Kong that China could do so militarily 'with a telephone call'.

Hong Kong island was annexed by Britain in 1841 and Kowloon, on the adjoining mainland, in 1860. Extensions inland from Kowloon, known as the New Territories, were obtained from China on a lease which runs to 1997.

In answer to past taunts from Moscow that Mao was applying double standards in tolerating this 'vicious survival of imperialist colonialism on China's doorstep while advocating adventurous policies to others', Peking had said it intended to settle matters peacefully. In their most formal statement on the topic prior to the 1967 riots the Chinese Communists said in 1963, 'With regard to the outstanding issues, which are a legacy from the past, we have always held that, when conditions are ripe, they should be settled peacefully through negotiations and that pending a settlement, the *status quo* should be maintained. Within this category are the questions of Hong Kong, Kowloon and Macao . . .'

In press commentaries during the months of rioting Peking said: 'Hong Kong is Chinese territory . . . the present is no longer the old days when British colonialism forcibly seized Hong Kong. Our fellow countrymen there are now backed by their powerful socialist motherland. Is it conceivable that Hong Kong will for ever remain under British Imperialism? Of course not, a thousand times no, ten thousand times no!' More recently in the autumn of 1969 China Watchers in Hong Kong got wind of an alleged new slogan which promised that 'the Chinese people will present Hong Kong as a humble gift to Chairman Mao in the 1970's'. It was not published officially in Peking. But since it was the first such slogan of its kind reported since the 1949 Communist take-over more attention was paid to it than to run-of-the-mill party slogans. Its exact interpretation, nevertheless, remained an open question. The fact is that Hong Kong's continued colonial existence is of considerable advantage to Peking. It is estimated that China earns at the very least £250 million of foreign exchange annually from the colony in direct trade and remittances of money to families and friends in China from Overseas Chinese. And not the least of the disadvantages involved in the return of the colony to China would be the necessary take-over by Peking of nearly 4 million free-thinking minds used to a non-Communist way of life.

Perhaps it can be said briefly that it appears that in the immediate future Peking has better and more pressing domestic things to do than take over Hong Kong from Britain. A stilted, slightly infuriating phrase often used by Foreign Ministry officials in Peking when turning down correspondents' requests for interviews, visits to factories, communes or in fact anything at all, can perhaps be accurately employed here: 'It is at present inappropriate.'

It is for these reasons, I believe, that reprisals and ultimatums over Hong Kong were still the chosen course in Peking in 1967, rather than any outright attempt to take back the colony.

In late 1966, as the Cultural Revolution boiled up, Peking put pincer-like pressure on Macao. Influential Communists in the tiny Portuguese colony south-west of Hong Kong were supported by Communist Chinese gunboats sailing threateningly off-shore and the Portuguese quickly submitted to humiliating demands which gave virtual control of Macao to Peking. But interestingly, I have since heard from Western diplomats that Peking allegedly refused an offer by Portugal to hand back Macao to China completely. China, it seems, was satisfied with a visible and humiliating victory over the colonial power.

This may have led local Chinese Communists in Hong Kong to believe that the dosage could be repeated as before with the British Crown Colony.

The trouble began in mid-May, 1967, with what appeared to be innocuous labour disputes at a plastic flower factory and a cement factory. Possibly the later riots were fostered independently by the Hong Kong Communists in the belief that they needed to demonstrate their Maoist purity against the background of mounting hysteria in China itself. Or possibly they were encouraged from Peking, to provide a distraction and a rallying cause to counteract the growing dissension and factional violence at home. In any event it appears that the bitter struggle that developed got beyond the control of all three parties concerned, the Hong Kong Communists, the Peking Government and the British Government in the shape of the Hong Kong administration.

Peking became involved in a battle of face with Whitehall and when Whitehall refused to kowtow to order in Portuguese fashion, the British diplomats in Peking in general and myself in particular were the easiest targets on which Mao's government could pick with impunity. That it took two years to persuade Britain to release all the news workers against whom I was held hostage probably surprised the Chinese leaders a little and eventually, I believe, embarrassed them, at least privately, quite a lot.

Six months of unrest in the Wai Chiao Pu reached its zenith in

August. For a few days the Ministry was under the control of a hot-headed extremist who apparently ordered both the invasion of my house and the sacking of the British Mission. I have learned since my release that this man was himself later dragged before a 'struggle meeting' and made to lower his head and admit his guilt as a 'swaggering law-defying mischief maker and a demon'. He was said in Red Guard newspapers to have exceeded his authority, disregarded the international repercussions of his actions and taken steps which had an 'irreparable influence on China's international reputation and foreign relations'. He appears to have been supported by a group of ultra-leftists near the top who were purged later in 1967.

He was Yao Teng-shan.

Foreign Minister Chen Yi was under constant attack from Red Guards during the spring and summer of 1967. He allegedly refused to allow Red Guard groups to be formed in the foreign affairs system. On many days I saw large groups of youths crowding round the gates of the Foreign Ministry compound with loudspeaker vans and I cabled reports of running fights with fists and blunt instruments in the street outside. The Foreign Ministry apparatus like that of the party throughout China was having to defend itself against the onslaughts of radical Red Guard groups who had been told by Mao, 'rebellion is justified'. This may help explain some of the Ministry's actions of that summer.

Then the intensity of attacks on the Foreign Minister heightened as the scale of disorder throughout China mounted in response to the new Maoist-inspired campaign against President Liu Shao-chi. I saw posters on the Ministry walls reporting that Red Guard groups barred by Premier Chou from taking part in meetings to criticise Chen Yi had broken in, fought with Ministry officials and broken open secret archives shouting 'What's so terrific about secrets anyway? To hell with them!'

The Wuhan Incident seemed to strengthen the hands of the 'ultra-leftists' in the leadership around Mao who advocated force and extreme measures to overcome opposition. One of these, Wang Li, who was kidnapped with the Public Security Minister, is reported in the Red Guard press after his return from Wuhan to have pursued an ambition to take control of the Foreign Ministry from the beleaguered Chen Yi. He apparently chose Yao Teng-shan to act as his lieutenant in the Ministry. Yao was an unknown diplomat until he was expelled from Indonesia in April after the trouble involving Overseas Chinese there. From then onwards he is said to have championed the Red Guard groups attacking Chen Yi.

I was at Peking airport to see him emerge from the airliner which brought him from Djakarta. He held a framed portrait of Mao, garlanded with red flowers, above his head as he walked down the plane's steps. He had been chargé d'affaires in Djakarta and was hailed as a 'red diplomatic fighter' on his return. An official of the Information Department had telephoned inviting me to the airport for the welcome, saying Yao and another expelled diplomat would be 'returning home triumphantly'. A high-powered delegation of party and government leaders, including Chou En-lai and Chiang Ching, Mao's wife, were there to greet him.

I saw Yao again at a three-hour press conference on the Indonesian situation on May 13th. I sat a few feet from him in the Peking Hotel as he smashed his fist repeatedly on the table and shouted a quotation from Mao, 'If we are attacked then we will certainly counter-attack'. He was answering a question as to whether China would break diplomatic relations with Indonesia.

A tall, heavily-built, square-faced Chinese with heavy jowls, Yao Teng-shan had an air of menace. Looking back to my report of that day I find I wrote: 'Yao Teng-shan thumped his fist repeatedly on the table and in a voice that often rose to a shout said the whole of Indonesia was dotted with concentration camps and millions of Indonesians had been slaughtered.' From this memory of him I can well imagine him ordering the Red Guard mob into my house – and the attack on the British Mission.

He is reported to have functioned as Foreign Minister for some fourteen days from about August 7th, at a time when perhaps the Party's top leadership was too preoccupied with domestic troubles to restrain him and his backers. I have already described the outbreak of anti-foreign attacks in August in an earlier chapter and for these Yao was probably responsible. But his career seemed to end abruptly after the British Mission burning, although how he or Wang Li, his backer, who also disappeared from view were dealt with by the leadership is not known.

Red Guard newspapers reported Yao's downfall. One report in early November said: 'Yao Teng-shan, an individual adventurist of the Khrushchev type and a political pickpocket has at last been dragged out for trial by the proletarian revolutionaries. This is gratifying, very gratifying indeed! On the morning of October 26th Yao Teng-shan was dragged back by the Second Foreign Languages Institute Red Guards to be struggled against. In the afternoon he was dragged out for criticism and repudiation . . . In the evening he was dragged up to a platform by our Red Guard fighters for trial before the masses.

'Under the cloak of a red diplomatic fighter he was once a swaggering law-defying mischief maker. However when the revolutionary masses fired questions at him he simply opened his mouth, seemingly tongue-tied and utterly disgraced. He had to lower his head and admit his guilt. The pipe dream of Yao Teng-shan, the demon, came to an abrupt, disastrous end!'

In another newspaper report Yao was described as 'a typical hypocrite, a thug sneaking here and there undermining the great Cultural Revolution and an out-and-out big political gambler with personal ambition'.

Moderate influence was gradually reasserted in the Foreign Ministry, in keeping with the general trend in the Cultural Revolution throughout China. Chou En-lai was reported in the Red Guard press to have deplored the burning of the British Mission and Mao's wife labelled it 'extreme anarchism'. On October 7th the party's Central Committee and the State Council issued a directive banning unorganised, hostile demonstrations against foreigners. Struggle by force against Foreign Ministry personnel was banned in a directive by Chou En-lai. This reversal of ultra-left influence was reflected in tough, nationwide directives from the party, government and army forbidding Red Guard seizures of arms and equipment from the People's Liberation Army and giving the soldiers orders to fire to defend themselves. The violent phase was damped down.

The Wai Chiao Pu returned to a semblance of order and Chen Yi up to that time survived – although twenty-seven pounds lighter according to Mao Tse-tung. He is reported as saying 'How can Chen be struck down. He has been with us forty years and has so many achievements. But he has lost twenty-seven pounds in weight. I cannot show him to foreign guests in this condition.'

Although the August excesses were clearly later regretted to some extent by the Maoist leaders, they had been committed to holding me in harsh solitary confinement, presumably by the rashness of Yao and his Red Guard followers. So although the conditions under which I was held were eased slightly in November – as were restrictions on the movements of British diplomats in Peking – after the purges of the ultra-leftists, they never felt themselves able to correct the situation and appear to back down. In October 1969 when I was released I saw the gutted ruin of the British Mission still standing stark and untouched. No move had been made towards repairing it and there was never any hint of the sense of embarrassment, betrayed in wall posters and Red Guard newspapers, being expressed to Britain.

So although the frenzied events of the 1967 summer should not be seen as the outcome of carefully-considered foreign policy planning by an efficient, smoothly-functioning government, the opportunity to set things right afterwards was never taken by those who purged the men directly responsible. Thus they added their sanction and authority to the acts.

There is one last factor in this hard luck story. I was one of the last foreigners living in a house mixed up with the general population of Peking away from the two diplomatic compounds. The Chinese authorities had been waiting until leases on such houses outside the compounds expired, then compelling the occupants to move into apartments within the compounds. The lease on my house expired some eight months after my house arrest began. The house, with a high-walled courtyard, made an ideal prison, and it had a small enclosed space for exercise, far away from other foreigners. Had the lease expired nine months before I should certainly have been moved into a flat in one of the two compounds where, if I had been put under house arrest, I would have been living cheek-by-jowl with other foreigners. I would have been much more difficult to guard without attracting embarrassing attention and it would have been impossible for me to take outside exercise without being seen. The rigorous solitary confinement would have been impossible, unless I had been taken off to a real prison. This the Chinese never seemed inclined to do. And the flats didn't have the kind of small rooms where I could have been isolated from my belongings either.

How's that for a hard luck story?

CHAPTER TWENTY-TWO

Red Book

The twelve-foot square room in which I was to spend nearly two years had bare brown floorboards that squeaked when I walked up and down. One window looked into the courtyard and the other window faced a blank, grey wall three feet away – the high wall of the adjoining restaurant. Two blackboards were propped on chairs under the courtyard window. They bore Mao's quotations in white chalk. First they faced the bed then later they were moved to face the chair on which I sat. They were just five feet away at eye level when I was seated.

I ate my meals from a wooden typing desk. Its top measured about five feet by two feet. It had three drawers and these were the only storage spaces in the room. I was allowed no wardrobe and had to hang my few clothes on the door. I was allowed no curtain at the large courtyard window. This came to mean that when dawn came up around four thirty a.m. in the summer sleeping was difficult. One of my single beds from upstairs with a comfortable mattress had been brought down. Each morning the boilerman, Lao Chiao, briefly swept and dusted the bare room. The distempered walls were an ugly mess of slogans in black Chinese characters. Paint and glue had been spattered around in the process of applying the slogans and portraits of Mao. There were two portraits of him, one large coloured one over the door to the washroom and one small coloured one which was pinned to the wall near the typing desk so that it was inches from my eyes. This small one had a reddish-brown smear on it, down one side away from the image of the Chairman and I often wondered if this too might have been, like that stain on the cell bunk, from Ming Ming. There was no portrait in the washroom and lavatory – the only room not graced with the picture's presence. There was a curtain at the window facing the high grey wall. A glass fanlight above the door leading into the passage allowed the passage light to shine into the room at night, serving the dual purpose of keeping me awake sometimes and allowing the guards to see into the room from the courtyard after I switched off my light.

I was allowed to close the door into the passage only while I ate my meals at around ten a.m., one p.m. and six p.m. – and to sleep. The cook went home immediately after delivering the tray at six p.m. and the dirty dishes stayed with me on a chair in the corner until the next morning when he collected them.

Hour after hour I walked slowly back and forth. From the passage door into the washroom, turn left and up to the space between bath and lavatory, turn and back again. On the return trip I would be face to face with the guard sitting on a chair in the dining-room watching through the door into the room. The typing desk at which I sat was set against the wall away from the line of the two doors so I was not constantly in the guards' vision. But frequently the duty guard left his chair to come into the room to see what I was doing.

And I always contrived to be doing nothing interesting. I came to recognise by the squeak of the guards' boots on the floorboards whether or not they had passed the point where they normally turned to go out into the yard to visit the outside lavatory. Whenever I heard a guard's footsteps I prepared to hide what I was doing until the footsteps hit the 'sounding boards' that indicated they were bound for the outside door. Since my door was next to the outside door it was a fine distinction but I learned to make it very accurately. My sense of hearing became very acute in isolation. So too did my sense of smell. I learned to recognise what the next meal would be from the faint smells emanating from the kitchen in the basement below. And I came to dislike the body smell of the guards when they crowded into the room all at once on occasions to look at me or inspect something. My eyes, too, I noticed became hypersensitive but in a different way. I would often think I saw one of the many paint spots on the walls dart sideways and would quickly turn my head thinking it a spider, a gecko or a cockroach. I got used to noticing the paint specks dashing around, especially when I was walking slowly back and forth at night in the light of the single neon-strip tube which lit the room with an uncomfortable glare – and a constant irritating buzzing noise.

On November 6th I wrote in my diary: 'After three days the new accommodation is becoming as oppressive as the old.' I asked the cook to ask the guards if I could get some old copies of the *Peking Review* from upstairs to read. He told me I would have to wait. The guards had telephoned the 'Wai Chiao Pu'. This was the first firm admission that the Foreign Ministry Information Department, not the Public Security Bureau, was ultimately controlling my every move. The guards later even checked with the Ministry by telephone when I asked if I could send a pair of shoes to be repaired.

The courtyard window was opened in the morning and closed at four when the boilerman left. It had a lock specially fixed to the outside. The wire screens were not allowed open. My diary records: 'The overall impression of the last three days in the new 'cell' is one of settling down again to a terrible empty routine. But I have maintained my calm absolutely and intend to continue to do so. I have considered going on a hunger strike for something to read.' But I never got any further than considering it. There already seemed enough to contend with in the way of physical discomfort.

On Wednesday, November 8th another long silence was broken. 'This has been one of the happiest days,' I wrote, 'because this morning I got a letter from Mother after eighty-two days. It was wonderful and I was so happy to hear from her.'

A few days later there was another providential act. After writing some figures for money he required, one of the domestic staff left a pencil on the window-sill. I snatched it up and hid it away and when its owner returned a few minutes later I said that it had not been left in the room, perhaps he'd mislaid it downstairs. Perhaps my guardian angel had been hovering around again, as she might have been on the occasion when I secretly got my first ball-point pen and when I got the new refill for it in the nick of time. I say this because a day or so later the refill of the ball-point pen broke and flooded and the only writing implement that remained to me was the newly-won pencil! I continued writing my diary with it, hiding it in my slipper in between times.

Eight days after my request the cook was allowed to go upstairs to my office and bring down some old *Peking Reviews* for me to read. I eked them out one a day, thirty or so pages of turgid propaganda, but it was better than nothing.

I told my diary: 'I long for newspapers and books without Mao in them. The newspapers have begun now to put Mao's picture on the front and sometimes on every other page with the rays of the sun glowing from it. It gets crazier and crazier. Otherwise the days are flat and quiet and long.'

To fill these days I cast around desperately for things to do. I cut strings of paper dollies from the pages of the *People's Daily* with my nail scissors, tearing the pages out very quietly in case the guards heard and came in to accuse me of insulting the sacred writings. But cutting out paper dollies is not an occupation that stimulates for long. So I turned to something else. There was a broken alarm clock in the room and I tried to mend this with the only material at my disposal. I undid the back, cleaned it thoroughly and greased its works with a bottle of mouthwash! It went for a few hours then stopped, never to go again, its works gummed up in a sticky mess. I was scraping the bottom of the barrel again for diversions. A thermometer put on the wall when the room was the office for my Chinese translators was left there. And as I walked back and forth hour after hour I converted Centigrade temperatures to Fahrenheit and back again endlessly, multiplying by nine over five and five over nine, adding and subtracting thirty-two and checking my answers against the two scales shown on the thermometer. This gave me the feeling I was exercising my mind and not letting it rot.

On November 13th I had my first contact with Chinese officialdom since my house arrest began four months before. I was sitting on my bed in the afternoon when the small, bespectacled, English-speaking cadre of the Public Security Bureau who had escorted me home from the Foreign Ministry in July, entered the room and motioned me from the bed with a perfunctory gesture. The shift leader I had mentally named 'Stone-face' because of his sharply-chiselled, impassive features led in his team of two behind the interpreter.

'Get out your red book,' said the interpreter. 'You are to read with us.'

I said I would listen. Had I got a red book? Yes I had. Then I must read with them. I didn't wish to read with them. If they wished to read Mao Tse-tung's quotations I had no alternative but to listen. But I declined to read in chorus. After this conversation was repeated several times, the attempt to get me to read with them was dropped. The interpreter with one red book in Chinese in one hand and another in English in the other hand proceeded to chant quotations in unison with the other three.

They wore round khaki caps with red badges of the Tien An Men – Gate of Heavenly Peace – on them. There were red flashes on the lapels of their loose, khaki jackets. Rumpled, blue cotton trousers and heavy British police-style boots completed their uniform. They tossed their chins and clipped their words and glared at me as they intoned the quotations.

Then the English versions read by the interpreter alone: 'The enemy will not perish of himself. Neither the Chinese reactionaries nor the aggressive forces of U.S. imperialism in China will step down from the stage of history of their own accord!'

A pause and then the second, seemingly spelling doom to my way of life. 'The Socialist system will eventually replace the Capitalist system: this is an objective law independent of Man's will. However much the reactionaries try to hold back the wheel of history, sooner or later revolution will take place and will inevitably triumph!'

Both quotations had been among those chalked on boards while I was in the eight-foot square cell and at that time I knew them both from memory. I resisted the urge to surprise them by reciting the words, sensing something important would follow.

Chairs were produced and all five of us sat down. I prayed inwardly that this meant a visit to the Ministry and release. Consulting his notebook the bespectacled interpreter said he had 'some points to make'.

Then he read them out. 'One. You must obey the guards.' He mentioned that I had disobeyed them on the morning I leapt up and closed the door of my room after 'Loud Lout' had flung it open. In future I must obey the guards. 'Two. You must have your hair cut. Three. You must keep yourself clean. Four. You must ask the guards if you want anything.'

I seethed when he said I should keep myself clean. Through gritted teeth I said the bath was covered in paint that I had not put there, but nevertheless I did not need to be told to keep myself clean. The insult was intentional and he added to it with the arrogance of his rejoinder. 'We have the right to remind you. We have the health of these men to think of.' He motioned towards my guards. I bit back my intended reply. If they were that concerned about their health let them leave my house and stay out of it!

I also said I had cut my own hair for nearly four months and would continue to do so. The thought of having it cropped and in that tiny room, too, seemed humiliating and I tried to hold out against it.

After consulting with the three guards the interpreter said I should clean the bath myself. I said nothing.

Then the interpreter asked if I had any questions.

'How long am I to be held here?'

'I have not been told that.'

It was cold, could I get some warm clothes from upstairs?

'Yes, that will be all right because you are to be allowed outside soon.'

I started at this. Outside exercise after four months meant a big change in my restricted life.

'When?' I asked quickly.

'That depends,' was the non-committal reply.

I asked to be allowed to send a reassuring cable to my mother, to be allowed to get some books and he said he would 'find out'.

Then the meeting broke up and I was conducted upstairs by the guards to the bathroom where I was allowed to collect all my toilet articles from the cabinet there. Previously, toothpaste, soap and other articles had been bought for me outside by the cook or boilerman. I was also allowed to get more warm clothes.

That evening I was so excited by the visit and by talking – although only briefly – in conversational English that I could not eat my meal. In my diary I wrote: 'I saw the visit as an excuse to give me concessions and they started with a reprimand about closing the door on "Loud Lout" only to save face. The visit occurred on a double thirteen – the 13th of November and the anniversary of the thirteenth week.'

In the evening 'Stone-face' came in making lots of quick gestures and eventually took away a box of Anadin headache tablets – and even packets of Coldrex pills for colds that I had brought down from upstairs. This was clearly to prevent me trying to use them to commit suicide.

The next day for the first time since the Red Guards had invaded me eighty-eight days earlier I stepped out into the fresh air of the courtyard. I was allowed to walk up and down for thirty minutes. The yard was twenty-two paces long.

I wrote of it: 'It was marvellous to feel the wind and see the sky and the tops of trees above the courtyard walls. It was beautiful, with the tip of one golden roof of the Forbidden City just visible in the sunlight, the sky blue and the berries red on the courtyard tree. The air was cold and crisp.'

On the afternoon of this same day I defied the guards openly for the first time, unadvisedly as it turned out.

A barber came to cut my hair. On impulse I refused, again feeling keenly the humiliation of the confined room, the watching guards and Chinese domestic staff – and the likelihood of being cropped. The guards gesticulated and ordered me to have it cut. I refused to sit down. They eventually withdrew without forcing me to have it cut. There was a lot of telephoning. I almost felt sorry for the barber who kept saying in English, 'But the Government has sent me, the Government has sent me'. He seemed appalled at the prospect of returning to say he had not been able to carry out a government order.

Almost immediately I had qualms about refusing. The intimidation I felt at that time came out clearly in my diary. I wrote that night: 'I have cursed myself for my foolishness and know not what tomorrow will bring in the way of a reprisal. I shall never get my requests for books and permission to send a cable now. I have thought I might get beaten up again by the Red Guards, be taken off to the Public Security headquarters or otherwise punished for disobeying the Government order to have my hair cut.'

The next day outside exercise, begun only the day before, was stopped, and in addition the courtyard window, normally un-latched from the outside each morning, was kept tightly closed all day. No haircut, no exercise or fresh air. It was the expected reprisal.

It was clear my recalcitrance on this occasion would get me nowhere and it seemed, in the light of reflection, a foolish thing to have made a stand on. More so because it had halted the longed-for outside exercise, curtailed my fresh air supply and jeopardised my request for books and permission to send cables. After struggling with an uneasy mind and my pride all day I told the guards through Lao Chiao I had changed my mind and would agree to have a haircut.

Scenting victory they crowded into the room. I must apologise in writing. A pen and paper were brought. I gritted my teeth and wrote a single line saying I regretted the previous day's refusal and was fully prepared to have a haircut now. The paper was borne away triumphantly to the Public Security Bureau head-quarters. It was the nearest I came to a written 'confession' during my confinement.

The next day the window was re-opened and I was allowed out again for half an hour.

But still my days were empty. The entire guard was changed except for one man and the new ones took to giving me ridiculous orders to close the window soon after it was opened, simply to assert themselves.

On Sunday, November 26th I wrote: 'I want to record my complete feeling of emptiness at the moment. Often in my prayers, said now kneeling at the side of the paint-spattered bath, I ask to be delivered from this "vacuum of hell". I pray frequently now and have come to look on Sundays as a special day and one from which to review the past week and look forward to the next. There have been no letters for nine days. Each morning I have hoped and been disappointed. I have somehow developed a dead feeling which makes it hard for me to make my mind to do anything active. In some moments I am seized with despair but most of the time I can contemplate long weeks ahead as empty as this without any feeling. It now seems as if I shall never get out of here. Life seems to be totally concerned with being a prisoner now ... My days are: rise around nine fifteen, do Yoga, shave, dress, go back into washroom to pray, breakfast, walk inside, allowed out into courtyard, walk inside again, lunch, brood and lie on bed thinking, walk, read or think, pray, dinner, lie on bed, walk, read or think, Yoga at 23.00, bed ... it is becoming in-creasingly difficult to remain enthusiastic about Yoga – or anything else for that matter ... Oh God please help me! My life seems becalmed in a flat sea never to become mobile again. Yesterday I was struck by the great length of time I have been under house arrest. From the heat of July to the freezing days in the "prison" courtyard. I try to tell myself that in the future you will look back on this with a smile but it is very difficult to see that now.' (Typing those words into the manuscript of this book in January

1970 I gladly smiled to justify that optimism of November 1967.)

About that time I discovered some new reading matter. Each evening as I ate my solitary meal I would look up at the empty window-sill and try to imagine seeing books on it. Perhaps next Sunday will see them there, I often told myself. I was desperate for reading. Then in the bathroom I found it. I noticed, one afternoon, an elastic band round a bottle of T.C.P. liquid antiseptic I had brought down from the bathroom. Turning it round I discovered a little instruction leaflet tucked inside the elastic band. My first impulse was to sit down and read it immediately. But then I checked myself. I would keep it to read with my supper at six o'clock.

I have always disliked eating alone. Forking food into one's face is a fairly base activity when robbed of all its civilised trimmings and I always tried to keep what little pleasant reading I had for meal times. At least that way I was slightly preoccupied. But I had long since exhausted my small collection of literature.

So that evening as I punted my chopsticks I eagerly absorbed the literary elegance of such phrases as: 'Influenza, as a precautionary measure during epidemics, use night and morning as for colds.' And 'Mouthwash: use daily diluted with about five parts water after meals.' And 'Chilblains, aching feet, athletes foot: freely apply undiluted.'

My reading made it a memorable meal!

One guard, soon after I was moved into the twelve-foot square room, made great dumb-show play of defining its limits. I had been walking right up to the open doorway as I paced back and forth. He came very deliberately and planted one large boot down beside a crack in the floorboards that ran across the doorway. The boot was on his side of the crack and he shook his head and hand to indicate it was forbidden. He banged his boot down on my side of the crack. And nodded contemptuously. Thus it was indicated to me that the crack in the floorboards was the new boundary of my permitted living space.

CHAPTER TWENTY-THREE

Relief Supplies

But into my confined world of bare, brown floorboards and slogan-daubed walls some light was soon to fall in the shape of books.

My diary for the last day of November sets the scene.

'The days have grown colder. The guards now wear fur hats and today the temperature was twenty-seven degrees. My mood is nondescript. I am looking forward to Christmas but mostly because it will be more time past. There have been no letters since November 17th – thirteen days. It is difficult to know why they have stopped. This is a tremendously empty period. I am glad to see November go. It failed to fulfil early promise.'

I drew up my Third Twenty-Three-Day Plan on that day, formalising my earlier slogan 'Calm to Christmas' as its title. Its subtitle was 'Dominate circumstances and endure emptiness'.

The rest read: 'The main method to be employed is Yoga. Absolute self-control for twenty-three days is the target. Pray. Be your own encouragement. Be more disciplined, allow no daily hopes and expectations. Ignore the daily arrival of the paper. Material targets from upstairs: suits, shoe brush, scarf, gloves and chess set. Neutralise relations with the guards. New intensive study of Yoga. Don't swear.

'Good luck, boy!'

Having allowed me a dribble of letters from Shirley in the early months, some from a friend in the British Mission and just one from my mother, my mail had finally dried up and was to remain so until Christmas. This was the first phase of a long tantalising game which those supervising my confinement played with my mail. Every single letter that arrived was tremendously important to me because it was the only link I had with outside reality. Deliberate delays and the withholding of my mail in the succeeding months drove me into great states of anxiety and anger that

I was often hard put to conceal. It seemed the most sadistic, insidious form of mental torture to me then. This was why I included in my plan an effort to ignore the arrival of the newspaper instead of trying to see through the courtyard window whether a letter was tucked inside it. The cook or the guards fetched it from the gate after the bell was rung about four o'clock each afternoon. The daily disappointment became almost unbearable so I endeavoured not to think about it.

The anti-swearing proviso I put in as my language, muttered to myself under my breath, had deteriorated to a fairly foul level with my depressed mood. It was another exercise in self-discipline. I had decided to 'neutralise' my relations with the guards to avoid incidents like that of refusing a haircut because it upset my efforts to retain a calm mind.

Then on December 4th 'relief' arrived. The cook returned from what I thought was his afternoon shopping expedition. But on the carrier of his bicycle as he came into the courtyard I saw, instead of the usual pile of cabbages, a brown cardboard box bearing an inscription on its side in blue and red letters that was delightful to my eyes – 'Carlsberg Lager, Copenhagen'.

The cook carried the box into the dining-room and the guards closed the door. I attempted to contain my excitement as I paced back and forth trying to guess what it was. Possibly all the letters withheld in the past months, I thought. There was a lot of telephoning and checking. Then I was handed a few letters from John Weston, my chess-playing friend, and his wife Sally and other friends in the British Mission. A few minutes later the letters were followed by the delivery of the box itself into my hands – the one and only gift of any kind to reach me during the two years. The box from John and his wife contained ten books, packets of cheroots, bars of chocolate, sweets, a toothbrush, razor blades and screwed up pages of the *Daily Telegraph* and *The Spectator*. John had cleverly torn up the newspaper and magazine pages and stuffed them into the box to make it look like padding, to get them past the guards. I was able to piece them together to read.

My diary records my reaction: 'My joy was immense. It was Christmas come early. This is what I had been praying for and never expected from outside. After examining my gifts I went to pray and give thanks in the washroom. The box, sent on

November 14th, appeared to be a reward for my determination in the new twenty-three-day plan. Soon I was hiding some of the books like a squirrel hoarding his winter nuts, some under the mattress, others under the bath in the washroom, in case there was a sudden change of mind and I lost my new treasures. Their arrival came as a tremendous relief after so long with an empty mind. The afternoon sped by as I read the prefaces to the books and reviewed my treasure generally. Perhaps the most exciting things were the newspaper and magazine. I spent almost the whole of the rest of the day reading every word in them. New drink tests had been introduced in England with breathalysers. There had been a Cabinet reshuffle and all the beauty and greatness of Britain flowed back to me as I read *The Spectator* review of books, plays, etc. I more or less decided not to touch the eatable things until Christmas in case nothing else comes – and also as another act of will. Until they arrived I was still trying to make one *Peking Review* last a day. This had become very monotonous.'

The books were mostly light reading, some Dennis Wheatley thrillers, four books by George Mikes the Hungarian-born humorist, Spike Milligan's *Puckoon*, a Penguin book of 100 crosswords, Somerset Maugham's *Of Human Bondage*.

Ten days or so later I wrote in my diary. 'I have just emerged from a kind of euphoria after reading my books for more than a week. I didn't think much about my predicament.'

Three weeks after I reversed my refusal to submit voluntarily to a haircut, another barber arrived and did his work on me in the twelve-foot square room with a guard standing by his side. He sheared off great chunks of lank hair that had accumulated since July. I had only snipped gingerly at it with my nail scissors during that time. Before the barber began I had asked if I could pay for it and this was accepted. And although it was cut short I was not given a prison 'crop'. It was a relief to have a haircut after nearly five months.

About this time an incident occurred which remains starkly in my memory as an example of the Kafkaesque nature of my life. About eleven o'clock or later each night I closed the door through which the guards stared into the room. By this time they had settled down for the night on their camp beds in the dining-room with the lights out and the door closed. One of them had dragged a chair out into the passageway between their room and mine to watch over me through the night. The chair was planted down outside the thin, ill-fitting door of my room, a distance of only five or six feet from the foot of my bed which was right against the wall.

I was very conscious of the closeness of the guard. So each night to prepare myself mentally for sleep I closed the door and retreated into the washroom, closing that door too, spread out my blanket on the stone tiles and did a session of Yoga exercises. Afterwards I sometimes read in bed in an additional effort to summon sleep.

The light in the washroom was fitted into the ceiling. Its plastic cover was dirty and contained the remains of many long-dead moths that had somehow found their way inside it. It cast a very dull glow in that room where both windows were covered over with black paint. The crudely-daubed slogans on walls which had not been decorated for about three years and on which the plaster was crumbling in places, gave the room a dimly grotesque atmosphere.

One night around midnight I was lying on my blanket beside the bath quietly assuming the Plough posture. I was flat on my back bringing my feet and legs up to touch my finger tips, my arms being stretched out along the floor above my head.

I heard the soft footfalls across the twelve-foot square room and remained motionless in the Plough position as the door opened quietly. In the doorway stood 'Stone-Face'. He wore a heavy leather jacket over his khaki uniform, a short belted leather jacket, against the cold. His eyes flicked round the dim room then came back to rest on me. His expression was blankly unchanging, hostile. I remained motionless on the floor, toes touching finger-tips above head, looking back at him. I resisted the urge to scramble to my feet in embarrassment. I thought hard of the Yoga teaching to remain calm in the face of everything. My heart thumped but I managed to retain an outward show of absolute calm and we continued to look wordlessly at one another. After long moments he turned and walked out, half closing the door behind him. I came down from the Plough posture, lay flat and waited for my heart to stop thumping. I remember shaking my head from side to side at the weird unreality of my life.

A few days later new 'rules' were laid down for me, almost certainly as a result of this incident. When I closed the passage door at night the light was to be immediately extinguished. I was not allowed to close the door of the washroom unless I was using the lavatory. This cut out my reading in bed and my midnight Yoga session.

But Christmas was coming – the first of two in solitary confinement.

CHAPTER TWENTY-FOUR

Christmas 1967

Christmas began early on December 22nd when a guard walked into my room with a Christmas card held just above his knee.

I was sitting polishing my shoes. Spit and polishing them to be more exact. For a week or so before Christmas I spent each afternoon working away with a rag making tiny circles in the polish on the toe-caps of a pair of brown shoes. I did not wear them but worked each afternoon increasing the shine in the time-honoured style of the recruit 'bulling up' his boots. It was another time filler and I was going to wear them on Christmas day. A request to get a warm scarf, the shoes, shoe brushes and polish from upstairs had been granted a few days earlier. I had been accompanied up to my bedroom by two guards who watched eagle-eyed as I sought out these things.

As I heightened the shine on the 22nd in preparation for Christmas a young, fur-hatted guard entered with a small envelope held in his right hand. He kept his arm straight down at his side so the card was held at a level just above his knee. He stood before me with it in this fashion, motioning towards it with his chin, indicating that I should take it. In the Chinese mind this meant that I would have to bend to get it and so abase myself before him. I had seen this done at the gates of the British Mission when demonstrators were presenting a petition to first secretary Anthony Blishen. As he had reached for it the Chinese holding it had begun to move it lower and lower. But Blishen snatched it adroitly away before the game went too far.

Now with five weeks behind me in which there had been not a single letter delivered to the house, the sight of a small envelope bearing an English stamp before me was something akin to what the olive branch in the mouth of the dove must have been to Noah. The guard looked at me, then down at the low-held card and back. I stared at him for a moment in a way which I hope conveyed my contempt for his piteous foolishness, leaned forward and took the envelope. He practically skipped out, I suppose to report another victory over the class enemy to his comrades in the dining-room.

Inside the envelope was a Christmas card from Shirley with a coy-looking, blushing, pink girl-elephant on the front, fluttering long eyelashes at a rather bigger, clumsier-looking but obviously eager male of the species. It was my one Christmas card for Christmas 1967.

The next day cables from Reuters general manager Gerald Long and managing editor Stuart Underhill arrived – my first word from Reuters since my house arrest began. They sent good wishes and I searched in vain for some sort of grounds for optimism. The next day in answer to a request I was allowed to write brief cables to my mother, Reuters and Shirley. It was the first word from me allowed to go beyond the walls of my house since the Red Guard invasion four months earlier and I restricted my messages to simple statements that I was well despite difficulties so as to make sure they got past the Foreign Ministry's scrutiny. The cables were taken away on the 24th and although they contained not more than about thirty words all told, were held for three days before being returned for despatch on December 27th.

The bare details of Christmas Day 1967 are recorded in my diary:

'I rose at nine getting into the washroom under cover of the chanting and singing of the guards. After doing Yoga, washing and shaving I dressed in my suit for the first time for five months and put on a tie. When I appeared walking back and forth the guards who were having a nine-man meeting in the dining-room and who had never seen me in anything except my very scruffy leather jacket, looked twice and seemed "suitably" impressed. I felt very good. Breakfast was normal then after a walk outside, to begin my day's treat I sucked a Polo mint. The mints were among the eatable things in the December 4th parcel which I have not touched since then.

'I read and laughed a lot at George Mikes' book *How to be Inimitable*, a skit on the effortless superiority of the British temperament. I continued reading this after lunch then opened a bar of chocolate and had a cheroot. After this I walked again for one and a half hours. I offered the cook a cheroot and he refused

as did the guards whom he asked on my behalf. I offered the box
to them in a rush of Christmas good-will. Reaction was nil. I
then completed a *Daily Telegraph* crossword in the Penguin book
in one hour seven minutes and was proud of this achievement.
Dinner was a surprise. I got a dish of beef and a dish of fish,
presumably as a treat, without any explanation. Then I again read
George Mikes, laughing a lot. This and some quiet reflection took
me up to the regular walking time around eight forty-five. I smoked
one of my bigger cheroots during this time but this didn't seem to
impress the guards much! After this I sat down to read the sad
and sentimental opening of Somerset Maugham's *Of Human
Bondage*, which I'd been saving for Christmas. This carried me
quietly up to bedtime at eleven thirty. I prayed about five times
asking for Christmas happiness for my mother and relations and
friends and for release soon for myself. I whistled and sang some
carols during my walks – to myself softly – and knew a quiet kind
of joy. The chocolate and butterscotch tasted good but I didn't
eat much of either. On Christmas Eve just before I was told I
could send cables the quotation boards in the room were changed.
These said: "Imperialism will not last long because it always does
evil things." And: "All reactionaries are paper tigers. In appearance the reactionaries are terrifying but in reality they are not so
powerful. From a long term point of view it isn't the reactionaries
but the people who are really powerful."

'I had half expected them to say: "A HAPPY CHRISTMAS
TO ALL OUR READERS!"'

A week later I dismissed 1967: 'December 31st. Today a bad
year of my life will pass away and I am hopeful that 1968 will
bring better days. But I am also aware my ordeal may not be over
by a long way. Today I was allowed to go upstairs escorted to
get my tiny German fan heater and was able to abandon my
heavy coat which I have previously been wearing all day for
warmth.

'As I sit here on this last day of 1967 two boards face me from
the opposite wall. One talks of "Imperialism not lasting because
it always does evil things". The other says: "All reactionaries are
paper tigers." On the window-sill is a bottle of cold water and a
flask of hot water. The sill also has a dead telephone instrument
and a pile of unreadable newspapers lie there too. Also the dishes
from lunch are on the chair in the corner and my little electric

heater is purring away. On the bed are piled my blankets and sheets. On top a fur collared jacket. Slogans are daubed all over the walls. Furniture: a bare desk, two chairs and in the corner, clean and dirty washing and old *Peking Reviews* are on the empty Carlsberg Lager box from the British Office. On the window-sill are Mao's works, other books, a tin of butterscotch and an empty cigar box. Mao's portrait is on the wall and there are slogans in Chinese too. The windows are sealed up with paper strips to keep out the draughts. One pane remains broken from the night of the invasion. Two books are hidden under the mattress to escape detection in case I am raided again. The sun shines in through the window. Almost every day is bright with sun although the temperature has been as low as fifteen degrees. A few clothes hang on the back of the door. I have nothing to keep my clothes in. In this room I shall see in 1968. I hope to God I shall be out of it soon during 1968 and not see in 1969 in here.

'Writing this is extremely difficult. I have to keep putting it aside and hiding it in case the guards come in. My final diary for the year. God please help me early in 1968.'

I stayed up until midnight and as the year changed I stood and drank a silent toast in warm water to my mother, girl friend, family and friends at home. A few feet away outside the open door I heard the guard fill his mug from his vacuum flask. He had some tea in *his* mug, however.

CHAPTER TWENTY-FIVE

Operation Zhivago

By mid-January I had read the few books that arrived in the parcel from my friends and was again becoming desperate for something new to read. Each passing day I thought of the book a few feet above my head out of reach – *Doctor Zhivago*. It was still lying on the bed where it had been flung contemptuously on the night of the Red Guard invasion, banned from my eyes as revisionist heresy. The bedroom was directly above the twelve-foot square room and when I was escorted there to get warmer clothes under the ever-watchful eyes of the guards I had seen that Boris Pasternak's book was still there.

In late December I asked the guards if I could be allowed to have my own books from upstairs but by January 12th I had received no answer. It was on this day that I worked out a plan to get *Zhivago* despite the ban on it. I had often thought in desperation I would sometime try to slip through the door into the passage unseen and up the stairs to bring things down. But an unwavering watch was kept from just a few feet away on my open door. It was clearly impossible and the prospect of further reprisals, like that over the hair cut, made me reluctant to take risks.

I decided the only possible method was to go upstairs for something else under the usual escort and try to get the book without the guards noticing. To do this I calculated that I needed to get up the stairs six paces ahead of the first guard so that I could quickly turn into the bedroom, grab the book from the bed and hide it under my jacket a moment before he came into the room. From the few times I had been escorted upstairs I anticipated that I would be allowed to go first and would be followed by two guards and either the cook or the boilerman who would do any necessary translating with the few words of English at their command.

I decided to practise the movements of my plan before trying to put it into operation. I took Dennis Wheatley's *Mediterranean Nights* and placed it on the chair in the washroom between the bath and the lavatory, out of the direct line of vision of the guard on watch. Then for two hours I walked back and forth from the door into the passage where the guards watched me, to the chair in the washroom. Each time I turned into the washroom out of the guards' line of vision I took two quick steps towards the chair, snatched up the Wheatley book, thrust it inside my leather jacket and held it under my left armpit by pressing my elbow hard against my side. Then, without breaking the rhythm of my walk I turned and walked back towards the passage door where the guard watched me, still holding the book out of sight. This was to accustom myself to the slightly awkward posture of walking with my left elbow pressed against my side, to make it look as natural as possible, and to adjust to having the guard look at me while I carried something hidden from his sight.

As far as the guard on watch could see I was pacing slowly back and forth as usual for two hours. But each time I went out of his sight in the washroom I tried to snatch the book from the seat of the chair, faster and more cleanly and transfer it under my armpit with a smoother, more fluid motion. I could not remember what position *Zhivago* was lying in on the bed upstairs so I practised with the book lying on the chair at all possible angles. After tucking it under my arm and walking up to the passage door where the guard watched I would turn slowly and go back again, depositing the book on the chair again ready for a further practice snatch next time I returned.

Two hours of this made me confident I could carry out my ruse if I could just get up the stairs those few vital paces ahead. I tried to cover all eventualities, even falling down and having the book drop out of my jacket. I emptied both my jacket pockets and fitted books into them to see if it was reasonable to claim that I already had *Zhivago* in my possession legally and that it had fallen out when I tripped. So much practice, while making me proficient at book snatching, also made me nervous. I was worried about the risk of discovery. I thought about putting it off until later but my desperate mood made me decide to go ahead.

After some hesitation I took off my pillow-case, quietly tore it in two places then showed it to the cook and told him to ask the guards if I could go upstairs to get a new one from the ironing-room cupboard.

I had been careful to check that the chief guard that day was a ruddy-faced man with broad Mongolian-type features, a guard, who from my listening and observing, did not appear to be either too bright, fast-moving or unduly hostile. I had weeks before named him in my mind 'Mongol'. I felt the chances were better with him than any of the sharper, more hostile shift leaders.

The cook went through into the dining-room carrying the torn pillow-case and I listened to the explanation in Chinese holding my breath. Then I heard the cook coming back. '*Hao-la*,' he said. O.K. I had put on my soft-soled slippers to help increase my speed up the stairs and to minimise the risk of falling, instead of the heavier shoes I normally wore at that time of day.

At the words '*Hao-la*' I began moving through the door to the bottom of the stairs trying not to do so with unnatural speed. 'Mongol', bless his heart, was his usual slow-moving self and was reaching for his fur hat. The guards were funny about their hats. They never came into my room or allowed themselves to appear in my vision without their hats. This often led them to scramble their hats back on to their heads quickly if something arose unexpectedly.

'Mongol' was adjusting his hat and coming slowly out of the dining-room towards the bottom of the stairs. Taking full advantage of this stroke of luck I bounded up the stairs, trying to hide my haste a little so as not to arouse their suspicions, and managed to reach the top before 'Mongol' and the cook and another guard were halfway up the second flight.

I turned quickly into the bedroom. There on the bed was the genuine target of my morning's painstaking rehearsal. It had a blue and white cover bearing a picture of Omar Sharif who played the name part in the film. My jacket was half unbuttoned. My heart was thumping at my own audacity and the risk of getting caught in the act. I reached out to the book. A jittery fumble and a scramble to pick it up from the floor? No, a clean snatch! And it went straight under the left armpit. But the guards were now coming through the door so I dropped to my knees and pretended to seek a pillow-case in a bedside cabinet which I knew to be empty. Then hugging the book inside my jacket with my left elbow I turned to face the guards and mumbled something about pillowcases in the ironing room. I went carefully through, opened a cupboard and with the three Chinese crowding at my shoulder to see what I did, I picked out a packet of new pillow-slips. Then carrying these before me in my right hand I indicated I was finished and ready to go downstairs again. They stood back and I again led the way down, walking with great care so as not to stumble and drop my prize. Back in my room I whipped the book from my jacket and slipped it under the small pile of those I'd already read on the window-sill in case the guards should have noticed anything and come in to search me as an afterthought. But the plan went like clockwork. I went into the washroom to congratulate myself then came back to take a peep at it. I remember muttering to myself, 'Marvellous, it's very thick, at least 400 pages'. The quality was not important. That it was long and would occupy more time was important.

In my diary I recorded my elation at the success of what appeared to be my daring plan. 'I was exultant when I came down. Getting the book has made a tremendous difference to my morale, particularly since it was forbidden and I pulled off my trick.'

Later when I had read it I noted: 'One of the most splendid books I have ever read. Stimulating, beautifully tragic and tremendously encouraging in its humanness in the face of mindless Communism.'

In fact *Zhivago* had some 500 pages and by carefully rationing my reading to an hour or two in the evening as I had done with all my books, I read it at the rate of fifty pages a day for ten days. It helped carry me over ten bad days, which would otherwise have been very depressing, until I was allowed access to some of my own books for the first time. Having *Zhivago* for those ten days was important to me because in the bleakness of the Peking winter, despite all my efforts to remain calm and balanced I began to feel an increasing sense of panic at the prospect of having to cope with confined solitude indefinitely. I was slipping into greater and longer-lasting periods of depression that were beginning to frighten me. This was to reach a climax in late February. But on January 23rd after a renewed request I was allowed to go upstairs closely escorted by guards and select some of my own books from a bookcase in the lounge. It was practically a month since I had first made the request. I brought down sixteen precious books and the guards told me that I could read those, then take them back up and exchange them for some more. A request to take all my books down was refused.

I wrote in my diary on January 25th: 'Things have changed greatly since my last diary entry. I had decided to try to get permission to send a note to John Weston at the British Mission asking him to try to get a Bible and some more books to me. I thought even if it did not get past the scrutiny of the Foreign Ministry it would convey my mood. I had intended to say as part of my request to John "Each day is difficult to get through". But as a prelude to this I thought I would ask again for access to my own books. To my amazement after a telephone call to the Ministry and a reply a few minutes later the guard clumped off down the wooden staircase, called the cook who came back up with him and told me "O.K." I still didn't really believe it and went upstairs with them and picked out an armful of books from the lounge. I brought them down and immediately began making elaborate preparations to hide some in case there was a change of mind. I put some in my bed and others in the washroom. I listened carefully to see if there was to be another phone call saying it had been a mistake. But no, I still have them after two days. I thanked God repeatedly for my good fortune. This act of God came at a very desperate time. I was just beginning to feel a very serious danger of having a nervous breakdown of some kind. I was fighting it almost every minute of the day.'

Deepening depressions were coming thick and fast, despite the fact that my exercise periods had been increased from one to two a day, thirty minutes morning and afternoon, on December 27th, and despite the fact that letters were now arriving more frequently. Some from Shirley were reaching my hand four days after being posted in London. I had been confined alone for six months and was beginning to find the weight of isolation pressing on me increasingly. I cast around for new ways to improve my mood and at the end of January I relented in my stubborn refusal to clean out the remains of the Red Guard paint in the bath. During those intervening months since August 18th I had remained determined not to clean the mess out of the bath. Instead I had 'bathed' standing naked in front of the sink. In those days it was very cold and the operation was unpleasant. So eventually I realised that holding

H

out on the 'bath principle' was only hurting me if the confinement was to be a long one. I set to with some scouring powder and after several hours removed the last trace of the paint. The sensual pleasure of lowering myself into the warm water after five months without bathing was an ecstatic moment and I neither regretted holding it off for so long, and even more, did not regret my decision to clean it at last. From then I bathed quietly and carefully in the early morning getting into the washroom under the cover of the noise of the guards' slogan chanting. I did not wish to be stared at while in the bath.

But even the new pleasure of bathing did not help my deteriorating mental state. At the end of January I wrote: 'I could almost say all hope – apart from hope that remains with life itself – all real hope of early release has left me.'

CHAPTER TWENTY-SIX

Super-Ingredient

Lying in bed at night trying not to hear the regular thump of your heart in your chest. Trying to tell yourself it is ridiculous to think that because it is clearly and insistently audible you must be ready any moment for an overwhelming pain to strike through it and end your life. Sweating slightly as you try to rid yourself of this obsession.

Trying not to swallow the saliva that gathers in your mouth every few moments in order to avoid stimulating the glands that will produce more and fill your mouth to capacity again and cause you to swallow again, setting up an unbreakable rhythm that will have you swallowing saliva every few moments throughout the day. Trying to think of something that will let you forget swallowing but finding that the harder you try the more frequently you swallow.

Trying to ignore and dismiss as inconsequential tiny flecks of brown that float across the vision of the eye as you walk back and forth in the courtyard.

Trying to tell yourself it is absolutely impossible for a human being to commit suicide in his sleep. But nevertheless being haunted by the vision of being able to control yourself in the depths of wretched depressions by day but somehow losing that control to the subconscious as you sleep. And conceiving it might be possible that as the misery deepens into unimaginable dimensions, the desire to remove yourself from it will win through as you sleep and your body will take itself through to the washroom and take a razor blade from the shelf ... And believing it enough to put all razor blades carefully away in ejector containers or in their original wax wrappings in their packets so that if the subconscious tried, the conscious mind might have a fair chance of stepping in to the rescue during wakefulness brought on by fumbling with the packet or ejector container.

Clearing your throat constantly of an obstruction that seems too persistent to be imaginary although you are aware you are getting into a state where psychosomatic complaints can take free rein.

Becoming frightened of composing a poem even unwritten and in your mind, after a first line suggests itself so powerfully to you, unbidden, that it increases and compounds the gathering sense of fright felt after seven months absolutely alone in confinement. The line is:

Each day crouches huge and menacing at the window
And only at midnight does it steal reluctantly away.

Being frightened to put down your fears and feelings in the diary in which you have previously recorded all your moods because this time they seem potentially terrifying, and to express them in writing might give them a firm substance, strengthen them and make it impossible to overcome them.

Being unable to eat anything at all beyond the first mouthful of each meal although the cook, after many meals have been returned untouched produces only tiny plates of finely chopped meat or poached eggs on small beds of soft, boiled spinach that don't even require chewing. Being unable to sleep hour after hour through the night although the muscles in your back are fluttering with the sheer fatigue of your entire body.

These are some of the things you might experience after seven months totally alone under close guard. These are some of the things I experienced as February 1968 wore on and I seriously contemplated pleading with my guards to send me a doctor because my mind was going.

Each night as I tried to sleep the guard sitting only six feet away from the foot of my bed on the other side of a thin door kept me awake. I heard every creak of the chair when he shifted in his seat, every rustle of the newspaper he read, every sniff and every slurp when he sipped the hot water from his tin mug filled from a vacuum flask planted at his side on the floor. I heard the snap of his lighter when he lit a cigarette, I heard him when he yawned, I heard it when he belched, broke wind or went out into the yard and round the side of the house to relieve himself in the outside lavatory not far from the back window of my room. I heard all this and was helpless to remove myself from the torment of the sounds.

And during the day when walks of forty minutes morning and afternoon were allowed me, I had to endure the unending stares of these same guards as they stood at either end of the small courtyard. As I walked one way I looked into the eyes of the man standing at the top of the steps to the house. When I walked the other way the eyes of the man standing under the curved roof of the courtyard gate were on me. I looked at the grey flagstones of the yard, I looked at the sky, I looked at the buttons on their jackets, I looked nowhere and I looked into their eyes, returning their stares to show I was not cowed. But it was a fruitless pursuit and it proved nothing. The eyes were always on me for no reason.

The constant, wordless hostility and contempt on the faces of the guards led me to defy them on impulse again. They had developed the habit of motioning with hand or head for me to go in after about forty minutes outside. Usually a sign was made as I was at one end of the courtyard and I could walk back without changing pace or direction and climb the few steps to the door. Then one of them realised he could leave his signal to the last moment as I was passing the door and by making it suddenly, halt me in mid-stride and force me to turn abruptly to go in. This was a new way to exercise the minimal discretionary control they had over me. In my depressed state I seethed with anger at this new attempt to add more humiliation to my circumstances.

The next time the guard tried to halt me in mid-stride I pretended not to see his signal and carried on walking. The time after to make sure he suddenly stepped out in front of me in the middle of the yard and waved towards the door. I side-stepped him without changing pace and walked on to the end of the yard. The result was beyond my wildest dreams. The guard ran after me gesticulating and loudly ordering me in. Ignoring his existence I turned, side-stepped him again and walking at the same pace went back across the yard, up the steps and inside.

The shift leader, a man who appeared so conscious of his own dignity that I had named him 'Little Caesar' in my mind, stamped into the room and stood staring at me fiercely. Then he almost ran downstairs to get one of the Chinese staff to come and translate. He ran up again, flinging the door of my room back on its hinges with an almighty crash. His unconcealed burst of anger would have been very satisfying to me had I not been apprehensive of the results of my action. 'Little Caesar' made a lot of noises

230 HOSTAGE IN PEKING

about my obeying him. Next day I was prevented from going outside as a punishment for my disobedience.

Then another incident with the guards a few nights later showed how my self-control was slipping. As I tried to sleep, the guard on the chair outside my door began sandpapering the stem of his pipe. In the quiet of the night the jarring, insistent scrape, scrape, scrape of the sandpaper on the pipe stem brought the tension in me to screaming pitch. I felt the anger surge up the lining of my stomach and I stopped it once there with a rush before it launched me into some action I might regret. Then the scrape, scrape, scrape continued. I tried to remember my determination to 'neutralise' my relations with the guards and avoid incidents for the sake of my peace of mind. But the noise went on and on and suddenly, practically losing my head, I flung back the bed clothes, rushed to the door, ripped it open and almost screamed, 'Stop that bloody noise!' while pointing to his hands.

The guard's mouth fell open with first shock and then amazement. I had never opened the door in the night before. I got back into bed shaking from head to toe. The fur-hatted guard came in and stood at the foot of my bed staring down at me in the darkness. Then not satisfied with this he snapped on the light and continued staring into my face. I shaded my eyes against the sudden glare of the neon tube. After several minutes of this he ordered me in sign language to turn off the light he had switched on and close the door he had opened. He went out. I deliberately did nothing and he came in again, repeated his order and went out, this time closing the door after him, so rescinding half of his order. Still shaking slightly and with my heart still pounding at a high rate I put out the light and tried to calm down. I slept hardly at all again. Next morning there was an inquest on my act in my room with the cook acting as interpreter. His few words of kitchen English proved so inadequate that I escaped this time with an apparent admonishment, without my walk or access to fresh air being affected.

But these clashes with the guards emphasised anew my absolute subordination to their whims and plunged me deeper into a state of despondency.

My sense of unease had been greatly heightened one night when I woke suddenly to find that one of the guards had come into the room while I slept. The guard in question was a young, eccentric

Chinese with a turn in one eye. He often moved around the court-yard launching sudden high kicks like a can-can dancer, bringing one foot up to touch his hand stretched out above head level. Sometimes he would suddenly grin at me for no apparent reason or on other occasions stare at me oddly.

After waking to find him creeping quietly from the room I became extremely wary on the nights he was among the guard. I felt unwilling even to try to commit myself to sleep when a few feet away on the other side of an unlocked door an unpredictable, apparently erratic man was to sit whiling away three empty hours. I began to wonder whether he might try to kill me in my sleep and whether the fear and discipline of the organisation for which he worked would restrain any possible flaws in his mental make-up. The only defensive action I could take was to put an empty water bottle on the floor just inside the door before getting into bed so that if the door opened in the night the bottle would fall with a clatter on the bare floorboards and at least I might be wakened to defend myself. I put the bottle down every night after that but there were no further incursions.

As the second half of February wore on every fibre in my body seemed to reject food and sleep. At meal times I slumped forward, head on arms, on the table. I dare not define my feelings precisely in my diary. But the pages for February are spattered with phrases like '... sometimes worrying about going mad ... two difficult nights not sleeping with guards sniffing, coughing and hawking outside the door ... year terribly depressing prospect and some-times seem unbearable. It is only bearable because it has got to be borne ... I have known some very difficult moments recently ... it keeps occurring to me how long it still might be and my mind wanders to the difficulty of holding out ... this morning I feel a strong need just to see and talk to somebody ... I keep telling myself I shall undoubtedly manage to pull through ...'

The climax arrived on the morning of February 24th, 1968, a turning point for me, as it turned out, in the whole twenty-six months of solitary confinement.

I wrote in my diary that morning: 'The depression of the last two or three days this morning reached huge proportions. The obsession has been that I am unable to stand this any more because my nerve has given out. Thoughts of pleading for a doctor and to be allowed to leave this room flood through my mind and I feel absolutely desolate. At breakfast for the second day running I felt like eating absolutely nothing... Then after praying with a hopeless desperation I suddenly decided what I needed was "fight".'

What happened that morning remains vividly in my memory. I had already carried the untouched tray of food to the chair in the corner from which it would be collected. I had numbly put on my sheepskin coat to await the sign to go outside.

Abruptly I began to curse myself. 'Fight, you bastard, fight. —— you —— you, fight!' I abused myself roundly in four-letter words like this then picked up a slice of toast and scrambled egg and forced it into my mouth. Food was the last thing on earth I wanted and I had to push it in as if I was stuffing a taxidermist's dummy. I may have groaned at the effort as I stood in the corner of that bare paint-daubed room forcing the food into myself.

For what happened next I return to the diary written that day.

'During my walk outside in bright sunshine with the temperature at thirty-two degrees and bright blue sky overhead I discovered a new "ingredient" that I required to help me on from here – "Seven Months Plus Determination". This new super-ingredient is the answer to things. I told myself that if I wanted to avoid the personal disgrace of a nervous collapse and the consequent admission of failure, this was the answer. I am absolutely determined not to give in but to see this damned thing through to the end, successfully standing firmly and strongly on my own two legs. So this day has distinguished itself as the day on which "Seven Months Plus Determination" came into tangible being. This I feel has been God's way of helping me with my distress. Praise God.'

This childish return to the jargon and ideas of television advertising at the most desperately serious moment of my isolation is perhaps some reflection of the impact on our culture of the media. I don't explain it, glorify it or apologise for it. I simply record it as a turning point in my resistance to the pressure of being confined alone. This idea of having found something new in myself helped me go on. The fright of having come so near to the brink of some kind of appalling breakdown made me determined not to slip back towards it again. Never after that did I allow myself to put my head on my arms in an attitude of despair. I redoubled my Yoga effort. Each time hopelessness and the sense of despair grew I consciously checked it before it got out of hand. It was never easy but the experience of February 1968 and 'Seven Months Plus Determination' became something to look back on and avoid if I was to survive with mind and body whole.

Five days later I was able to record that my appetite which disappeared completely for four days was returning. 'Recovery simply comes slowly after a struggle,' I wrote. 'One of the things I have done in getting out of this depression is almost to convince myself there is a good chance of something turning up in 'Bountiful March'. I am now in the eighth month, perhaps something will turn up.'

Lovers of less prosaic things than washing powder television commercials will be glad to learn that two other factors around that time helped me draw away from the danger of a frightening mental collapse. I read Nicholas Monsarrat's *Three Corvettes* and wrote in my diary: '... tremendously entertaining factual stories of courage by British men at sea in the Second World War put new heart into me. What is my ordeal compared with those of the war?'

And Sally Weston, the wife of my friend John, sent a letter with a very encouraging and indirectly flattering extract from one of Browning's poems. I suppose it tickled my vanity and I immediately learned it. As I paced up and down the courtyard under the eyes of the guards, what they didn't know was that I was reciting these lines to myself.

One who never turned his back but marched breast forward,
Never doubted clouds would break,
Never dreamed though right were worsted, wrong would triumph,
Held we fall to rise, are baffled to fight better,
Sleep to wake.

CHAPTER TWENTY-SEVEN

Visit One

The first unbroken spell of solitary confinement lasted 249 days. From the night of August 18th, 1967 when the Red Guards stormed into my house until April 23rd, 1968 I was alone with my thoughts. Eight long months and two days. Then came a twenty-minute break before I began another spell of 217 days in isolation.

On the afternoon of April 23rd at four o'clock the red gate of the courtyard opened to admit the British chargé d'affaires in Peking, Sir Donald Hopson, and second secretary John Weston. For the meeting I had been conducted into the room normally occupied by the guards and through the window I caught sight of the two Englishmen as they entered. In the pale spring sunshine their fine, Western-style suits seemed to glow. When they came in and sat down I was forcibly struck by the colours in their neckties. For many months I had seen only the drab, rumpled cotton of the khaki-and-blue uniforms of the guards and the blue-grey cotton working clothes of the Chinese staff in the house. The dreary dirty surroundings in which I lived were practically devoid of colour. I myself had worn a faded leather jacket and old sports trousers most of the time.

The impact of colour on my eyes was immediate and lasting. I still retain the mental image of Hopson and Weston walking into the courtyard. Sir Donald wore an almost white tropical-weight suit and John Weston a darker grey, business suit. Neither of these creations would have excited any attention in normal circumstances. The second secretary's tie was a zig-zag green and mauve pattern, that of the chargé d'affaires was a quieter blue and white spotted affair.

The moment in which I saw my first friendly, non-Asian faces in nine months – I had been alone since July although in telephone contact for the first month – was an emotional one. The rich, resonant voice of the chargé d'affaires was booming 'Hello, Tony' even before he was through the door into the room. Then he was pumping my hand. John Weston was close behind him and since I couldn't get my right hand out of Sir Donald's grip I found John grabbing my other hand and we stood like this gripping hands for several moments. Somebody said 'How are you?' several times and eventually I managed to say 'All right' in a strangled sort of voice.

It wasn't until two years later that I discovered that I was not the only one who approached the meeting with trepidation. Both my visitors then admitted that they had spent a very jittery day after being informed of the arrangements for the visit. Back home Sir Donald told me that, though delighted at that time to get permission, he did not look forward to the meeting since he could not know in what state he would find me. But none of this was apparent to me on that day, obsessed as I was with the strangeness of seeing friendly faces again and trying not to appear to be taking the ordeal too badly.

I had learned of the visit only twenty minutes or so before it began when two Public Security Bureau interpreters entered my room. After motioning me to stand, one addressed me in clipped, heavily-accented English. 'I am instructed to tell you that today at four o'clock two officials of the Office of the British Chargé d'Affaires will visit you. You must abide by the following regulations:

1. You must use only standard English. 2. You must exchange no documents, letters or papers. 3. You must not record or take photographs. 4. We reserve the right to terminate the interview at any time.'

I asked for the rules to be repeated and the interpreter read them again. Both times he seemed to lay great stress on the last instruction. I thought this was to intimidate me in what I might say. The visit was to last a bare twenty minutes.

I sat down to wait the short time to four o'clock, my mind in a whirl at the prospect of suddenly meeting people again. I couldn't formulate much of a plan but decided to be circumspect in what I said in case I should incur further reprisals.

I was led into the dining-room which had been set up for the meeting with furniture from my upstairs lounge. I was directed into a deep armchair on one side of the room. On the wall in English above my head was a great black slogan in letters two feet high saying 'Down with A. Grey'.

The visit was agreed to by the Chinese in return for a special visit by Communist representatives to fifteen Communist newsmen imprisoned in Hong Kong for offences in connection with the riots there. The two British diplomats sat down on the other side of a low table placed between us and the chargé d'affaires began by reading a message from my mother and one from Reuters general manager Gerald Long.

Then he told me: 'Although your release is not just around the corner, things are better now than they were nine months ago.'

I learned that the Foreign Secretary, George Brown, had twice offered to exchange me for Hsueh Ping, the first New China News Agency man jailed in Hong Kong. Reuters had tried in vain to send a representative to discuss my case. A message from fellow journalists on the editorial floor of Reuters quite illogically caused my eyes to dampen momentarily. 'We hope to see the Anthony Grey by-line on the file again soon,' it had said.

Kindness and kind wishes after so long of steeling myself against hostility quickly found chinks in my emotional armour. John had been in touch with my girl friend Shirley by letter frequently since my house arrest began, and when he asked if I wanted to send her a private message my voice died away on me with the emotional effort of expressing some tender feelings in words.

But I insisted that however nervy I might appear my mother was to be told I looked all right so as to prevent her worrying unnecessarily. Then torn between the desire to convey some of my mental suffering and the equally strong desire not to appear unable to stand up to hardship, I eventually mumbled words to the effect that I had sometimes felt on the verge of a nervous breakdown, 'but that was probably only due to the isolation'.

I learned for the first time that Red Guards had burned down the British Mission. When asked if there had been any violence during my invasion, I hesitated, thought of the possibility of further reprisals, and said 'I don't think there is any point in going into that now'. But although I was enormously glad and relieved to see my own countrymen again at last, I was resentful too. Sir Donald Hopson's 'things are better' and the words 'constantly striving' in the cable from Reuters general manager clearly meant to me there was nothing concrete to tell me. Nothing was being done by the British Government or the organisation which

I represented. However powerless both these parties might have been and however illogical my resentment, I felt it very strongly. I was the innocent victim, I was suffering, why was nothing being done to help me?

Sir Donald asked whether I had a set of playing cards to use and of this I later noted in my diary '. . . . Hopson asked a stupid question about whether I could play patience . . .' He also told me that the Chinese prisoners in Hong Kong could send letters and that I should ask to do that. Of this I noted 'I got a bit angry here after saying I was intending to ask later. He appeared to be trying to tell me what I should do here. That's not the job of the British Government. They should get me out of here. What he doesn't know is that a cable of a few words to my mother sent off last week had been held thirty-six days at the Foreign Ministry before it was allowed to be sent.'

All these emotions were crammed into a fleeting twenty minutes, with two Public Security Bureau interpreters sitting beside us writing every word of our 'standard English' into their notebooks. Another guard sat opposite them, keeping his eye on the clock and on us.

After they had gone I wrote of my anger and resentment but added 'But, by God, it was wonderful to see them, their colourful neckties and suits, their English faces. Hopson looked incredibly suntanned, John pale. I shook hands with them very warmly again as they left. As he went out John made what I thought was a slightly nonsensical remark: "Keep it up." Keep what up where? My God, it was just wonderful to see them though. Hell, it has been nine months since I saw anybody like that. How incredible!'

I tried to sum up what for me had been a momentous experience.

'What does it mean? It means I am irrevocably linked with fifteen prisoners in Hong Kong and won't get out until they do. In psychological terms it was a wonderful boost just to see friends, shake hands, talk and look at them. It has been an encouraging day. It has broken the long, terrible, empty nine months of not knowing and thinking all kinds of strange things. It is a reassuring sign although it doesn't mean the end is near. I shall rededicate myself to endurance as a result of it.'

The entire conversation was recorded on tape through microphones hidden in the room I am sure, although the Chinese went

to great lengths to prevent me knowing this. Just after the interpreters had told me of the impending visit a guard had suddenly
come to stand in my room and had ordered me to remain sitting
on my chair and not to move from it. This made it impossible
from such a low level to see out of the window properly into the
courtyard.

I thought at first somebody important from the Foreign Ministry
was to attend the interview and that I should not be allowed to
look on his arrival. I saw civilians cross the yard and enter the
house. Their footsteps went up the stairs to the room above the
dining-room where the visit was to take place. I could just see
the tops of their bent heads as they crossed the yard and judged
from the jerky way they were walking they carried heavy cases
in their hands. Once in the dining-room waiting for my visitors I
glanced round and saw wires running from a waste-paper basket
and out under the door leading to the bottom of the stairs. This
door had remained locked and both I and the two British diplomats had been led into the dining-room through a door leading
directly into the courtyard that was never normally used.

After the visit I was again briefly ordered onto my chair in
my room by a guard who stood in front of me and the two civilian
heads moved jerkily across the yard again, clearly carrying their
heavy burdens. I concluded they could only be recording tech-
nicians who had taped every word in the room above. I guessed
they were from the Foreign Ministry where every inflection in
what the British diplomats said would be studied to help formulate plans in the continuing confrontation with the British
Government over me.

The Chinese authorities displayed a strange ambivalence in hand-
ling the visit. Clearly acting on the instructions of the Fat Cadre
(the high-ranking Public Security Bureau man who was always
around at important times), my boilerman came into the room before the visit and pointed to the large darn I had made in the
knee of my very scruffy trousers. I was also wearing, as usual,
the battered-looking leather jacket. My surroundings being so dismal and dirty, I had felt disinclined to wear a decent suit except
on Christmas Day. 'You change,' said the boilerman. I said no.
'I think you change,' he added emphatically. I said I always
looked like that and would continue to do so. This was evidence
perhaps of a directive from the Foreign Ministry that every effort

should be made to make the interview conform to civilised standards – but not to such an extent that it would prevent the British representatives realising in what wretched conditions I was being kept, or appear to reduce the pressure on the British Government to capitulate in order to ease my plight. Perhaps it is an example of great Chinese subtlety – or maybe the dilemma moderate thinkers face when trying to retrieve situations produced by extreme actions while still fearing to lose face or their own positions.

Tea had been served for the three of us by the boilerman during the brief conversation although it remained untouched on the table between us. Tins of my cigarettes from a drawer upstairs were on the table for the guests. Perhaps these are just additional, inexplicably-bizarre aspects of a situation for which there was never any precedented framework anyway.

CHAPTER TWENTY-EIGHT

More Nails

One evening late in May, as I sat reading, a carpenter rushed into the twelve-foot square room and began hammering six-inch nails into the woodwork of the window facing the sheer, grey wall of the adjoining restaurant. I watched horrified. The real heat of the Peking summer was just beginning and for the past few nights I had opened that window to try to cool the room.

The carpenter noisily banged in nail after nail, sealing off the window. When I was moved into the room from the eight-foot square cell the previous November I had been told by the guards I could open it myself at any time. But through the winter I had not needed it open. The guards who had followed the carpenter in stood watching carefully as the window was secured and the fresh air cut off. I was beside myself with anger at this apparently gratuitously vindictive act. The window faced a smooth sheer wall about fifteen feet high and there was no possibility of using the window for anything but fresh air. The window on the other side of the room was closed every day at four p.m. with a lock on the outside. I was quite unable to conceal my anger and stood up staring furiously at the chief guard. Words as always were pointless. He glared back. There had clearly been a decision to nail it up and nothing I could do or say would change it.

The nailing up of the window was the start of a long hot summer in which I had to sit sweating and listening to the whirr of my two electric fans being used by the guards in the next room.

A few days after the April visit of the British chargé d'affaires I had asked if I could write letters home. After an eight day wait I was told through the boilerman that I could write one letter a month to either my mother or my 'wife'.

I had been particularly glad to hear news of my mother during my consular visit since only two letters from her had been allowed to reach me in the nine months of my house arrest, although she had written frequently. My girl friend Shirley had established her right to send letters to me by sheer persistence. From the very beginning in July 1967 her letters had been returned but as fast as they were returned she sent off fresh ones, firing a veritable barrage of letters non-stop into the reading room of the Foreign Ministry or wherever they were read. (All letters that reached me had sticky glue marks on the edges of the back flap indicating they had been opened and scrutinised.) By the sheer weight of her correspondence over many months Shirley had impressed herself on the minds of the cadres of the Foreign Ministry as my leading correspondent and I am sure the volume of her letters alone had led to the few trickling through in my days in the tiny room, and the increased flow after that. Other friends wrote from time to time and these letters reached me sporadically until May. Then when permission was granted me to write once a month to my mother or 'wife' all other incoming mail stopped completely and remained stopped until my release a year and a half later. Why the 'wife' stipulation was made I don't know since it was officially known I was unmarried. But from May onwards I wrote alternate months to Shirley and my mother.

I wrote at the beginning of each month and handed the letter to the guards who spirited it away to the Ministry. The first letter was returned twelve days later and the boilerman was allowed to take it to the post office after I had inspected it and sealed it up. Each succeeding month the Foreign Ministry held the letter longer and longer before returning it. One was eventually held five weeks and the average time was one month. As the summer wore on the delays in my incoming mail grew and grew, sometimes reaching five weeks. This meant that the gap between writing and replying could stretch to ten weeks in all. This, I believe was all part of the insidious pressure exerted deliberately by the Foreign Ministry in the hope of influencing the British Government to release the imprisoned newsmen in Hong Kong out of humanitarian sympathy for me. Also I could tell from the English and Chinese postmarks that the guards added to the delay by keeping the incoming letters on the table in the dining-room for a week, ten days, a fortnight or even up to a month as the mood took them. That I knew letters were often just a few feet away from me, withheld by a whim, angered me greatly again and again. Often I had to clench my fists and grit my teeth to control the urge to rush into the guards' room in a fury and demand the letters.

One of the reasons for this may have been that the guards really had no power of their own over anything at all. They simply acted on strict instructions from the Foreign Ministry. Perhaps holding back my letters gave them some twisted personal satisfaction. Here was the 'reactionary Reuter newsman', as it said on all the posters that they could read every day on the walls. This was their class enemy that they read about in the *People's Daily*. Every day they were told to carry out class struggle, to attack bourgeois reactionaries, and to follow Chairman Mao's revolutionary line. Here they were living in the house of a bourgeois man, sleeping on his furniture. Perhaps this was just the tiniest thing they could do to exercise their own revolutionary initiative, here was another little screw they could turn. So they kept the letters on the table. Sometimes I would be walking backwards and forwards in my room and I would see that they had dropped a letter on the floor and they would hastily pick it up and put it out of sight. I also saw letters one day when in the yard. The papers came through the door-slit before my eyes while I was walking towards it. The papers fell down and two letters fell down too. One, I could see from the stamps, was from a friend in East Berlin. That letter was *never* given to me. So I knew there were also letters coming to the house that were not delivered to me at all.

Up to the time I was first allowed to write letters there had been a pattern of gradual concessions dating from the time of my removal from the tiny room. In late February I had been allowed to have my own fountain pen with which to write cheques. But it was made clear I should write nothing else privately. When I asked permission to draw up accounts for my expenditure of the past nine months, the guards brought chairs into the twelve-foot square room and sat at my elbow the whole of one afternoon watching me write as I did it. Then the sheaf of papers were taken from me and taken to the Foreign Ministry for inspection where they remained one week. I found the guards' close presence so intolerable that I never asked again for permission to write anything else.

In March my diet was finally normalised when I was allowed to have milk, tea and fruit juice again. I was also asked at the same time if I wanted a doctor for my throat. The guards could hear I was clearing it constantly. I believe this was all in preparation for the consular visit in April. But after the visit the hard line clamped down again with the nailing up of my windows and this set the tone of my treatment for the succeeding months.

After two weeks of stifling hot nights with temperatures in the room in the eighties I asked if the courtyard window could be left open all night. This was granted but the wire screens were nailed into place across it. So I was nailed into the room again. The windows in the washroom had remained securely nailed all the time. Because it was still very hot I asked if a small twelve-inch square section of window in the solidly-nailed up side could be opened to help cause a draught in the hot nights. This request was conveyed to the Foreign Ministry but never granted. They were determined to make me sweat it out, it seemed.

At the height of the heat and humidity in July and August I would sit motionless on my straight-backed chair with sweat oozing from every pore and soaking through my trousers and shirt. I often emerged for my forty-minute afternoon walk with my shirt as wringing wet as if it had been dipped in water. Once I noticed a young guard on seeing this, rush into the twelve-foot square room, while I walked in the courtyard, to check the thermometer there, as if he couldn't believe it was so hot.

In the dining-room the guards had the many windows on all four sides of the room open, and were basking in the breeze of my two large electric fans with their jackets and shirts off, wearing only trousers and vests. On the back of a couple of cable forms I kept a daily graph on which I plotted the indoor and outside temperatures. This helped me to endure the heat. I could see the peaks of temperatures and identify trends towards cooler times. I often longed for wind and rain which came frequently at the hottest times with monsoon intensity and cooled the air a few degrees. At times of peak humidity condensation, dripping from the rusty cold water pipes in the washroom, spread puddles on the stone tiles and plaster fell from the walls in chunks because of the damp. The room smelled damp and musty.

In that long summer of 1968 I used every possible pretext to convince myself time was passing, that I was making progress. I measured off time on the day I set aside for washing my socks. It was usually a Thursday and on this day I mentally ticked off another 'sock-washing week'. On Sunday I mentally ticked off a 'prayer week'. I ticked off calendar months and lunar months always seeking to assure myself I was steadily moving towards hope of release.

On Sunday I moved the wooden chair at which I knelt to say prayers, away from the bath into the middle of the washroom. I did this to give the day a different aspect. It was a small thing but very faintly ritualistic and made me realise how the need for a ritual, a ceremony, no matter how slight, is deeply embedded in us. It was a way of giving a comforting familiar pattern to the emptiness of time and space. It helped me understand how other much more complicated rituals and ceremonies had grown up from such beginnings many hundreds of years before. There was another moment too which made me intensely aware of the links of today with the long distant past. It came when I read in a book of old Chinese poetry which I had got from upstairs, a verse of the T'ang dynasty, written before the year 770, 'The Sights of Spring'. In it appeared the lines: 'And birds sing heart-rending songs of separation ... A letter from home is worth ten thousand pieces of gold.' That a Chinese twelve centuries before should have had precisely the same intense feeling about letters from home that I had in 1969 was a poignant comment on the unchanging quality of human nature despite all other material changes. And it was somehow encouraging.

The red, white and blue striped edges of airmail letters had become the most exciting thing in my life. I even had a dream in which old friends came to visit me – and the outlines of their bodies were edged in the red, white and blue stripes of airmail envelopes!

But despite my solitary state there were times when I felt glad to be alone. I had only myself to deal with. The thought of being closely confined with another prisoner in a cell, having the problem of another, possibly unpleasant, personality to contend with sometimes seemed a worse prospect.

Right through that summer the days and nights were often punctuated with the thump and clank of drums and gongs and the seemingly frantic yelling of crowds of demonstrators marching by in the street outside. The noise was all-pervading and almost drove me to distraction. In May it was particularly bad. One night I wrote in my diary: 'This morning, for the second day, crowds of slogan-chanting marchers streamed by in the street. As I walked in the courtyard a guard came in through the gate and I could see the demonstrators carrying slogans on signboards mounted on bamboo sticks. They shout 'Down with American Imperialism, Down with Soviet Revisionism, Long Live Mao Tse-tung.' They sound for all the world like hordes of demented, tormented, crazed souls being driven from hell. These are the cries of my world on this day of misery.'

Two days later the noise was still going on unceasingly. I wrote again: 'Outside the screams and yells rip and jar on my nerves. I feel very desperate again.'

A couple of days later I found out that this was a rather special demonstration in support of the anti-Government riots and strikes in France and this brought my apprehension about what was happening in the world outside during my long confinement to a peak. Perhaps the worst thing of all was not knowing. Having no information about events in the world generally and about my own case in particular. Both my mother and Shirley, the only ones allowed to write to me most of the time, avoided saying anything in their letters that might cause them to be kept from me. I had no Western newspapers, no radio, no reliable facts on which to base my thinking. In a sense I was living in a near-vacuum as far as information was concerned.

My sole source of information was the *Peking Review*, the weekly English-language propaganda publication which reproduces important editorials from the Chinese Communist press and takes a look at world events through blood-red spectacles. Although I had worked some time in Communist countries and was very much aware of the distorted nature of their publications, the effect on the mind over a period of time without anything to provide a balance is considerable. The descriptions of the spreading riots involving youths and workers all over France with pictures of street fighting and barricades and reports of workers seizing factories were very depressing reading from the *Peking Review*. And it became clear that the Peking millions marching in the street outside were doing so in direct support of the French 'revolutionaries'. Persistent reports of financial crises in the West, spreading student riots throughout the world and the devaluation of the British pound were larded with Maoist predictions that capitalist society was heading for collapse. Judicious quotes from

Western newspapers were used out of context. All this made me seriously wonder whether a repetition of the revolutionary uprush of the nineteenth century in Europe was coming about. If I ever emerged would I find Britain and the Western world I knew completely changed? The blackboards before me day and night carried the Maoist message into my mind, I suppose. Although I consciously felt it meant nothing, the fact that the people who wrote the words were all-powerful in my life lent weight to what they said as time went by. This added a new dimension to the simple despondency of solitary confinement. But into this starkly black and white world of Triumphant Communism and The Crumbling West a tiny speck of information fell which helped in a way to restore my faith and perhaps illustrates best of all the effect of totally one-sided information on the mind.

In her letters Shirley each week enclosed the crossword from the Sunday *Observer* to help me while away my time. At the time of the continuing chaos in France when my fears for the fabric of Western society were greatest I turned over the latest crossword and found some small advertisements on the back. One was advertising for youths to train as showroom salesmen for Ford cars in Piccadilly, London. I was immensely encouraged. Ford's wouldn't be advertising for salesmen in Piccadilly if Europe was plunged into chaos, depression and revolution, if money was valueless and the masses were marching on Westminster. And in the succeeding weeks whenever I worried about the persistent Chinese reports of deterioration in conditions in Europe and America I remembered that Ford's in Piccadilly still had enough faith in the future to train up young salesmen. And each week from then on I looked on the back of the *Observer* crossword for new faith. There would be advertisements for, say, the Chair of Economics at Salford University and even such nebulous things helped me believe everything was still in order back home and worth holding out for.

Keeping me cut off from meaningful information and contact with my own country was all part of the political blackmail which the Peking Foreign Ministry applied without let-up until May 1969 when it was learned that the last imprisoned newsman in Hong Kong was to be released early. Then and only then did they allow information to reach me through the use of my portable radio.

And though I was not interrogated or 'brainwashed' in the normal sense, the ban on all views except Peking's, the positioning of the blackboards with Mao's message on them right in front of my eyes, and the frequent changing of the quotations was a deliberate form of mental aggression calculated to have some effect on me – and on the British Government.

Shortly after my greatest time of mental distress in February when I decided I had found 'Seven Months Plus Determination', I hit on an idea to occupy my mind constructively. I found it was not enough to find a pastime to while away the hours. Even reading, though extremely important, did not seem to be mentally satisfying since I had no coherent library with me, only a spotted collection of novels, books on China, the odd biography and general light reading. And doing crosswords in the book of 100 hundred puzzles sent me in the December parcel was not in itself satisfying. But after studying the construction of crosswords I decided that I would compile them myself. I had never been very interested in these word-games before although one of my faults had always been punning.

I decided to compile one crossword a day, using the back of old account forms which I had been allowed to get from upstairs for listing my monthly expenses and the backs of cable forms which I had been allowed at Christmas when sending off cables. The most important thing about this activity was that I told myself I would compile them carefully to a professional standard and try to sell them to newspapers or magazines when I got out. This seemed to give me a purpose, a goal to aim at, a sense that each day I was doing something of value which one day would find its justification in their appearing in print.

Most crossword solvers probably never study the construction of the squares around the words. I looked at this and found stimulating mathematical and artistic variations in the endless way in which the black squares can be rearranged before words are inserted. They can be made to form crosses big and small, in the centre and at the edges, L-shapes, zig-zags and so on in a kaleidoscopic series of differing patterns which give a pleasing visual appearance to the puzzles.

The worst moment in each succeeding empty day was the instant of waking from the oblivion of sleep to the realisation that there was no point in the day to come. This had often been the time when depression began to engulf me afresh. So to obliterate the effect of this awful daily period I began soon after the February crisis to get out of bed immediately on waking, creep through to the washroom, wash, exercise and dress then creep back and with the door still illegally closed, sit down at the desk bent almost double so that I could not be seen from the courtyard. The high window-sill made it possible to remain hidden from the view of a guard of average height in this position.

Then I would work intensively, drawing out the crossword square, marking off fifteen by fifteen smaller squares inside and devising a pattern of squares into which to fit the words. For this I used the pencil I had 'stolen' from one of the domestic staff when he left it in the room inadvertently. When I had completed the square I shaded the black squares with ink and got enormous artistic satisfaction from the resulting patterns. Once I had fitted the words in I would memorise them. Then as I walked back and forth in the yard later in the day I occupied my mind working out clues for them in the groan-provoking humorous style of crossword compilers down the ages! It allowed me to forget the watching eyes of the guards, occupied my empty mind, eased the tension in me as I walked. I would compile clues like 1 across in one of the early puzzles. 'What an irritated deep sea diver must do to make the grade?' (4.2.2.7.) And the abysmally unfunny answer would be 'Come up to scratch'. There were even worse puns than that in the thousands of clues I compiled over the succeeding months.

The pencil which had been vital for keeping my diary became a vital element in my crossword compiling too and as it became shorter and shorter I had to husband the dwindling lead carefully. It eventually became so short that the remaining piece of lead slipped back into the minute piece of wood surrounding it when I tried to write so I had to poke my nail scissors into the top of the wood to prevent the lead from slipping back. The pencil was one of my few precious possessions and I treated it with great care.

The small india-rubber originally attached to the end of the pencil I used too in compiling the crosswords until it became a speck as large as a grain of sand. At this point I reluctantly bade it farewell. But by this time my crossword-compiling skill had increased until I could work without rubbing out. My first cross-word took me six hours but when I eventually ceased doing them towards the end of the year in favour of learning Chinese I could dash one off in half an hour or so.

As that long summer wore on I added another activity to my survival effort – writing short stories. Getting paper was difficult but I did this by carefully timing requests for paper on which to write my monthly letters. When permission to write letters was first given I was escorted upstairs and allowed to get one exercise book. I kept my letters fairly short. Then waiting until the guards had changed and those on duty did not know what paper I had got before, I pretended I had no more paper, hid the remainder of the exercise book and asked to be allowed to get more. This way I built up a reserve of three exercise books in my possession in which I eventually wrote a dozen or so stories. Many of them were humorous as a relief to the deadly serious nature of my life.

I was able to occupy my time while walking in the courtyard under the gaze of the guards devising plots, characters and situations for my stories. I had been a dismal failure as a short story writer at the age of nineteen before becoming a journalist. I wrote one or two and sent them to editors and received only rejection slips. Eventually what I thought was my best one got lost in the post so taking this as an omen of their worth I gave up the idea, and the only writing I did after that was in newspapers. Now in the silence of my Peking room I dug back ten years and wrote a couple of what I'd thought were my best ideas then into story form, and I devised new ones. By the autumn I had run out of ideas but I had occupied several difficult months in this way.

I always feared I would lose my diaries, the stories and the crosswords if a search were made. That they survived seems something of a miracle in retrospect. One explanation occurs to me. The Foreign Ministry in overall charge of me may have assumed that the watch on me was so close that I would not have been able to write anything without the guards knowing. Therefore no search was necessary. The day-to-day guards may have felt that since they were never given explicit instructions to make a minute search, and would not have understood English anyway, they were to leave me more or less alone. From time to time they came in while I was there and looked around at things, pulled my pile of clothes about or looked at the books on the window-sill. Sometimes they entered the room and looked around while I was walking in the courtyard and I tensed at the prospect of losing the creations on which I spent so much time. But since I was never detected writing by the guards, except when doing my monthly letter which I wrote openly, possibly it never occurred to them there could be anything worth finding. It is just possible, too, that nobody in authority would have cared anyway but I doubt this since every other feature of my daily life was controlled with such capricious vindictiveness. In any event there was no search and on release I managed to have my diaries and other materials brought out safely in luggage where they would not be associated with me.

One of the first things I wrote in my confinement was a reconstruction of a perfect day at home which I had created in my imagination during the days in the eight-foot square cell. With great concentration I tried to set down in simple words the idyllic scene. When reading the first paragraph I was struck by what I imagined was its lyrical quality. I thought it fell very neatly into the opening lines of a poem. So I rewrote the first paragraph line by line in verse form. This was in April. I put it away in a pocket of my jacket meaning sometime later when in a more confident mood to add a few more verses. In June I took out the five lines again and added some extra verses of shamelessly nostalgic sentiment about my own country which I longed to be in. I also wrote a prediction into it, to bolster my optimism, that the autumn of the year would see me home. I had never tried seriously to write poetry before and apart from a bit of doggerel later in the year never tried again. Perhaps it was written unconsciously in the spirit of Anything-Mao-can-do-I-can-do-better, because my poem, like his most famous one, is coincidently about snow.

Snow in England

It is Sunday morning in winter
Snow has fallen freshly during the night
And now, in the early dawn
The English countryside lies quiet and beautiful
Beneath a coverlet of white.

The birds are hushed in awe
Black branches bear their bright burden with pride,

No foot's left its print
No eye roused from sleep yet beheld the joy
Of the cold winter outside.

There is enchantment in snow
Its very presence thrills the soul although unseen
And coming on first sight of it
By chance, the heart delights, exalts and cries out
At its beauty pure and keen.

The magic quilt settles soundlessly
Comes, like love, with quiet mystery about the door
And in its silent embrace
The earth, a willing mistress, an enraptured woman
Is more lovely than before.

But now the summer sun burns down
On me, perhaps on her for we're far apart,
But when the snows return to England
To embrace her I, too, will return to settle
Once more quietly in her heart.

June 1968

CHAPTER TWENTY-NINE

Visit Two

In my mind I divided the long haul through the hot summer into four parts to be dealt with one at a time. May, June, July, August, each represented a quarter. I almost ceased telling the time by hours and began to think that it was now quarter past June, half past June, quarter to July, and so on. The days and weeks passed with a slow tedium that would be impossible to capture on paper. I hoped always that the autumn would bring release.

In September occasional pains I had felt in my chest for several months seemed to become more frequent but I tried not to notice them, telling myself I would hold out until the autumn and have a medical check-up once free. I also still felt forced to clear my throat loudly every few minutes. In a letter Shirley had managed by a clever allusion to indicate that Hsueh Ping, the Chinese newsman imprisoned in Hong Kong was due for release in November if he earned the full eight months remission on his two year sentence. I allowed myself to become very hopeful.

Meantime there had been another change in the rules governing my books. I had decided to get through the summer with the twelve books I got from upstairs under escort in May. When I asked again for more books in the autumn I was told I must write out the titles of those I wanted. I said I couldn't remember the titles, could I go upstairs under escort to take note of them. No. So in effect my books were out of bounds again without reason. Like the nailing up of the windows this illogical turnabout caused me to suffer another bout of impotent fury which I was hard put to conceal. By mid-November nothing had happened about my release and because the chest pains appeared to be more persistent and my throat was still troubling me, I asked for a doctor. Having sweated through the summer I was worried about the possibility of tuberculosis. After a wait of two days a young woman doctor came. Seeming distinctly uneasy in the slogan-daubed room, she gave me a quick examination with a stethoscope and rushed out. I asked the interpreter with her what the diagnosis was and he said 'Maybe you have bronchitis'. I asked if I might have an X-ray and was told this was not necessary. I was given some pills and some liquid medicine. The examination was fairly perfunctory. I tried to control my misery and hoped against hope for release after the sixteen long months alone. On November 21st I saw in the *People's Daily* a news item in which the Chinese characters for 'journalist' and 'Hong Kong' were clearly visible to me. In my diary I wrote: 'Probably the release. But how many had there been. Does this mean I am to be released? I am very hopeful but I am trying not to discount the possibility of having to stay on.'

But at a quarter to three on the afternoon of November 26th, 217 days after I had last seen friendly faces, that possibility became harsh reality again. A Public Security Bureau interpreter entered the room and, ordering me to rise, intoned the familiar litany that made my heart sink.

'The Information Department of the Chinese Ministry of Foreign Affairs has informed us that today at three o'clock two officials of the Office of the British Chargé d'Affaires will visit you. You must abide by the following regulations...' The standard English, no exchange of documents, no photographs, we-reserve-the-right-to-terminate-the-interview-at-any-time rules were as before. I sank down into my chair as he went out. I was stunned and hugely disappointed. A visit meant no release. The visit of Sir Donald Hopson and John Weston in April had put new heart in me since it had meant the end of nine months isolation. In the fifteen minutes before my new visitors arrived I tried to fight down the anger and bitterness I felt because still nothing was being done from London to bring about my release.

I was escorted through to the dining-room again. Again I saw the wires running from a waste-paper basket under the door and up the stairs.

The gate opened to admit the chargé d'affaires, by this time Mr Percy Cradock. Sir Donald Hopson had earlier been granted an exit visa and had left for home. Percy Cradock had been a senior member of the Mission staff when I arrived in Peking and was well known to me. Quietly-spoken, thoughtful and widely respected for his considered approach to diplomacy and affairs in China he was a man I liked personally. Yet so great was the turmoil of unreasoning bitterness in me that although glad to see him, I was immediately rude to him.

'Tony!' He called my name as he came through the door and shook hands. He introduced second secretary Roger Garside and sat down. The note-scribbling interpreters sat at one side and a poker-faced guard sat on the other watching the clock. The time set was twenty-five minutes, five minutes more than before.

Percy said he would read some messages to me. I broke in: 'Before you do that can you tell me if there is any chance of my getting out of here soon! I've been in solitary confinement for sixteen months and am not really interested in platitudinous messages!'

Percy began to say things were improving. I butted in again: 'That's what I was told seven months ago!' And I sank back in my chair, knowing that there was little else tangible for me in the visit.

Percy went on to say gently that he hoped that the publicity of the visit and the fact that Hsueh Ping and other Chinese newsmen had been released would bring some improvement. Then the messages. My fierce resentment boiled over into my diary later: 'I listened without enthusiasm to the messages. Long (Gerald Long, Reuters general manager) came again with the rubbish that they were "Doing everything for my release and thinking of me every day!" Crap! ...'

Then Percy read from a written draft details of the political background to that stage of my confinement. All eight correspondents originally mentioned in the Chinese Foreign Ministry statement made in July 1967 when I was put under house arrest, had been released. I interrupted quietly to ask how many newsmen were left in prison in Hong Kong. Several, was the answer. And when was the last one due out? Percy paused and pretended to think about what he knew would be an unpalatable piece of news. Finally he said he believed one finished in 1971.

I remember involuntarily muttering 'Oh my God' and slumping back in my chair at the horrifying thought of perhaps three more years.

Percy went on to say relations were improving and added that the publicity would show how badly China treated foreigners. I was amazed to hear him say this so openly and I noticed the interpreter scribbling furiously. In the intimidated state into which I had been forced by sixteen months of solitary confinement I was incapable of uttering such a forthright expression of the facts and I envied him his freedom to do so.

Later in the short interview I attempted to explain how I had tried to fight down my bitterness and anger when I heard I was being visited and not released. I didn't mean it personally. But my hopes had been badly dashed, I said.

Realising I had little to lose, I revealed for the first time the precise details of my living conditions. The room twelve feet square, the windows nailed up through the sweltering summer, the door ever open in the cold winter despite my diagnosed bronchitis, my first cell the eight-foot square room, the washroom windows painted black, the guards watching through the door constantly, my fear of tuberculosis, the ban on my books. I told all – or nearly all, only hinting that there were things I still couldn't say. Percy won my admiration immediately by adding, 'I think I have some conception. Nobody dare show you a generous spirit.'

Not until a year later did I see the press cuttings of the reports of that meeting. The chargé d'affaires' diplomatic telegram to the Foreign Office in London was published in full in the newspapers – a rare departure from normal practice by Whitehall. 'He was obviously agitated at seeing the British officials and, as might be expected, under considerable general nervous strain as a result of his long solitary confinement.' After listing the living conditions in my house Percy had concluded with a sentence which went round the world in headlines: 'He lives in a void.' A French news agency correspondent present at a press conference given by Percy Cradock and Roger Garside in Peking the same evening wrote: 'Both visitors seemed to be having difficulty in controlling their emotions.' Gerald Long put out a statement in London: 'My reaction is one of horror at the conditions in which Mr Grey is held. I appeal once more to the Chinese authorities to release him immediately and I count upon the press, radio and television of the world to renew this appeal daily until he is released.'

A storm of publicity through newspapers and broadcasting systems was about to break. For the past sixteen months there had been little reporting of my confinement. The British National Union of Journalists had accepted the advice of the Foreign Office and

Reuters that too much publicity might worsen my plight, perhaps lead to a faked trial. What publicity there was had been low key. But now it was admitted this tactic had failed and journalists in many countries pitched in to do what they could to help.

All this was unknown to me in my twelve-foot square room. I wrote a bitter diary entry three days later – the first time I could bring myself to write of the visit. 'On the 26th all my hopes of release were shattered by a sudden and unexpected visit. The effort of trying to change my thinking back to long-term misery has left me almost completely inactive for three days. I have been most deeply miserable and hardly know how to carry on. Now what? If the worst happens it may go on for a time too horrible to write.'

During this second visit I sat in the same armchair as before. But the slogan on the wall behind and above me 'Down with A. Grey' had this time been covered up with no less than fifteen portraits of Mao! The portraits showed him walking, standing still, sitting, smoking, reading, chatting – and doing nothing. During the interview I noticed that Roger Garside, who had never been in the house before either in normal times or since it was taken over, was staring agog at this incredible wall decoration.

The resentment which burst through my self-control during the visit often extended beyond representatives of the British government and Reuters. I even once felt viciously resentful when Shirley described in a letter a picnic at which she'd had strawberries and cream and champagne. This was as completely unreasonable as the resentment felt towards Sir Donald Hopson, Percy Cradock and Gerald Long, who were clearly men of goodwill and who personally wished only to help.

In the days following the visit Fleet Street journalists formed an Action Committee to campaign for my release. Some 2,800 journalists signed a petition asking that I be freed and this was taken to the Office of the Chinese Chargé d'Affaires in Portland Place, London. There for the first time a Chinese diplomat who received it linked me openly and formally with thirteen remaining Communist newsmen jailed in Hong Kong. Britain could not expect my release until the last of these men were free, the diplomat told a representative of the Fleet Street men.

The International Federation of Journalists representing 60,000 journalists in twenty-three countries cabled a protest from Brussels to the Chinese premier, Chou En-lai, and sent a copy of the protest to U Thant, United Nations Secretary General.

The Reuter board of directors and general manager Gerald Long appealed repeatedly to Mao Tse-tung and Chou En-lai by cable for my release. The International Press Institute, Danish journalists, Australian journalists and the Berlin Foreign Press Association, of which I was once a member, were among organisations which sent cables to the Chinese leaders. But these and cables from other organisations and individuals, including my mother, met with silence or a message – 'telegram rejected'.

One unique contribution was made to the release effort. An electronics man jammed the telex of the Chinese diplomatic mission in London with an endless punched tape saying repeatedly 'Release Anthony Grey. Release Anthony Grey. Release Anthony Grey . . .'

The Fleet Street Action Committee collected money from journalists and arranged to have a leading psychiatrist standing by to fly to Peking to see me at a moment's notice. A request for permission to allow the doctor to visit me was made to the Chinese chargé d'affaires in London but no answer was given.

A French journalist Jacques Marcuse, who had long experience of writing on China, publicly offered to exchange himself for me. He wrote to Chou En-lai saying he would hand himself over at the Hong Kong-China border if I were allowed out at the same time. M. Marcuse had often written critically of China, had spent fifteen years there and had told Chou En-lai in his letter: 'I am willing to hand myself over in exchange for the freedom of Anthony Grey, I who am guilty in your eyes while he is a mere hostage.'

All my fellow journalists in Reuters joined the campaign and sent a cable to Chou En-lai asking for my release. Later they petitioned the Prime Minister, Harold Wilson, who received a deputation. The Fleet Street Action Committee also later met with Mr Wilson.

Foreign Secretary Michael Stewart promised to 'look again at the matter of Mr Grey'. In a guarded statement following the uprush of publicity Mr Stewart said: 'In a matter like this you have to judge very carefully, sometimes from week to week what kind of action will produce the right results.' It was to be almost another year before Mr Stewart's 'right results' were produced,

I

and then I sat by his desk in Whitehall at his invitation listening to his explanation of why it had not been possible before.

But in December 1968 I continued to sit in my room in Peking waiting for a doctor.

I had asked for a doctor again a few minutes after the visit on November 26th and fifteen anxious days elapsed before one came. This time it was a man and after a more relaxed examination he informed me I had no bronchitis but was suffering from pharyngitis, inflammation of the cavity of the throat.

Then inexplicably two days later a small medical army descended on my room. First two doctors wearing white caps, face masks and long white coats to their ankles, entered – they looked as if they had come to operate not to examine me. Another white-coated orderly arrived with microscope slides and test tubes. Two others carried in a tall wooden stand with peg holes in it and large amounts of electrical equipment, the main item of which looked rather like a small, battered underwater camera of the kind used by aqua-lung explorers.

In the next hour I was given a rigorous medical examination. The two doctors tapped and searched over my body, checking their impressions with each other. Several guards crowded into the room to watch. The orderly pricked my ear and took blood samples, the other men set up what turned out to be X-ray equipment, suspending the 'underwater camera' on the peg pole. It was the kind of equipment used to take X-ray photographs in Britain in the early part of the century. It had clearly been specially mobilised to take X-ray films of me without having to move me out of the twelve-foot room. I noticed sticking plaster held two parts of it together. I had seen modern equipment in an up-to-date X-ray theatre on my arrival in Peking when I had chest X-rays as part of the medical examination for my Peking driving-licence, so I knew this was not standard equipment.

The doctors peered at my chest through a thing which looked like a wooden megaphone with an opaque end. It was moved around different areas of my chest by hand while the electric gadget operated behind me. Then I had to hold large plates, first front and then back, in a sitting position to enable the films themselves to be taken. Despite myself I couldn't help being somewhat amused by the fantastic contortions that some of the medical people were going through as they clambered around the room over wires and stands and chairs and sign boards and Public Security Bureau guards to carry out this Thurberesque medical check. I wrote in my diary later: 'Today I have become convinced that the Chinese genius could stage the entire Olympic Games in this twelve-foot square space if they really felt it was necessary.'

I could not understand at the time why I was suddenly the object of so much expert medical attention – and so ostentatiously expert at that. In retrospect I believe it may have been that the great welter of publicity in the Western world about the way I was being treated eventually stung somebody like Chou En-lai into seeing that the situation was recovered a little, and a clear cut attempt was made to see if I was really seriously ill.

The next day the sign boards in the room were abruptly changed. For almost six months one board had faced me saying: 'If anyone attacks us and if the conditions are favourable for battle we will certainly act in self-defence to wipe him out resolutely, thoroughly, wholly and completely (We do not strike rashly, but when we do strike we must win).'

If anything seemed explicit this did. Until the British Government meets our wishes Grey stays. Now, the day after my medical, the new board said simply: 'Lifting a rock only to drop it on one's own feet is a Chinese folk saying to describe the behaviour of certain fools. Reactionaries in all countries are fools of this kind.'

Once again looking back this may have been an expression of spleen from somebody in the Foreign Ministry immediately after it had been found I was not seriously ill. This could have been a way of saying that the publicity that had been given to me would not help get the British Government off the hook. The same quotation was used a few days later in the first Chinese Government statement on me since my house arrest began seventeen months earlier.

Six days later I was told through an interpreter I was suffering only from pharyngitis and that the chest pains were muscular, caused by the constant chest action involved in clearing my throat.

There was one other sign that the outburst of publicity caused some embarrassment, albeit temporarily, in Peking. The monthly letter I wrote on 3rd December in which I spoke openly of my great disappointment and near-despair was confiscated by the Foreign Ministry. It was clearly seen that such a letter might be used to add more fuel to the flames of publicity already burning bright around the world. It was simply never returned to me to be posted. My January letter seemed for a time to have suffered a similar fate but turned up mysteriously at my mother's home in Norwich, open and unsealed and without a stamp or postmark, not apparently having been through the British mails. This may have been an attempt to surround the previous one that 'went astray' with confusion. How the January one arrived is a complete mystery. Could it have been through some network ending up with a local Chinese restaurant?

CHAPTER THIRTY

Christmas 1968

Some 3,000 Christmas cards were sent flooding through the mails from Britain to 15 Nan Chihtze, Peking, in December 1968 – but by Christmas not one of them had reached me. Hundreds were also reportedly sent from Australia, the United States, France, Germany, Belgium and other countries, even from India and Pakistan. All were carefully fielded by the Peking authorities and what exactly happened to them is not known. But the point was made. The address of my one-man prison was printed in newspapers in many countries and some newspapers and television stations made direct appeals for cards to be sent to show the concern felt for an innocent individual held for reasons beyond his control and responsibility.

I was unaware of this at the time and after my release it was very moving to find many of those people who had sent Christmas cards or postcards from their holiday resorts writing to me to tell me why and to express sympathy, concern and good wishes. In a way I believe my individual personality was not involved. The letters and cards from all kinds of people in many countries showed that they had identified in me, perhaps unconsciously, a husband, a son or a friend of their own or simply looked on me as one man from a society whose sense of justice was outraged by this act of harsh imprisonment without cause.

And although the cards did not reach me at Christmas 1968 I think they probably made their impact felt somewhere in the hard heart of Communist Chinese officialdom. Because there occurred during that Christmas one small, otherwise inexplicable act of generosity from my jailers. And it was offered without any request from me.

I had asked to send cabled messages to my mother, girl friend and Reuters and this was granted on Christmas Eve. I handed them to the cook to take to the guards in the next room. Immediately he came back and began gesticulating and looking around among my books. After several long minutes of painstaking dumb show I began to guess what he was getting at. I folded a piece of paper and stood it up on the typing desk and he nodded eagerly. I was being offered the opportunity to send greetings cards – and I hadn't even asked or dreamed of asking for such a thing!

But how? 'I go buy,' said the cook, obviously conveying the instructions the guards had received from the Foreign Ministry. I gave him money and he went out immediately. It was an unprecedented concession and the only time I was offered something for which I didn't ask. I think this must have been a result of the thousands of cards flooding into the Peking Post Office from the West. A small humanitarian gesture perhaps to counteract the damaging impression being made by my confinement.

Soon the cook was back with a dozen New Year cards in Chinese. One to my amazement was different to the others. It bore on its front in lurid colours the billowing mushroom cloud of a hydrogen bomb explosion. Underneath in Chinese characters was the legend 'Mao Tse-tung's thought is a spiritual atom bomb.'

I couldn't help smiling at a greetings card so ludicrous in our eyes. I longed to address it to Harold Wilson with the simple greeting 'Happy New Year – or else!' with my name and Peking underneath. But I thought there was slim chance of it passing scrutiny in Peking. I spent a great deal of time trying to work out a cryptic, satirical message for the card. Eventually I addressed it to Mr Long, Reuters general manager, with words to the effect that I hoped the year would see 'a solution to all problems'. It was meant to be a sort of reference to the finality of the mushroom cloud as well as an expression of hope for myself. I wasn't very satisfied with my attempted humour. But the comic nature of the card so struck me that I felt compelled to try.

It was returned from the Foreign Ministry with the others – which bore simple thoughts of Chairman Mao in his own calligraphy – only eight hours after I handed them to the guards on Christmas morning. This contrasted sharply with the thirty-five days some of my monthly letters were held at the Ministry. The cables were also returned in under twenty-four hours and went off on Christmas Day. I had deliberately written the words 'Christmas Eve' into all three cables to my mother, girl friend and Reuters and appended the date so as to show the receivers how long they were delayed. But on Christmas Day I was instructed to change the date on them. The Ministry seemed particularly anxious not to obstruct my Christmas greetings. Some of the cards I sent were photographed and printed in newspapers in Britain, so perhaps the Chinese made a little public relations point with them.

For Christmas Day I dressed in my grey suit which had gathered dust on the back of the washroom door since the previous Christmas. There was a cable and a letter from Shirley handed to me at breakfast. The letter was one month old, written on the night of my visit, and gave me the first news of the reaction. Harold Wilson had referred to me in a speech that same night I learned, but I didn't know what he said. There was a *Sunday Times* crossword in the letter and this was my entertainment for Christmas Day 1968. No parcels were allowed although several ways were tried of sending parcels to me. After a lunch of fish and cauliflower two cables arrived from Reuters – one from Gerald Long, the other from editorial colleagues.

I ate little or no breakfast or lunch but in the evening hungrily devoured an ordinary meal of meat balls and rice. I read in the evening, sang a few carols to myself as I walked back and forth and penned a few lines of quiet resignation. 'I can't bear to think of spending Christmas 1969 here. I've just looked back to last year's entry and found that is exactly what I said then. I suppose if it is to be, it is to be. I can only accept what comes. . . .'

In my Christmas cable to Reuters I had said after long deliberation: 'Feelings inexpressible that those Londoners who should and could meet their responsibility to help me continue after a year and a half to do nothing.' By 'those Londoners' I meant the British Government. I remember thinking an uncharitable Christmas thought. 'Those Londoners' were enduring my ordeal very staunchly behind their desks in Whitehall.

CHAPTER THIRTY-ONE

Chinese Lessons

Four days after Christmas I was sitting huddled in my sheepskin overcoat in the twelve-foot square room waiting for my six o'clock meal. The door of the room was open as usual and the courtyard temperature beyond the ill-fitting outside door immediately adjoining my room was well below freezing.

The cook brought the food and the *People's Daily* as he did every day at that time. I flicked idly over the pages which I couldn't read. The few Chinese characters I knew included 'Hong Kong' and 'journalist', and I always scanned the news items to see if there was anything likely to be connected with me. Suddenly my eye hit two other characters I knew very well. I knew them because they were splattered all over the room I lived in. '*Ger-lai*'. The ideograms for my name leapt at me out of a thick, black headline. I scanned the text and saw it several times more after the words '*Liu To She*' which is the nearest the Chinese can get to Reuters. The R sound always comes over in transliteration as an L. I was startled, puzzled and suddenly filled with new apprehension. What on earth did it mean? Was this the prelude to the trial on some faked charge that I had always half-feared? Was this some unthought-of spying accusation that would result in a hopelessly long incarceration without the slightest chance of release? Bad as it was not knowing when I would be freed, my strange predicament was better than a firm, long sentence without hope.

I stared helplessly at the meaningless symbols. I was beside myself with the frustration of having firm information about myself in front of me that I couldn't understand. Among the books on my shelf was a *Teach Yourself Chinese* text book. I had got it from upstairs in May and had made several abortive attempts to begin learning. But I had hoped for release in the autumn, and could not convince myself there was any point in trying to learn

the very difficult language without tuition or help. I had shirked
the tremendous mental effort and application required. I had sometimes felt guilty to myself about it, but my depressed state of
mind had seemed to defy the kind of concentration required. I
had tried to tell myself it would be at least a good intellectual
exercise but I had somehow remained unconvinced by this line of
argument.

But so great was the feeling of impotence generated by the vital
news item I vowed there and then to devote myself to learning
Chinese so that I might discover what it said. And in any event
the sustained effort would help carry me sanely through several
months. Another factor which had prevented me from getting
started before was the lack of paper on which to write the
characters, so essential to a coherent study of Chinese. But I hit
on the idea of holding on to the *People's Daily* instead of letting
it be taken away in the daily clean-up and practising the symbols
in the white margins around the edges of the print. The new
strict rules of the guards had meant for several months that I was
not allowed to be escorted upstairs under any pretext. Escapades
like the *Zhivago* one were now impossible and no further exercise
books were obtainable.

I frantically scanned the index of 1,200 characters in the text
book for more than an hour trying to catch a glimmer of the
sense of the *People's Daily* article without success. My meal went
completely uneaten. I could only pray that the news item didn't
mean some awful deterioration in my life. Over the next couple
of days I prepared myself mentally for the task ahead, tried to
shake off the lethargy and, on New Year's Eve, as well as drinking
another silent toast in warm water to family and friends back home,
I resolved that in 1969 I would learn Chinese.

I set myself an intensive programme to complete the forty-
chapter book in four months. And from January to April I rose
almost every morning in the grey, early morning light and crept
into the washroom. There, wrapped in my overcoat against the
cold dusty winds that blew in through the tiny cracks in the
windows, I sat next to the bath scribbling the tortuous Chinese
hieroglyphics in the margins of the *People's Daily* and chanting
them quietly to myself. I learned every one of the sentences in the
book by heart, repeating them from memory as I walked in the
yard or in the room. I drew the characters out in the air with a

forefinger as I held my hands behind my back. And I scribbled away at my desk too, always being ready to hide the book and paper when a guard approached. I didn't want to lose the materials since I was not at all sure my jailers would approve of my learning their language. I hid the newspapers that were covered in my scribbled characters in the Carlsberg Lager box under my bed.

Chinese characters are tremendously difficult to memorise and write at first. But great intelligence is not required, just industrious, constant application. I slogged on devoting all my waking hours to the task. Crossword-compiling, story-writing, ant-watching, paper doll-cutting, soap-carving, antiseptic label-reading were things of the past. The great drive was on to learn Chinese! And the satisfaction was great as the scales fell from my eyes and I began to be able to read the slogans splashed around on the walls of the courtyard, some in letters several feet high. 'Long live Chairman Mao, Long Live the Great Proletarian Cultural Revolution, Long Live the Chinese People's Republic.' 'Those who oppose China will come to no good end.' 'Down with British Imperialism.' 'Down with Grey.' 'Long Live the Chinese Communist Party.' There was for me an excitement in reading these hackneyed phrases in the original language for the first time.

The job of learning was made doubly difficult for me because the text book was written in 1949 and the Communists had since greatly simplified more than 500 characters in their campaign against illiteracy. I had to use a hit-and-miss system of deduction and guesswork to link those characters I had learned with the simplified version used in the People's Republic.

But then the *People's Daily* slowly began to yield up the secrets that had remained hidden to my eyes for so long. Eventually I read of the resignation of General de Gaulle in Chinese from the *People's Daily* – and imagined for some time my study must have been faulty to translate a news item in such an unlikely way. But I checked and double checked and decided it was true, though amazing, and was greatly satisfied to have it confirmed later in the *Peking Review* (which I think added the explanation that a referendum was a bourgeois trick for exploiting the masses).

The details of the *People's Daily* news item which had launched me on the study of Chinese in a dither of apprehension at the end of December became known to me much earlier than I expected. A translation of it was printed in the *Peking Review* which reached me some two weeks later. The magazine had obviously been delayed as the Foreign Ministry reflected on whether to allow me to see it or not. But having committed themselves to the one and only considered defence of their action that they ever made in cold print, they clearly had eventually decided I should be allowed to see it. The black headline which had leapt out of the page at me had in fact said 'British Government will Gain Nothing in using Grey Question to Whip Up an Anti-China Outcry'.

It can perhaps be imagined how frantically I ran my eye through the long 1,000-word article fearing to find at last some definite term of imprisonment, fearing to find myself described as a spy or a 'dangerous element' or even a reactionary. But to my great relief no epithets had been used. I was still a simple hostage. I read it over and over again and sensed between the lines a defensiveness, an underlying feeling almost of embarrassment in what amounted to an attempt to justify taking a hostage in the face of the outburst of indignant publicity in large sections of the world's press.

The item, a wonderful example of the view of life through distorted Chinese spectacles, began: 'To mislead public opinion and divert the resentment of the people at home the British Government, beset with difficulties at home and abroad, recently stood facts on their head, called black white and used the question of Reuter correspondent Anthony Grey to whip up an anti-China outcry. Not only had it set off its entire propaganda machine to raise a hue and cry but British Prime Minister Harold Wilson and Secretary of State for Foreign and Commonwealth Affairs Michael Stewart have personally stepped forward to attack China. These abject actions on the part of the British Government will, despite all its pains, only show its utter stupidity. On December 3 British Prime Minister Wilson told the parliament that "Grey's detention is totally unjustified". This is sheer nonsense.'

The statement recited the arrest and sentencing of Communist newsmen in Hong Kong – 'brutal suppression' were the words used – and added that for the Chinese Government to have adopted the measures against me was entirely justified.

Then there was a paragraph that made me gasp in disbelief and I repeated it to myself many times over the next few days always shaking my head incredulously. 'Grey is treated leniently. He still lives in his house and conditions for his everyday life are in the main the same as they were before his movement was restricted.'

This rejoinder was made in reply to a published comment by Michael Stewart that I was being held 'under inhuman restraints', and to other criticisms made in Hong Kong that China was not showing respect for the normal standards of civilised behaviour. 'This is downright fabrication and slander. The fact is just the opposite...' the newspaper item said and went on to say how leniently I was treated in my own house. The two British diplomats who visited him could not but admit that Grey looked physically quite well and this served as a forceful slap in the face of their superiors, the statement added. It was hard to believe that the item was issued by the Foreign Ministry where it was known that all foreign affairs statements are based on evidence of a country's own representatives on the spot. There was talk of 'a dark concentration camp and prisons' in Hong Kong although it was known that prisoners in the colony had access to television sets, books and newspapers, were allowed to play football and watch film shows at weekends and were not kept locked in their cells by day.

But despite the ragged nature of the attempt to justify their actions the statement made clear there was still no possibility of China backing down. 'Since the Hong Kong British authorities continue to keep the thirteen patriotic Chinese journalists in jail the Chinese Government is fully justified in continuing to restrict Grey's freedom of movement. This is the consistent stand of the Chinese Government.' That was it, apart from the quotation about the British Government lifting a rock only to drop it on its own feet.

I thought wryly that the British Government had lifted a rock only to drop it on *my* feet – and still showed no signs of moving it for me.

But I noted in my diary that I was pleased that Mr Wilson and the Foreign Minister had spoken out. 'At least the case is now in the open. It gives me hope even if it is in the distant future. I hope this year will see my release.'

By the end of April I had learned some 1,200 characters. In mainland China today where a high proportion of the population is still illiterate, literacy is defined as the knowledge of 1,000 characters. Although I couldn't read the paper fluently I felt considerable pride at being the equivalent of literate in China plus a little bit more. The growing sense of achievement in learning the language of my captors was worth the slow, daily grind of repetitious learning by rote. The spoken language is very difficult because of the different tones employed and I was rarely able to understand more than an odd word I heard spoken by the guards.

As my knowledge of the language increased I began studying more closely the pink posters pasted around the two rooms. They were identical copies of the one pasted on my back on that night the Red Guards raided me 100 years before. One copy was even pasted on the headboard of my bed. I began to recognise more and more characters in it as my study progressed.

My overriding ambition soon became to translate the poster word for word to see exactly what I was accused of and how. I did not know until after my release of the reference to me as 'the big spy Grey' made at the struggle meeting against my driver – thank goodness! Had I known of it the worry of being put on trial would have been a great additional burden.

I deliberately refrained from looking at the poster for some weeks while I concentrated hard on the slow process of adding new characters to my growing mental store.

Then in mid-April, with *Teach Yourself Chinese* mastered several days ahead of the Four-Month Plan made in January, I went through to the washroom one lunchtime and began a detailed attack on the secrets of the pink poster pasted up by the mirror, peering intently at each character in turn. Over the next few days I gradually worked out all the faint, handwritten characters on the poster which had been run off on a duplicating machine. I could translate it all! It was perhaps the greatest satisfaction of my whole twenty-six months confinement to have mastered it. I have a strong lazy streak and to have worked with such concentrated industry and to have won such a satisfying result was very gratifying to me.

I then determined to carry a translation of the poster to freedom with me as evidence of the illogical hysteria of the night it was employed. It had never been officially published and I had sensed from the tone of the *People's Daily* statement quoted earlier in this chapter that it was something that already Peking would not be proud of in the cold light of day. I thought of copying it out but judged that if they searched me and the house my efforts would be wasted. So I decided that if my belongings were finally confiscated, no matter what else I lost, I would carry out the poster where it couldn't be found – in my head.

I set out to learn and memorise every character in the poster. I learned a phrase and then a line at a time. Soon I had the whole poster by heart and each day as I walked up and down the courtyard with my hands behind my back I would practise drawing out the characters with one finger in the air. I learned it until I could say it in my sleep backwards. Towards the end of my confinement the posters were removed and the room cleaned up and I carried on reciting it carefully each day to keep it fresh in my mind until I could write it in safety. Then the night I was released I wrote the characters of that poster in a flat in the British part of the diplomatic compound. The translation follows. It will be seen that the only 'crime' the Red Guards accused me of in writing was being an Imperialist element and a reactionary newsman. The quoted authority for the action was Mao's statement that we were all paper tigers anyway!

Mao had originally used the paper-tiger image to pooh-pooh the West's atomic bomb. It has taken its place in history alongside Lenin's analogy that imperialism is a colossus with feet of clay. The paper tiger idea is a succinct one for intimating that the apparent superiority or strength of an opponent is only superficial. In pondering over what to call this book I thought that if the subject were less serious it might be called 'News Paper Tiger in Peking'.

最高指示

一切反动派都是纸老虎。看起来,反动派
的样子是可怕的,但是实际上并没有什么了
不起的力量从长远的观点看问题真正强大
的力量 不是属于反动派而是属于人民

勒令

首都无产阶级革命派对英国帝国主义分子路透社反动记者格雷勒令如下:

一 格雷在找方警卫人员管制下必须老"实"不许
乱说乱动

二 格雷必须在我革命群众规定的范围内活
动,不得超越

三 对我革命群众在格雷住所张贴的毛主席象,
语录及标语等,不得涂抹撕毁

四 格雷必须了格遵守我国政府的一切规定不
得有丝毫违扎,听候我国政府处理

以上所望格雷必须照办,如有违反一切 后果由反动记者格雷本人员全个责任.

上纸簧北京照相机厂红色造反委员会

北京中教育战线"红旗"

北京小教联总部

一九七年 九月十九日

The poster that the Red Guards pasted to my back. I memorised
the Chinese characters and wrote them out in my own hand after
my release.

Here is the translated text of the poster.

Highest Directive

All reactionaries are paper tigers. In appearance the reactionaries are terrifying, but in reality they are not so powerful. From a long-term point of view, it is not the reactionaries but the people who are really powerful.

Order

Proletarian revolutionaries of the capital, Peking, strictly order British Imperialist element Reuters reactionary correspondent Grey as follows:

1. Grey must always be 'reliable' under the control and supervision of our Public Security Bureau men and may not step out of line in word or deed.
2. Grey must live and remain within the limits defined by our revolutionary masses and must not go beyond them.
3. The portraits of Chairman Mao, the quotations and slogans, etc., stuck on Grey's house by the revolutionary masses must not be erased or torn down.
4. Grey must strictly observe all the decisions of our government and must not contravene them in the slightest degree; he must await further notice from our government.

Grey must act according to the above commands and should there be any contravention, reactionary correspondent Grey himself must bear the entire responsibility for all the consequences.

Peking No. 1 Photo Machine Factory Red Revolutionary Rebels Council and all revolutionaries of the capital

Peking Middle Schools Fighting Line 'Red Flag'

Peking Primary Schools General Liaison Office.

August 18th 1967.

CHAPTER THIRTY-TWO

My Guards

> The East is red,
> The sun rises,
> China has brought forth a Mao Tse-tung
> He is the people's great saviour.
>
> Chairman Mao loves the people,
> He is our guide
> He leads us onward
> To build the new China.
>
> The Communist Party is like the sun,
> Wherever it shines there is light
> Where there's the Communist Party
> There the people will win liberation.

Every morning for two years I was awakened by the singing of these words in their original Chinese form. They were sung by my guards a few feet away in the dining-room at anything between six o'clock and eight o'clock and the fact that they knew I would be wakened by it made them sing all the more loudly, I believe. The song 'The East is Red' became the anthem of the Cultural Revolution and was sung as a prelude to work all over China in factories, schools, farm communes and in any place where a few people gathered each morning.

In my dining-room the guards who had slept overnight on their camp beds or my sofa got up to join members of the incoming shift who were to take over from them. The singing took place before a portrait of Mao that was hung in a gilt frame on the wall above and to the left of my sideboard in direct line of vision through the open door of my twelve-foot square room. On the floor beneath the portrait, standing just against the sideboard was a spittoon which the guards had brought into my dining-room for their use. It was used constantly day and night with loud accompanying noises.

273

When the guards finished 'The East is Red' they launched into reading several quotations from their red booklets, still drawn up in two ranks looking reverently up towards the portrait. The leading guard would recite that Mao was their 'great teacher, great leader, great supreme commander and great helmsman'. Then he would call out a snatch of Chinese that remains ingrained in my mind: *'Mao chu hsi chiao tao wo shou'* – 'Chairman Mao teaches us' – and then all together the assembled ranks would chant the quoted teaching. There would be anything up to twelve guards in the line up. For the second year of my confinement, I, a solitary prisoner, was guarded all day by no less than nine guards. They all sat around in my dining-room taking part in endless sessions of what we would call cross-indoctrination but which they called the study of Mao Tse-tung's thought.

Study materials included *People's Daily* editorials about the current phase of the Cultural Revolution, Mao's *Selected Works*, articles from the Communist Party's theoretical journal *Red Flag* and Mao's own 'Latest Instructions' which consisted of a few well-chosen phrases issued in the style of an imperial edict. Senior Public Security Bureau men gave lectures and each day the whole thing was flung open for each man in turn to give his own Maoist testament, his own expression of the faith. The others would criticise each man's version and the whole thing often developed into a noisy free-for-all with everybody shouting at once. The newspaper editorials were invariably read out at the top of the voice of a selected guard and since these sometimes covered the whole page of a newspaper could become a nerve-wracking experience for me sitting a few feet away with the doors of both rooms open. Even with the door of my room closed before I rose in the morning the loud noise of the ceremonies and editorial-reading bore in on me in a way which left me infuriated and helpless as I tried to cling to the last vestiges of the night's sleep.

These sessions went on all day, almost every day, and sometimes late into the evening too. The sign that they were at an end and that I could reasonably hope for peace and quiet for a while was the singing of 'The Helmsman'. Start with 'The East is Red', finish with 'The Helmsman'.

'The Helmsman' went like this:

Sailing the seas depends on the helmsman
All living things depend on the sun for their growth,
Moistened by rain and dew young crops grow strong,
Making revolution depends on the thought of Mao Tse-tung

Fish can't live without water,
Melons can't thrive off their vine,
The revolutionary masses cannot do without the Communist
                                                        Party,
Mao Tse-tung's thought is the never-setting sun.

I heard these two songs so frequently they became ingrained in my mind. I would find myself humming or whistling them as I washed. And I found myself making up my own sets of rather rude words to them in my mind to counteract the tedium of their presence.

After my second consular visit in November 1968 the guards 'redecorated' the dining-room where the meeting had taken place, sticking up pieces of coloured paper all round the walls with slogans on them and fixing sheafs of song-sheets on to the walls too. These reminded me of my childhood. They were like Christmas pantomime song sheets that were lowered to the stage in the interval so that the audience could learn and sing the simple song quickly. From then on each afternoon the roomful of guards would devote several hours to learning and singing in unison from these sheets which also carried the tonic sol-fa notes to help them learn the tunes by the doh, ray, me method.

The song with which they annoyed me most and I believe quite deliberately so, was 'The Internationale', the world-wide Communist rallying song. They usually got round to this after six o'clock while I was still eating my meal with the door of my room closed. They roared it out, ten or so voices in hoarse unison, time and time again, louder and louder. After finishing my food I had to open the door myself to let in the noise of their 'singing'. When they saw the door come open the singers usually pulled out a few odd decibels to add to the uproar. I would often sit on my chair with fists clenched tight as they sang on and on, clearly taking delight in the discomfort they knew the noise would be causing me. The giggles and laughter as they paused for breath between renderings betrayed this.

For many months, two guards clumped off down the wooden

staircase to the kitchen every day after lunch to teach revolutionary songs to the cook and boilerman and engage them in the
study of Mao's quotations and newspaper editorials. This activity
invariably produced noise that jarred my nerves. The kitchen walls
were also decorated with portraits of Mao and blood-red posters
with black characters written on them quoting Mao's most per-
tinent teachings. Every day before starting work the cook, boilerman and wash amah had to gather before their portrait and posters
and sing 'The East is Red'. Their voices filtered up to me through
the floorboards of my room directly above. Each morning loudspeakers mounted in the streets nearby boomed out the strains of
'The East is Red' across the rooftops at six thirty or seven
o'clock. This early morning noise was often swelled by the thud
and clump of the guards' boots on the stairs as they went to wash
themselves in the kitchen. And because I was allowed no curtain
at the large courtyard window the combined effects of the noise
and light woke me constantly. I was so incensed by this that it
spurred me to work with great determination to re-enter the precious oblivion of sleep. Having failed with a request to Shirley to
try to send me ear plugs in a letter, I developed the knack of
closing off the ear that wasn't next to the pillow with one finger
for long enough to allow me to get back to sleep. I suppose the
finger dropped away after I fell asleep but the temporary respite
from the noise was enough to allow me to leave the state of wakefulness. To counteract the light from the window in the early
summer dawns, I put a rolled-up handkerchief with short pieces
of string tied to each end at the side of the bed the night before,
then when I woke, without opening my eyes, I groped for it and
tied it round my head with the handkerchief covering my eyes.
So, often blindfolded and with a finger in one ear I would force
my way back to sleep. The early morning period was the worst
to face, as I have already said, and to gain an hour or two of
extra unconsciousness each day was worth a great deal of effort.

The behaviour of the guards varied somewhat over the twenty-
six-month period, possibly reflecting the intensity of the Cultural
Revolution campaigns inside the organisation. During the first six
months the shift changes were accompanied by only casual quotation reading with the guards lolling against the table and sideboard in a loose group. Around Christmas 1967 they began to

form up regularly to sing 'The East is Red' and 'Helmsman' but still the days were relatively quiet. Three guards were on at a time and there was no propagandising as a rule. A few times a week the twelve or so guards taking part in guarding me would gather for a general meeting that would last all morning and they would discuss anything connected with me too I think, especially if I had done something that required disciplinary measures – stopping my walk or closing off the window – or if I had made a request for something from upstairs. Their hot water was at first brought in vacuum flasks from headquarters just up the road, and the guards rarely went into any other rooms in my house except the dining-room they occupied. The guards changed frequently over the whole period. A total of seventy or eighty different men in all took part in guarding me at one time or another, maybe more. But in the second year after the entire guard was changed overnight they began to use the whole house. All clumped upstairs to use my private bathroom and lavatory before settling down for the night. Nine guards remained on duty by day and four at night. Just before my first visit the practice of watching over me during the night from a chair planted down directly outside my door stopped. From then on my door was watched at night from the daytime guard position – a chair placed at the side of the dining-table. This move, although only a few feet back from my door did lessen the claustrophobic feeling of the night. The change of the entire guard for the second year led them to bring in their own small enamel spittoon. The sight of this in my dining-room was very offensive to my eyes. Previously the other guards had simply opened the windows to spit through. The new guards also suspended a curtain on string halfway across the dining-room so that those sleeping were shaded from the light of the standard lamp at the dining-table. Those on duty at night usually whiled away the time reading papers and political materials. The guards also began using my upstairs lounge and office for smaller offshoot meetings during the day. They also used the kitchen downstairs for washing and boiling up water for making their tea. They used my refrigerator in the summer. The sound of its door being constantly opened and closed in the basement annoyed me intensely. They brought fruit to put in it, cooled their drinking water there and also used my ice-cube containers to make ice. I saw one guard bring up ice cubes in one of my soup dishes and cram a handful into his mouth one hot night. It made my teeth shiver to think of it – and I also wondered what their superiors would think if it was known they were indulging themselves in such bourgeois luxuries as ice-cubes, made in a refrigerator.

The sound of the refrigerator being used annoyed me and so too did the sound of my drinks cupboard being opened in the dining-room. It was fairly well stocked with full bottles of spirits, liqueurs and wines and after the complete change of guards it was used also to house the tin mugs and drinking glasses of the guards themselves. The sideboard was being constantly opened and closed and for many weeks until I got used to it this sound infuriated me beyond all logical bounds. They also used my large, old fashioned radio set in the dining-room, frequently playing revolutionary Peking opera at a deafening pitch. One guard I am sure developed a taste for *Playboy* magazine. In a cabinet in the room above the twelve-foot square room was a pile of magazines, *Punch, Private Eye, Playboy, Life,* and so on. And one particular guard made a practice of slipping upstairs very quietly in the middle of the night. I noticed this often when I lay awake unable to sleep. I would hear his rubber-soled canvas shoes shift quietly up the stairs. Then the creak of the door at the top of the stairs was just audible in the quiet house. Then I tried to trace his movements in the room above by listening and staring at the ceiling. As far as I could guess he always seemed to make for the side of the room where the magazine cabinet was. It can only be imagined with what goggle-eyed amazement the guard would have turned over the pages of photographs of naked female pulchritude. In the starkly puritanical atmosphere of the People's Republic of China such a magazine must have exploded like a bombshell on his eyes. I think none of the other guards had discovered the magazines. He and only he made such clandestine excursions upstairs when his two shift fellows were asleep and this was the only explanation I could reach. Unless he liked the jokes in *Punch* or *Private Eye.*

For a time the guards decided to hold their little red booklets of Mao's quotations in the 'present arms' position, as they watched me exercise in the yard. Normally they held nothing in their hands. Then they began standing at the top of the steps leading from the house, stiffly to attention with the diary-sized red-covered book held exactly and formally in an upright position across the front of their jackets. My first reaction to this was to laugh. I walked back and forth in the yard and as I came towards the guard I often looked first at the little booklet held in front of the stomach then up to the face of its holder. The expression was always an intent scowl as if to say 'You'd better watch out now I'm holding this book'. This went on for two or three weeks, then some of them started to dangle the book rather listlessly at their side during my forty-minute walking periods. Then abruptly it stopped. I think somebody's over-zealous idea had been dropped when the ludicrous nature of it finally dawned on them.

The guards also wore farthing-sized Mao badges on their jackets at first – little red badges with a golden profile of Mao Tse-tung superimposed. As time went by they began to get bigger and increased to the size of a half-crown. This trend continued and I amused myself by predicting that if this craze continued unchecked the people of China would soon be disappearing behind cart-wheel sized badges. Only top of head and feet would be visible. I had to smother a laugh therefore when during the momentous ninth Communist Party Congress in the spring of 1969 one guard turned up wearing a massive lapel badge of Mao that was literally the size of a saucer. And soon they were all wearing them.

The worst aspect of the guards' behaviour was the constant, mute hostility which most of them felt obliged to turn on me. This found its expression mainly in endless staring with eyes showing a mixture of hatred and contempt as I took my walks in the courtyard. There were often, although not always, two guards in the courtyard with me, one at either end and this practically made the walk a misery. After wearying of staring grimly back at them I attempted to ignore their stares but nevertheless in such a closely confined space it was unpleasant to feel the constant attention of hostile eyes. When eventually some of the conditions of my confinement were relaxed towards the end I was allowed to walk alone in the yard without supervision and this was a great relief.

Hostility was expressed too in another way. Until my conditions were relaxed in the twenty-second month I was never given a definite time at which my two daily periods of exercise should be taken. I always had to await a sign from the guards and they took a vindictive delight in keeping me waiting for this. From the time when I could walk only within the room I had paced up and down to the washroom morning, afternoon and night. Since from very early on the guards had taken to stopping my walking as a disciplinary measure if I stepped out of line, I determined never to ask to be allowed out lest I gave them the chance to affront me by refusing. So I paced up and down each morning and afternoon, ready to go into the yard when I got a sign. Very often I would be kept pacing back and forth for a long time before one deigned to give the signal. Sometimes I would be kept waiting so long that once outside for the regulation forty minutes I would run well into the next meal time period and food would be taken into my room to grow cold while I finished my walk, waiting for the sign to go in again.

I tried to rationalise this hostility, and perhaps in a sense it is not too difficult to understand. In the nineteenth century Western imperialist countries, with Britain in the van, were doing their best to carve up China into colonial divisions, in effect. China became a semi-colony and Europeans often behaved in a supercilious and arrogant way as if they had conquered and occupied her. Foreign gunboats moved in the coastal water and rivers and the Peking embassies of the West were turned into embattled fortresses guarded by their own troops. In 1967 one Chinese leader addressed himself to Britain in a speech: 'We hereby warn the British Imperialists: the old debt you owe us for launching the dirty Opium War and forcibly occupying Hong Kong by taking advantage of the corruption in the Ching court is not yet repaid. Today you are again perpetrating fascist atrocities in Hong Kong . . . the 700 million Chinese people absolutely will not tolerate it.'

This kind of sentiment has been constantly expressed and no doubt over-expressed by China's Communist propagandists to inculcate an indelible awareness of the evils of the non-Communist world into all Chinese. The humiliation of the nineteenth century, however, was indeed a very deep one to the ancient Chinese civilisation which previously had seen itself, as the name of the country implies, as 'the middle kingdom' with all else beyond barbarian. The frenzy of the Cultural Revolution and the resulting Hong Kong trouble intensified these emotions and my guards, subjected as they were to a blanket barrage of anti-British, anti-Western propaganda, could perhaps hardly be blamed individually for behaving the way they did. Being told that every minute of every day is the time to fight the class war and having so clearly-defined a class enemy before their eyes left them with little alternative but to be hostile.

But although I could reason this way I could not easily forgive their apparent hatred of me. I made up names for them, some extremely insulting, in my effort to provide myself with mental opposition to their intimidating presence. Only one guard was present off and on for the whole twenty-six months and he was a particularly untoothsome-looking individual. I feel it is uncharitable to hold anybody's appearance against them in itself and would not have done so with this man if he hadn't gone out of his way to be consistently offensive. With his aggressive, prolonged staring and contemptuous gestures when ordering me around he endeavoured to outdo all others in showing his enmity towards the class enemy. I named him 'Pervert Jaw' in my mind because of his prominent jutting jaw and lower lip and a slightly effeminate walk. And when he pointedly ignored me and kept me pacing back and forth in my room for three quarters of an hour when I should have been allowed outside I would make up insulting rhymes about him to the tune of a popular romantic song and sing them quietly to myself to fight down my helpless fury.

I dubbed my guards with other titles like 'Loud Lout', 'Little Caesar', 'Hulk' – a vast man with broad drooping shoulders and pendulous jowls, 'Rickets Face' – a thin man with not absolutely symmetrical bone structure who never ceased for a second to stare balefully at me as I walked, and 'Basket ball' – an athletic type who when he took off his jacket in summer revealed a red figure nine on the back of his vest which he clearly wore on the basket ball court. There were others like 'Cat,' 'Lofty' and 'Angela' for reasons that should be fairly clear from the nomenclature. One I named 'Sinanthropus'. This was the Latin term for 'Peking Man' given to an early mammal skull found near Peking. The skull was believed to date from the earliest days of man. The guard in question was particularly ponderous and lumbering in his movements. At the time when the rules about my getting books were changed he repeated monotonously, despite all my reasoning, 'Write the titles, write the titles'.

In late January, 1969 these illogical regulations about my not being able to get books from upstairs without submitting the titles for approval were inexplicably reversed. I was escorted upstairs for another look round and took a few of the remaining books down with me. But when I asked a few weeks later if I could go up again my request – once more quite illogically – was ignored. But by this time I had become so accustomed to the capricious behaviour of my jailers and had so few worthwhile books left anyway that it made little difference to me.

In the first summer one shift of three guards played draughts constantly. Stripped to their vests and baggy blue trousers they lolled on top of my dining-room table banging the counters down loudly. I sat quietly in the twelve-foot room trying not to wince at the infuriatingly repetitive sound.

But if the guards provided the most objectionable feature of my confinement they also provided me with material for character and personality study. Even though I understood little or nothing of what they said it was not difficult to analyse the characters of the men from the way they conducted themselves, quietly or loudly, in a controlled manner or erratically, whether they commanded the respect of their fellows or were looked down on, whether they were bright or dull, sympathetic or repellent to each other. I came to be able to recognise all their voices from a distance when they were out of sight. I could recognise a man too from the loud hawking noise he made preparatory to spitting, even if he were in the yard or downstairs in the kitchen. I could pick out those likely to advance to higher positions in the Public Security Bureau, which were the respected party members among them and which were obviously rankers destined only to do menial tasks for the rest of their days. To be fair there were a few who were not aggressive in their demeanour and for them by contrast I felt something akin to a liking. One I remember particularly I dubbed 'Little Chou En-lai' because he was spruce and neat, with quick movements like China's premier, who has considerable personal charm. He was young, not a shift leader, but carried himself with dignity, almost never spat and was the only guard in whose blue cotton trousers I ever saw a crease from a flat-iron. He never smiled at me or made the slightest gesture of sympathy. But neither did he glare nor stare unduly. He conducted himself intelligently and efficiently doing the job of giving me the minimal instructions to go in and out of the house without any overtones of hatred or any other emotion. Perhaps as a result of his sensible approach I dreamed one night that I took him for a drink in an East Berlin café and was delighted to find he spoke English!

At the other end of the spectrum was a young guard who joined the team watching over me towards the end of my confinement. He could only have been sixteen and must have been a school-age Red Guard when I entered China. From the moment of his arrival he was clearly determined to make his mark by his uncompromising attitude towards the prisoner. At night as I paced back and forth he would set himself feet astride, arms folded, in the doorway of the dining-room to stare needlessly at me. His eyes blazed with ferocity. Here was a Red Guard who wanted to set the world on fire. When later I was allowed to go upstairs for a short time each day he would come and stand over me as I sat at my desk, staring hard. One day after returning his stare for several long uncomfortable minutes I decided to try the effect of my voice on him. I had never spoken directly to any of my guards alone until then. I said simply 'What do you want?' He seemed momentarily taken aback but continued to stare insolently at me and only after several more minutes did he return downstairs.

Next morning he arrived with another young guard and they both pulled up chairs on the other side of the desk where I sat reading and leaned forward to stare into my face. On this occasion I sensed there was an attempt to provoke me so apart from an occasional glance I tried to ignore the two guards and pretended to concentrate wordlessly on my reading. Later in the day an interpreter arrived and the young guard came into the twelve-foot square room with him.

The guard started spitting words at me tossing his head angrily. 'Yesterday you were arrogant and shouted at this guard,' the interpreter said. I denied this quietly.

Then came the only attempt to extract a 'confession' from me in the whole twenty-six months. 'You should confess to being arrogant and impolite to this guard. It would be better if you confess now....' I declined to confess to arrogance (although on reflection much later I suppose it would not have been an uncomplimentary thing to confess to after nearly two years solitary!)

The interpreter asked me to repeat the words and show him the tone of voice I had used. Then he persisted in his confession efforts repeating that 'it would be better' for me if I did confess. Since I seemed to have a choice I decided to risk not 'confessing', and insisted that I had not behaved with what they imagined was arrogance. I tried to say as little as possible in reply to the ridiculous accusations of the teenager. Eventually the interpreter seemed to hit on a compromise formula. He asked me to remember and bear in mind for the future the warning about my behaviour. I agreed to bear it in mind and the incident ended. There were no reprisals. I think the revolutionary fervour of the young guard was misplaced. I had noticed a civilian cadre in the dining-room during the interview and fancy he had come down from the Foreign Ministry to investigate the report. This was shortly after it was announced that the last Hong Kong Communist newsman would be released in a few months time. Hard-line action against me therefore was by then inappropriate. But it illustrates how some guards were at that late stage still unable to let slip the chance to try to heap humiliation on me.

One last anecdote about my guards. One of Mao's most famous exhortations is 'Do not take a needle or a thread from the people'. This was one of the maxims of the Red Army in the civil war and this attitude distinguished the Communist fighters from the looting, raping army of Chiang Kai-shek and was an expression of the basic appeal of the new forces to the Chinese masses. It is still frequently quoted and held up as an ideal. So I was particularly pleased to find that the Chinese, who to the outside world sometimes appear as 750 million living personifications of Mao's theories, don't always abide by them – even Chinese uniformed men!

When painters came on the Foreign Ministry's instructions – and at the Ministry's expense – to cover over slogans in the house just before my release I saw one guard creep out into the yard one afternoon. It was quiet and the painters were away at lunch. Taking a quick look round to see if anyone was watching – he did not see me in the shadow of my window – he raised a lid of a paint can with a coin and ladled out enough paint to put a fresh white strip on the tail-end of the mudguard of his bicycle. Next day all seven of the guards' bicycles parked in the court-yard had bright, fresh, white tailpieces on their rear mudguards. Never take a needle or a thread but the people won't miss a spot of paint!

CHAPTER THIRTY-THREE

To Romance

The faintest shadow of romance flitted through the stark, all-male world in which I lived early in the year of 1969. I use the word 'romance' advisedly since according to my dictionary it can mean 'to embroider one's account or description with extravagances'. And as you will see the romance was all in my mind.

In November I had been visited by a doctor, a woman. She had seemed distinctly uncomfortable examining a foreigner in such grim, prison cell-style surroundings and had made a guess at bronchitis which later examinations had not borne out. At the time, hoping against hope for release and worrying about the possibility of a chest complaint I had not paid much attention to her. But she was very small and pretty, I had noticed. I had remembered standing in the centre of the room, towering above her it seemed at six feet nothing, wearing a shabby leather jacket and much-darned scruffy trousers trying to place a thermometer under my left arm to take my temperature for her and feeling the greatest loutish oaf on earth beside her petiteness.

Her dark hair was held back from her face with a single schoolgirl clip and she had kept her eyes modestly averted from mine all the time. She wore the proletarian-style trousers and a rough navy blue jacket, but the trousers were not baggy and shapeless like those of most Chinese women. They were slightly tapered and tucked neatly into small, zip-up canvas boots. She was so small she looked for all the world to me like a girl of nine or so. After the briefest of examinations as I lay flat on my back on the bed with guards and interpreter looking on, she practically fled from the slogan-daubed room, seemingly very glad to be out of it. I had asked the interpreter for the diagnosis and the answer was 'Maybe you have bronchitis'.

Later examinations proved this not to be so but I continued to suffer with pharyngitis and so much so that I again asked for a doctor in January. Eleven days after my request the little doctor appeared one morning immediately after breakfast, with an interpreter. She was more relaxed this time. I guessed that she might have been assured officially by the Foreign Ministry that she was to treat me normally without concerning herself with the ideology of the situation.

This time the guards did not come into the room with her, just the interpreter. I stood up as she entered but immediately sat down again since I was towering over her and this was clearly embarrassing. She had brought a big torch to look at my throat. To me she looked enchantingly petite as she stood beside me putting questions through the interpreter. Standing up, she was not much taller than I was seated. She wore exactly the same clothes as before but again looked neat, almost pert.

I had remembered this second visit as a pleasantly unique moment in those twenty-six months starved of feminine companionship. But I had forgotten the heady impact made on me by her visit until, in order to write this chapter, I looked up my shorthand diary entry written that night. Here it is in full:

'After breakfast that delightful little lady doctor arrived again. She had another look at my throat and I asked through the interpreter what caused my pharyngitis. She said it was probably dryness of the atmosphere. She almost smiled a few times. Her wide almond eyes were very pretty. She stayed on with the guards in their room after she had finished and I was ordered out to walk in the courtyard. I was walking slowly in her direction as she made to leave. As she came down the steps into the yard our eyes met and I imagine I must have started to smile very slightly and I thought I noticed an almost perceptible smile start on her face (I could be imagining it of course). But she was absolutely lovely. So tiny. When she leaned over me to examine my throat as I sat on the chair I could breathe her smell which was so fresh and fragrant. She wouldn't dare to use such a bourgeois thing as perfume but she must have bathed very well with sweet-smelling soap this morning. I closed my eyes and breathed deeply and inhaled the fragrance. I have hardly stopped thinking of her since.

'Later the interpreter returned with three little bottles of inhalant and two packets of pink tablets. Before lunch the cook came into the room and fixed a tray of water on top of the radiator inside its recess to dampen the atmosphere on the doctor's instructions. I think the sweet angel really wanted to help me.

'When she went out of the room I thanked her in Chinese and she acknowledged it with a little nod of the head. She was much more friendly and self-controlled this time. Her age I could make no estimate of. Her hair was lovelier this time – slightly longer or perhaps she'd just washed it.'

The diary entry ends there but I can remember for a few hours having that slightly foolish feeling that approximates often to falling in love, and I seriously contemplated for a time pretending to be greatly in need of a doctor again soon in the hope of getting another visit from her. But I didn't.

This incident perhaps illustrates the obvious – that it is highly undesirable for a man to be alone for two years without a female of the species. But total isolation dulls and blunts the edges of the emotions somewhat while the isolation lasts, puts them on ice to a degree, and this is perhaps a saving factor.

The early months of the year slipped by occupied mainly with the study of Chinese but my diary was still recording bouts of despondency – and flashes of anger.

In March the Foreign Ministry apparently thought that perhaps another tweak of the thumbscrew might help their case along and my mail was curtailed. Letters sent by Shirley suddenly started ostentatiously arriving back in London in batches marked 'undelivered'. They contained nothing different to those previously delivered safely.

In mid-April I wrote: 'Now it's twenty-six blank days without mail and I know letters are being written constantly. How wretched these —s have become. I promise myself to write all this in detail if ever I get the chance. I shall write too about the guards' tantalizing method of holding letters day after day on the diningroom table.'

In my study of Chinese I came across a number of old Chinese proverbs and longed to include them in Chinese characters in my letters home so that those in the Chinese Foreign Ministry might ponder on the wisdom of their ancient civilisation. But I did not want to give away that I was learning Chinese. One I liked particularly for its succinct expression of the dilemma in which some Chinese must have felt themselves to be over my case. It was 'Ch'i hu nan hsia' – 'Once you are mounted on a tiger the difficulty is getting down.' I felt the embarrassment that had showed through the December public statement indicated that somebody in the Chinese hierarchy might have liked to get down gracefully if they could from the tiger they had mounted in taking me as a hostage.

Another that struck me was '*Ya tzu ch'ih huang lien, sui k'u pu neng yen*' – 'When a dumb man eats the yellow lotus he is unable to describe its bitterness.' I had often felt, with a touch of self-pity, like that dumb man in the long months alone. Yet another found me agreeing heartily with its sentiments. '*Tsai chia ch'ien jih hao. Tsai wai shih shih nan*' – 'A thousand days at home is all right. But when you are away there are always difficulties.'

But when I felt self-pity beginning even slightly to assert its influence I deliberately tried to counteract this with a rational appraisal of my plight. Nobody had forced me into China. I was not a soldier who had been drafted there. All Reuter correspondents are offered their assignments and may refuse them if they wish. I came with my eyes open and knew that I was exposing myself to a risk in committing myself to living in such a country without any formal protection such as that diplomats normally enjoy. My plight might have been worse. There was no defined sentence hanging around my neck. Count your blessings!

During the long time alone I felt very keenly the lack of anybody to talk to and naturally turned to talking to myself. I found that I did this most frequently in the washroom in front of the mirror. It only happened when I had the door closed and the guards would not be able to hear. Frequently when washing my hands I would catch sight of my pale face, my grubby leather jacket, perhaps a woollen scarf wound round my neck against the cold – all this against the background of dirty paint-spattered walls. And often I would shake my head and tell my reflection aloud such complimentary things as : 'You are an extremely bizarre-looking character, Grey.' And I was often unable to suppress a smile. I talked to myself too in different accents. I had always liked mimicry and was amused by my own efforts at it. I often spoke to myself in the clumsy guttural English of some Germans I had known in my time in Berlin, I tried to capture too the lilting charm of the English spoken by French friends, the endearing accents of Indians and Pakistanis, Cockneys and Yorkshiremen, Scots and Welshmen.

To brighten my daily prayers I sometimes switched to an Irish

brogue when saying the Lord's prayer. I frequently added a rider
expressing the hope that it would not be thought irreverent. I
traced the pleasure I got from this to visits made with friends to
Catholic churches in England where I had been charmed by the
pleasing voices of the often-Irish priests.

During my mimicry sessions I often fell into an imitation of the
Public Security Bureau interpreter informing me about a visit. I
would stand before the mirror, screw up my eyes and with the
exaggerated severity which he seemed to feel was appropriate,
would spit out the words 'We have been informed that today at
three o'clock two officials of the Office of the British Chargé
d'Affaires will visit you. You must abide by the following regulations. . . .' My impersonation would sometimes please me so much
that I would have a quiet chuckle over it.

I was rarely ever near to weeping in my confinement, having
early on decided to try to avoid self-pity, but was strangely
moved just once. It was in mid-January 1969 when the only Christmas cards I was allowed – from my mother, sister and girl friend
– arrived. In a letter delivered with them Shirley had enclosed
the Christmas general knowledge quiz from the London *Times*.
This was not of so much interest as a report on the back of it of
the American Apollo moon shot made at Christmas 1968. It was
staggering, eye-opening news to me in itself. The astronauts had
read the story of the creation in Genesis back to earth by radio
while orbiting the moon. But as they came out of the lunar orbit
to head back to earth one of the astronauts told mission control
on earth, 'We feel like the crews of old time sailing ships. We shall
be very glad to reach our home port'. The reply from earth was
'We shall be glad to get you back'.

A lump came to my throat and my eyes dampened. I felt I
could understand very intensely the feelings of the quietly courage-
ous astronauts as they turned their sights for home with so much
distance and possible danger between them and safety. And I
could not avoid identifying this emotion with my own. So much
political complexity, negotiation, time and sheer distance halfway
round the world seemed to stand between me and home.

Perhaps in a chapter about romance I should mention my plans
for escape. They were very fanciful but I think an inevitable and

K

essential part of the protective thought processes of a man enclosed in a confined space.

It did not take much time for me to arrive at the conclusion that escape from my house and China too, was impossible. Even if I could have got clear of the confines of the house a non-Asian foreigner stands out like a sore thumb anywhere in China and unaided movement would have been impossible without attracting attention that would certainly have led to recapture. But I did comfort myself, at the times when the awfulness of solitude pressed in on me most strongly, with the thought that I might take a desperate chance to escape – and return to my prison! And I even took one or two precautions to make it possible to put the plan ino effect. After the courtyard window of the twelve-foot square room was allowed open at night the wire screens were nailed in place with a single four-inch nail. I loosened this a little each day while pretending to stand idly at the window until I think it could have been pulled out at night without much effort. I then planned to climb out and drop down into the courtyard, steal round the side of the house and into the back area where the coal was stored. There a wall about six feet high adjoined the low roofs of surrounding single-storey Chinese houses that stood between my house and the willow-fringed moat of the Forbidden City. I thought I could scale the small wall, cross the rooftops and either drop quietly into the moat and swim across or scramble round the moat's protecting wall until I came up against the road running under the high grey battlements of the Forbidden City itself. Once well clear of my house in the darkness I thought I would steal one of the many bicycles which clog the streets of Peking by day and ride to the British Mission a few miles away.

There I would make contact with British diplomats who would be amazed at my bold stroke in escaping and I would have a much-needed whisky and demand to be told what the facts of my case were and what was being done. After perhaps another whisky or two to fortify me in the alcohol-free days to come, and an hour or two of desperately-needed conversation, I would return before dawn and re-enter my house by the way I left it with the guards none the wiser. This was a highly fanciful idea but it was in a way a comfort sometimes to think that there was a possible way out if things became so bad as to be otherwise unbearable. And I did, during one visit upstairs to my bedroom to get clothes, take pains to seek out my rubber-soled tennis shoes and take them downstairs. These I thought would be indispensable for the quiet stealth and agile movement required in my 'escape'. In fact at no time did I ever wear these shoes and never in reality came close to putting my escape plans into action.

In this connection, too, perhaps my deceiving the guards by doing things unknown to them – keeping a diary, getting the banned *Doctor Zhivago* – was another expression of this 'escape' idea. It was very important that I should be able to do even the smallest thing that could escape their notice. It gave me a satisfying feeling that they were not, as they believed, all-powerful in controlling me.

I 'escaped' too, in my dreams. I had two dreams which constantly recurred over the entire period reflecting my two greatest desires, to be free and to have access to information. But so great was the wearying deadness of each empty day that it impressed itself into my dreams and even while dreaming I was free I would come to know with a sudden and familiar sense of dread that I was in reality still a captive.

In the first dream I would be in the streets of my home city, Norwich, or in London and would be walking or travelling in a bus. I would look up at the names of the shops and realisation that I was still captive would dawn when I found that the names were not in the right order or the right names were not there at all.

Again later I would dream the same dream and this time for a short distance the names of the shops would be in the right order but after a time they became jumbled and the sickening knowledge of reality would descend again.

In the next version I would be looking at the shop names and thinking that before, I only dreamed this but now it's true, and I would walk on. But suddenly I would remember I had no recollection of how I got home, no memory of a journey, no idea how I had got a passport to travel with (my passport was among my belongings left at the British Mission and was eventually destroyed in the fire). It was at such a stage in the dream that I would know unmistakably I was still captive, was in reality still asleep although the dream was continuing. In the dream I would tell anybody that I met I was dreaming and that really I was still a prisoner. This dream extended itself too, to the point where

I would be explaining in the next dream how once I had only dreamed I was free and here and now I really was free – and then I would suddenly stop in the middle of a sentence with horror when realisation dawned again that because there was no memory of a journey it was *still* only a dream. I would again explain to whoever I was addressing they were only taking part in a dream. This dream extended itself time and time again like a mirror reflected in a mirror, reflected in a mirror and so on to infinity. It was as if my subconscious mind in its effort to free itself was managing each time to push the illusion a little further, to make it last a little longer before the inescapable fact of my confinement rushed back to flood my mind totally again.

The other dream involved newspaper shops and news stands. As a journalist who had always been obsessively interested in newspapers from a professional viewpoint I felt the lack of them most keenly. And in my dreams they came to symbolise the moment of freedom. I dreamed of approaching a news stand on which I could see the British daily papers spread out for sale. I would draw close and try to scan the headlines, looking first for news of my own release. But the mastheads of *The Times*, the *Daily Mail*, *The Observer* and others which had seemed clear from a distance would blur into obscure women's weekly magazines and other irrelevant journals and the shelves would somehow become bare of all except totally unwanted, unreal periodicals.

The dream would fade but later I would have a similar dream in which I would be running towards the shop again thinking: 'I remember dreaming this before but now it is reality and I'll buy one of each newspaper this time.' Again they would dissolve and while still dreaming I would become aware that it was a fantasy of my sleep. Again, later, I would dream that twice before it had been a dream but this time, look there they all were, the daily and Sunday newspapers and it was only a matter now of buying them all. But the few people in front of me in the queue would take their share leaving the same useless remnants. This dream projected itself through the mirror-like succession of disappointments as did the other homecoming dream until I approached the shop or stand with a weary recognition that the likelihood of the newspapers remaining real was remote.

In October 1969 in Camberwell where I stayed for a time after reaching London I went out each morning with great deliberation

to break this dream forever. Each day I bought every daily newspaper published in London as well as a few American dailies,
plus all the news magazines as well for luck! The newsagent
grinned in a puzzled way as he selected one of each for me and
I turned back home with the great bundle under one arm. And
there was for the first few days often news about myself in them!
Only when I related this connection with my dreams to a friend
was it pointed out to me that by coincidence the name above the
door of the newsagent to whom I was giving so much obsessive
custom was 'Tony's Corner Shop'.

Part 4

CHAPTER THIRTY-FOUR

Getting Hopeful

On an afternoon in late May 1969 the gate of my courtyard suddenly opened and a gang of men carrying boards on long poles entered. On their boards they carried large sheets of sandpaper. And with their sheets of sandpaper they brought me my first real grounds for hope of release in nearly two years of solitary confinement in my house.

I watched with great excitement as the two-feet high Chinese characters scrawled in black paint on the lime-washed courtyard wall opposite my window disappeared in clouds of dust and grit. The gang of workmen were applying sandpaper boards to the Red Guards' handiwork of August 18th, 1967 and obliterating the slogan that said 'Long live Chairman Mao, Long live the great proletarian cultural revolution'. For the authorities to order the erasing of such a slogan there must have been some tangible cause, I knew. It was the first real sign of retreat. I became very tense as the possibility of release after so long alone seemed to grow before my eyes. Then the gang moved into the house and began work on the walls of the passage outside the door of my room and on the walls of the staircase and the upper landing. I couldn't sit still. The door of my room had been closed and the painted slogans on its outside were being taken off with sandpaper.

I listened to the clatter and scrape of the workmen's tools and became so tense at the prospect of an end to my ordeal that I developed a blinding headache. Then gradually I became aware of another sound coming through the noise in the normally quiet house. It was the persistent and purposeful pounding of hammer and nails on woodwork upstairs. After several minutes of careful listening I reached the inescapable conclusion that all the windows in the upper part of the house, my lounge, office and bedroom were being nailed up.

My hopes that had rocketed not long before plummeted suddenly back to zero. Or perhaps not quite zero. But I knew that nailed-up windows upstairs meant no release, just possibly another move to different quarters. After the sudden rush of hope of release this left me dejected again.

The next day the workmen came again, with distemper this time. Over the patches where the black paint daubings had been erased, clean white distemper was applied.

Next morning, on May 30th, a Public Security Bureau interpreter entered my room with the chief guard.

'We have several things to tell you this morning,' the interpreter said. Both men were reading from sheets of paper. First one in Chinese then the other in English. 'Each day between ten thirty and midday and four o'clock and five thirty you will be allowed to go either to the courtyard or to three rooms upstairs. But you must first tell the guards. You must not open the doors or windows yourself, you must not go on to the balconies. You may take your radio and your books with you. You may close the door of your room. Have you any questions?'

The reason for the nailing up of the windows was clear. It was to ensure that the upper storey was as secure a prison as the lower, to ensure I didn't try to get out on to the surrounding low roofs between my house and the Forbidden City moat.

The cleaning of the walls had stopped short of my room. All the upstairs rooms, the staircase and the guards' room were now slogan-free. But I continued to live among Red Guard graffiti, Mao portraits, pink posters and chalked quotation boards and would do for another three months.

The partial cleaning away of the slogans and the easing of my strict confinement came, I learned later, as a direct result of a move in Hong Kong on May 9th. It was on that date that the Hong Kong Government announced reductions in sentences on a number of Communist prisoners, including one man vital to my freedom. He was a certain Wong Chak, whose sentence had been originally scheduled to end in February 1971. He was one of a number of prisoners of different occupations whose sentences were reduced on May 9th from five or four years to a maximum of three. At the end of 1968 my fate had been linked with a total of thirteen imprisoned news workers in Hong Kong. Two had by this time been released, ten were due for release by September 1969, leaving Wong Chak the sole survivor of the thirteen to carry on to 1971. But the reduction of his sentence from five to three years meant that with maximum remission he was due out in October. A spokesman for the Hong Kong Government said he was authorised to state that the action in reducing Wong Chak's sentence was 'in no way connected with the unfortunate plight of Anthony Grey'. It was said that Wong Chak being involved was a coincidence. The decision to cut the prison sentences was the result of a general review made possible because of improved conditions in the colony. The Hong Kong Government had all along opposed a 'deal' to secure my release.

But despite these obscurantist utterances in Hong Kong the cadres of the Wai Chiao Pu in Legation Street, Peking, saw that they had won. In some four months the last news worker was to be released two years ahead of time. Hostage-taking had after all paid a dividend, although a very small one and the price in embarrassment to China had been high. Nevertheless it had paid. So the order went out to begin easing my thumb out of the thumb-screw. My conditions were improved.

But for the time being these details remained unknown to me, although I guessed something important had happened.

That morning in late May I was able to walk to the door of my twelve-foot square room, point my finger up the staircase and when I got an affirmative nod from the guard on watch could, for the first time in nearly two years, climb the stairs *alone* to the upper floor. I looked around and with delight found that my Zenith transistor shortwave radio still worked, despite having been tossed around by the Red Guards. I looked out at the magnificent view over the roofs of the old imperial city again and later wrote in my diary: 'During my first trip upstairs I noticed the view of the golden rooftops and the East Gate of the Forbidden City and with something of a thrill I saw Chinese characters in red and white around the gate that I could read "in the flesh" as it were after studying the dead texts of my book and newspapers in the closed off room below. They are the first Chinese characters I have read outside my house.'

I took my radio back downstairs with me and at three o'clock that afternoon succeeded in tuning in my first English-speaking voice. Apart from the two visits of twenty and twenty-five minutes by British diplomats it was the first time in twenty-two months I had heard English being spoken as a native tongue. But I could

barely understand a word of it! I had tuned to the American
Forces Network station in Tokyo and as the voice warmed up in
the set I identified the subject matter as a report of the latest
Brooklyn Dodgers baseball game – which was all Greek to my
uninitiated ear! But nevertheless hearing the rich American drawl
was a memorable moment. The news followed and I heard about
the Paris peace talks on Vietnam, the current truce in Vietnam
itself and the planned investiture of the Prince of Wales. A few
hours later I got the B.B.C. World Service news and from that
moment on rarely missed a news bulletin during my waking hours.

On the domestic front in China, April had seen the convening
of the Ninth Congress of the Chinese Communist Party at which
the loose ends of three years of Cultural Revolution chaos were
tied up. The purging of President Liu Shao-chi and many other
prominent leaders was confirmed, a new Central Committee, Politburo and Politburo Standing Committee were elected comprised
of staunch Maoists to a man. Defence Minister Lin Piao was
designated as Mao's eventual successor in the new Party con-
stitution. I had followed this in the newspapers in Chinese and
had felt vaguely hopeful now that the turbulent movement which
led to my imprisonment was moving into a quieter, saner phase.

The improvement in my conditions of life gave me added hope.
I could walk for an hour and a half in the yard unsupervised or
go and sit upstairs during that time, or do a little of both. The
guards still came upstairs to stare at me from time to time but
the relief from the one room and the constant watch of the guards
in the courtyard was indescribably welcome. By another stroke of
luck the Peking summer of 1969 was cooler and with the improved conditions I did not suffer from the heat as I did the year
before.

I began to fill in my gaps of knowledge from the radio news.
The Suez Canal was still closed two years after the Arab-Israeli
war of 1967, de Gaulle had been replaced by President Pompidou,
King Constantine was in exile from Greece. I listened avidly to
every news and current affairs programme and every commentary,
gradually piecing back together my view of the world after nearly
two blank years. Even long after I returned home I continued to
have blind spots about news that had passed me by. I heard
occasional references to myself in news and current affairs programmes. I heard a commentary on the Derby from Epsom, tennis

from Wimbledon and Test Matches at Lords. I soaked up these individual proofs of the continuing normality of life at home like a parched sponge would soak up water.

A few weeks later I heard in a news broadcast that British Defence Minister Denis Healey, during a visit to Hong Kong had said he expected my release in October when the last of the Communist news workers, Wong Chak, was freed. My hopes were high and only my impatience was greater. I had ceased all activity other than listening to the radio each evening and a little reading. My learning Chinese had fulfilled its purpose as a vehicle for carrying me sanely through the first half of the year and helping me decipher the posters and slogans around me. It had indeed been a satisfying intellectual exercise too.

I heard a broadcast message from my mother on the B.B.C. and journalists on the magazine programme 'Outlook' sometimes sent their good wishes over the ether to my twelve-foot square room.

On July 14th I received my third and last consular visit. A few days before, the painters had moved in to redecorate the dining-room which the guards occupied and I was able to meet there with the British chargé d'affaires, Mr John Denson and second secretary Roger Garside in comparatively clean surroundings with no anti-Grey slogans on the walls around me this time. Only the scribbling interpreters and the watching guard were unchanged. The rules were the same and the wastepaper basket with the wires running from it was there too. Mr Denson told me that it was hoped my release would follow the release of Wong Chak on October 3rd. I had a definite date to work towards for the first time. Because of the easing of my restrictions and the use of my radio I was able to go into the meeting with the British diplomats in a much calmer frame of mind than at previous visits. And on the radio that night I heard it reported as the first item on the B.B.C. news that I had appeared more relaxed. The meeting that had been scheduled to last twenty-five minutes was allowed to meander on for nearly forty-five minutes.

July 21st, 1969 was a memorable day – not only because it marked the two year anniversary of my house arrest. That humid Peking morning with my ear glued to the radio I heard Neil Armstrong talking to my twelve-foot square room from the moon as he took his one small step for man and one giant leap for mankind. But the 750 million Chinese living in the vast country all around me were never told of this historic feat.

Two impatient months later the painters appeared again and I was moved upstairs for a day while the slogans were removed from the walls of the twelve-foot square room and the washroom. They were redecorated a gleaming white. The quotation boards of Mao's thoughts were removed too. The pink posters were also removed – but I kept repeating the Chinese text to myself each day, still determined to keep it in existence in my mind until I could write it safely on release.

It was just over two years since the Red Guards with paint brushes, hammers and nails had turned my house into a garishly-decorated prison – a one-man prison in which the prisoner paid all the expenses! I paid out just over £4,000 – an average of over £150 a month – for the privilege of twenty-six months solitary. This was the basic cost of paying the rent, the upkeep of the house, the wages of the three Chinese working in it, their food during working hours and my own food and living costs. Reuters London office was allowed to continue sending money to the Bank of China in Peking for me. The Chinese authorities demanded all payments from me as if I was living a normal life, including the quarterly licence fees for my car which stood in a locked garage for the two years. The garage had holes in the roof and the car gradually disappeared under several inches of windblown grit during the two years. When I finally opened the doors the car looked like a Volkswagen-shaped sand hill.

CHAPTER THIRTY-FIVE

Getting Released

There were no bars at the windows of my one-man prison, just six-inch nails in the frames. The sound of the nails being hammered in was audible above the tumult of the Red Guard invasion on that night of August 18th, 1967 when my house arrest became solitary confinement. More nails had been driven into the windows of my twelve-foot square room in the following May and before I was allowed the brief use of upstairs rooms in May 1969 the frames of the windows of my bedroom, office and lounge had been nailed up too.

It was fitting then that the end of my imprisonment should be signalled by the sound of subdued hammering and quietly splintering wood as the nails were levered out and removed.

This happened on the morning of Saturday, October 4th, 1969. Chinese workmen in blue cotton drabs had arrived at the house shortly after nine o'clock and I heard the noise of the unbarring of my windows upstairs as I sat eating my breakfast in the twelve-foot square room below. My heart did not leap with excitement or elation. For me it was not a sudden and unexpected end. I had been curbing my impatience for four months since hearing of Defence Minister Denis Healey's expressed hope that I would be released in October. Since my last meeting with British diplomats on July 14th I had been counting the days to October 3rd. This was the day on which the last imprisoned Communist newsman in Hong Kong, Wong Chak, was to be freed. There had been no precise promise of my freedom on that date and as the days slipped slowly by I hoped against hope that nothing would go wrong.

On October 3rd I spent a tense day listening to news bulletins on my shortwave radio. The walls of the twelve-foot square room now gleamed with fresh distemper and there was not a slogan or poster or portrait to be seen. The floor, however, was still bare and the brown floorboards still squeaked underfoot as I walked across them.

That night, sixteen hours away from freedom, I wrote what was to be the last entry in my diary.

'Friday, October 3rd eleven fifteen p.m. A day of some tension. The first mention about my release was on Radio Newsreel on the B.B.C. last night at eight o'clock with Hong Kong correspondent Anthony Lawrence's despatch saying "Anthony Grey may be free soon". This wasn't mentioned in the later news bulletin and was dropped from the Newsreel at eleven p.m. and I was annoyed and wondered whether it had been a mistake. I was up for eight o'clock this morning to hear the news (midnight the previous evening, London time) but there was nothing in the bulletin or on Radio Newsreel. I did my Yoga exercises early and had a bath and wondered whether I would be interrupted to be called to the Foreign Ministry.

'While I was walking in the courtyard this morning there was a buzz at the bell of the courtyard gate and three guards came out of the dining-room looking excited and buttoning up their jackets – rather in the way they would have straightened their ties if they wore them. But nothing happened. I got a slight headache again through the tension.

'In the afternoon I managed to get a London news bulletin at three o'clock and heard halfway through it that Wong Chak had been released in Hong Kong. Then at four o'clock there were more details of his release, waving a red book of Mao's thoughts and so on but I lost it halfway through because of bad reception. Then on the main news at five o'clock I learned as I sat in my upstairs lounge that British diplomats who had come to see if I was free, had been turned away three times from my courtyard gate during the day. This was obviously one occasion when the guards went to the gate straightening themselves up. I was very excited at hearing on the radio how near I had been to friends just a few steps away beyond the courtyard gate. At six o'clock I tuned in the Voice of America news from Washington and I was mentioned on there too in connection with the Hong Kong release. By the seven o'clock bulletin I was still the first item on the B.B.C. news and this time it added that my telephone was still cut off although the last Chinese newsman was free.

'By the eight o'clock Radio Newsreel there was the added snippet of information that the Foreign Ministry in Peking was closed today for part of the National Day holiday. By nine o'clock the "still no news of Anthony Grey" item was holding on as the headline item in the bulletin. At ten o'clock in the news magazine programme "Outlook" the B.B.C. Commonwealth correspondent John Osman was interviewed and he said attempts had been made to influence China over my case through Tanzania and Pakistan who enjoyed closer relations with Peking but some diplomats thought this hadn't helped. Osman also said that no journalists "expected help from the government"!! A review of the Fleet Street papers followed – "all papers headline the story of Anthony Grey's possible release". God, why don't they shut up until it happens I thought.

'At eleven o'clock I was still the first item in Radio Newsreel with the announcer saying "still no news of Anthony Grey's release". Then I nearly had heart failure when he broke into the middle of the programme with a news flash, in a very excited voice saying Reuters correspondent in Moscow, who had contacted Peking by telephone, had come through with a report that the Chinese would speak with British diplomats about Grey tomorrow. This alarmed me because the announcer said it so dramatically. I am waiting for the midnight news now to hear it again. God please let it be tomorrow. (Anthony Lawrence in Hong Kong said it was not known whether Grey would leave immediately or what route he would take. Talk about counting chickens before they hatch!) Dear God let it be soon.'

And there endeth the diary.

The midnight news bulletin didn't enlighten me any further and I went to bed and to my surprise slept well until next morning.

Just after nine o'clock workmen arrived and began unnailing the windows. I tried not to let myself begin to feel the relief I had longed for during two years until it was indisputable. During my walk in the yard more workers arrived and went into the twelve-foot square room and began fiddling with the dead telephone instrument on the window-sill. As I paced back and forth for what turned out to be the last time in the yard the telephone began ringing upstairs and down as the engineers tested it. These telephones had stood silent since the Red Guards put them out of action two years before. The bustle of activity went on in the house with everybody ignoring me. But I didn't care, my spirits were rising. By lunch-time nothing had happened and I began to wonder whether anything would that day. Then while I was eating lunch I heard an almost forgotten sound – the chatter of a news teleprinter. It came from my basement. The telephone engineers had also restored the New China News Agency service which was supplied to the house as part of an agreement between Reuters and the Chinese agency. The sounds of normality were returning to the house.

After lunch the moment for which I had waited so long arrived. The chief guard and interpreter walked into the twelve-foot square room.

'The Foreign Ministry summons you,' the interpreter told me translating the guard's words. 'You must prepare yourself. You will be taken there in fifteen minutes.' That was all. They left me.

I was allowed to go upstairs to change. I took from my wardrobe and put on a navy blue suit, a blue and white striped shirt with a button-down collar and a navy knitted tie. If my description of this sounds rather self-conscious, like an actor about to go on stage, it is because it was the first time in more than two years that I had needed to put on clothes for some practical purpose in which appearance mattered. I put on my sheepskin overcoat and went back downstairs to wait for a few more minutes.

Then the guards took me to the gate and I stepped into the street for the first time since July 1967. The car at the kerb was again a Polish-built Warszawa, biscuit-coloured and newer-looking than the one I was driven home in two years earlier. Once again squeezed in between two Public Security Bureau guards on the back seat I was driven to the Ministry in Legation Street. The sun shone and I was immediately struck by the incredible cleanness and quietness of the streets. No wall posters! When last I had seen them the seething streets were plastered with an all-embracing ugly mess of paper. We turned out of Nan Chihtze on to the broad avenue Chang An – Boulevard of Eternal Peace. I could see away to the right the broad expanse of the Square of Heavenly Peace, quiet and empty in the autumn sunlight.

Inside the Ministry compound the guards remained with the car, directing me towards the Information Department door. In the same comfortable reception lounge where the July 1967 meeting had taken place a small, bespectacled official wearing a neat, greenish cadre's suit buttoned high at the neck sat waiting for me in one corner of a long sofa. His face was expressionless and he didn't move. I took off my overcoat, put it over a nearby chair and sat down in an armchair at the side of the sofa which he had indicated with the faintest of gestures. There was a table in front of us with sheets of paper and a jar of sharpened pencils.

There was a pause and I sensed we were waiting for something. Then the large double doors of the room opened and a familiar face entered. It was Mr Chi. Smiling slightly in no particular direction, he came briskly across the room to take his seat at the opposite end of the sofa to the other man, who I learned was a Mr Shen. Mr Shen took out a piece of flimsy paper with his speech written on it. He read from it in Chinese pausing for Mr Chi to translate. Again I found myself breathing tightly as I waited to learn the details of my immediate fate. Expulsion within twenty-four hours, forty-eight, seventy-two hours? Deportation? A return to normal in Peking? Or something I hadn't thought to anticipate?

'We have called you here today to make an announcement.' Mr Chi was doing the translating for Mr Shen. Their voices were modulated, quiet, courteous. 'On July 21st, 1967 your freedom of movement was restricted because of the illegal and unjustifiable detention of correspondents in Hong Kong.'

The statement was coming in several helpings as before with a pause for the Chinese before the next translation. It was just sufficient to add more suspense to the moment.

'On many occasions the British authorities were told that if they were all released your freedom of movement would be restored.' Another pause to give added weight to the next short sentence to which Mr Chi added heavy emphasis as he looked across at me. '*And we must make it clear that what we say counts.*'

Then almost an anti-climax: 'All the correspondents have now been released. Your freedom of movement is therefore now restored.'

Mr Shen sat back, Mr Chi sat quiet, looking across at me. They had finished. It was all very simple.

Mr Chi looked tolerantly amused when I ventured a question, what exactly did this mean? The attitude of both men in the second part of the interview was that of people dealing politely with a slightly stupid child. But perhaps their smiling at each other as I asked questions – as if they found my simplicity endearing – was a cover for some embarrassment at the actual personal confrontation with their hostage.

Mr Chi answered my question. It meant that all conditions for me were as before July 1967. I pointed out that my card of accreditation as a foreign correspondent in Peking had expired in September 1967 and was told with a smile: 'That is your affair.'

I had no desire to stay in China but wanted to have an exact definition of my position before leaving the interview. Was my house arrest to end with an order to leave China? I formulated the question in a different way. Could I apply to have my accreditation renewed?

'You may apply,' said Mr Chi.

'Will it be granted?' I asked.

'You may apply,' said Mr Chi, exchanging another indulgent smile with Mr Shen.

What was the position of Reuters?

Another laugh and another glance to Mr Shen as if to say what incredible questions. 'All is as before.'

The lease on the house at Nan Chihtze expired nearly two years ago, I persisted. What about that?

I should take that up with the department concerned.

What about visas? Use the normal channels. I could make enquiries of the Information Department later if I had any questions.

I had been too taut to take notes while the statement was made to me. Now I asked if I might make one or two notes. With an almost exaggerated courtesy Mr Chi made an expansive, smiling gesture towards the pencils and paper on the table. I jotted a few shorthand symbols and the two Chinese sat quietly by, still apparently faintly amused at my behaviour. But again perhaps it should be remembered it is an Asian, if not worldwide habit, to laugh or smile in embarrassment.

I prepared to leave but again decided it safest to get a definition of my 'freedom of movement'. Was I now free to walk out of the door, I asked.

Mr Chi smiled again: 'We suggest you go in the car.'

'Am I not allowed to walk?'

'The car will take you to the door of your house.'

'Then I am not free to walk?'

'We *suggest* you take the car.'

There was sufficient emphasis on the word 'suggest' to make further enquiry pointless. I walked out to the car, got in the back seat between the two guards and was driven back to 15 Nan Chihtze.

Earlier that day the British chargé d'affaires had been summoned to the Ministry and told I was to be freed but had not been informed where. British diplomats had therefore waited in their cars outside the Ministry, outside my house and in between to follow my progress. I did not notice this. The Public Security Bureau car drove slowly back to my house. It stopped. The guard on the pavement side got out. I climbed out. He got back in, closed the door and the car drove off. I stood alone on the pavement outside my gate, free to step away in whichever direction I chose for the first time in 806 days.

My feeling was not one of joy or elation or great emotion. It was simple and overwhelming relief that the great span of time alone in confinement which had sometimes seemed likely to be unending was finally at an end.

Second secretary Roger Garside from the British Mission had been sitting in a car at the kerbside as I arrived back at my house. He got out quickly, came over and we shook hands. I have no recollection of what we said. Then leaving the diplomat briefly I used my own key to open the courtyard gate that had been controlled so long by my guards and went in. I ran upstairs to my office and sat down to write a detailed note of everything said to me at the Ministry while it was fresh in my mind.

Then I went down again. The house was empty, I suddenly realised. No guards. I looked into the dining-room, their 'operations' room. They had removed their camp beds and telephone and portraits of Mao. The once-polished top of the dining-room table was dull, scuffed and worn after two years' use as a desk. The chair covers were worn thin and tattered by constant use. I walked freely into the twelve-foot square room, the washroom and the adjoining eight-foot square room whose door now stood open revealing the office equipment stacked in it. But I didn't linger in those confined spaces. I went downstairs to the kitchen where the cook, boilerman and wash amah were. After a brief, friendly word with them to tell them to take the rest of the day off I went back up to the courtyard and out to the street where Roger Garside's car waited. I asked him to drive me to the main telegraph office on Chang An boulevard.

There I sent an urgent cable to Reuters general manager, Gerald Long. As I wrote on the cable form I noticed the Chinese counter girls, to whom I had frequently handed cables two years before, whispering among themselves excitedly, nudging each other and nodding in my direction. It was nice to be remembered. They spent a lot of time poring over the words I wrote:

'Urgent. Reuter Hong Kong. 61545 Ex Grey Peking Onpass Gerald Long. Summoned Foreign Ministry 15.00 local time and told freedom of movement restored as per prior July 21, 1967 Stop Am well please reassure my mother Tony Grey.'

Then I paid for it, returned to the car and was driven to the diplomatic compound to meet the chargé d'affaires, John Denson. In the flat of one of his second secretaries I sat down to drink coffee – and talk.

I tended to hog the conversation, I was reminded later. Talking over coffee cups was a luxury in which I had not been able to indulge for some time.

There was one final irony on the day of my release. When I returned to my house from the Foreign Ministry I found a brown-paper parcel on the desk in my twelve-foot square room. I was too excited to bother to open it at the time but the next day I found it to be a Christmas parcel sent by my mother in 1967, some books and a sweater. It had arrived nearly two years late!

Later that night the New China News Agency put out two brief items to the world in their English language service reporting the end of the affair. I found them on the teleprinter in the basement of my house at 15 Nan Chihtze when I returned there next day. This is how they looked:

'0040 – patriotic chinese journalists unjustifiably imprisoned by hongkong british authorities all leave jail victoriously.
'hongkong, october fourth (*hsinhua*) – supported by the great socialist motherland and following persistent struggle by patriotic compatriots in hongkong, the patriotic chinese journalists who were unjustifiably imprisoned by the hongkong british authorities at various times in 1967 had all left jail victoriously by october third. the patriotic chinese journalists in hongkong welcomed them

warmly and extended best wishes to them. the latter pledged to continue to hold aloft the great red banner of mao tsetung thought and make still greater contributions to the patriotic journalist cause. they have all returned to their work posts. end item'

'00402 – chinese foreign ministry information department announces restoration of freedom of movement to reuter correspondent anthony grey

'peking, october fourth (*hsinhua*) – the information department of the chinese foreign ministry on october 4 summoned the british reuter correspondent in peking anthony grey and announced to him that, since the hongkong british authorities had already released all the patriotic chinese journalists, his freedom of movement was restored to him as of this day. it was again pointed out to him that it was the hongkong british authorities' unjustifiable persecution and imprisonment of patriotic chinese journalists that had brought about the restriction of his freedom of movement. end item'

CHAPTER THIRTY-SIX

Getting Back From There

At a state banquet that same evening China's premier Chou En-lai said: 'Well, Grey's out, he's free.' And he was speaking in English, a rare departure from his normal practice.

Mr Chou did not make this odd remark in a formal speech but in an almost jocular aside to the British chargé d'affaires, John Denson. The state banquet was being given for the visiting prime minister of Congo (Brazzaville). As Chou moved informally among the diplomats present he made a special point of approaching and addressing Mr Denson. It was the first time a prominent Chinese leader had spoken to the head of the British Mission since it was burned down two years before – or some time before that even. Mr Chou's once proficient English has grown rusty, probably from lack of use and his attempt to use it in talking to Mr Denson seemed to indicate a conscious effort to add some diplomatic nicety to the moment. Mr Denson himself is a fluent Chinese speaker.

'Well, Grey's out, he's free,' said the premier.

'Yes,' replied Mr Denson, 'But he's not out of China yet.'

'Well, he can stay here if he likes,' said Chou lightly.

'I'm not sure he'd want to,' Denson replied.

The premier, seemingly in very good humour began moving away then stopped, came back and gesturing towards the group of foreign newsmen attending the banquet added with a smile 'Is he here this evening?' 'No, not this evening,' said Denson and the odd little conversation ended there.

After the banquet when Mr Denson returned to the diplomatic compound, he related the conversation to me. Chou En-lai had seemed to make a tremendous effort to use his English in the conversation. It would be easy to lend too much significance to the remarks either in the context of Sino-British relations or Chou's attitude towards the affair. After all, other Britons remained imprisoned without trial and some were still held in mysterious circumstances at the time of writing. It did, however, indicate his close awareness of the details of my case and its repercussions. My remark about whether there was a possibility of renewing my accreditation made earlier that afternoon at the Foreign Ministry may have been made known to him and it may have seemed to him that offering the possibility of my staying on would make a good showing for China – exactly the opposite effect of expelling or deporting me. Perhaps he was genuinely anxious to make it clear there was an opportunity for a British correspondent to remain resident in China, as China had an interest in maintaining its agency journalists in London. Perhaps it showed that Chou, who is reliably represented as a moderate influence in the Chinese leadership, and is at his best as a diplomatic negotiator, was not altogether pleased with the course events had taken. But at least it can be said with certainty that Chou is not in the habit of making jocular, meaningless asides in foreign languages to Western diplomats. Whatever his intention, it seems the gesture was personal and conciliatory, no matter how slight and no matter how incongruous it appeared in the light of what official action had gone before.

At another reception before I left Peking Chou again asked foreign correspondents present whether I was there.

Meanwhile back in the diplomatic compound, I had been sending and receiving messages to and from family and friends in England. The Foreign and Commonwealth Secretary, Mr Michael Stewart, sent a personal message saying how glad he was that my 'unjustifiable detention had come to an end'. I remember smiling at the irony of seeing that word 'unjustifiable' used to me for the second time in a few hours from two vastly different Foreign Ministries.

That evening there was the first meal that I had shared with human company for twenty-six months. And there was the first drop of alcohol in that time too. Roger Garside's fiancée, a French girl, cooked me a fillet steak, and there was *pâté de foie gras* to begin. The fourth at the dinner table was second secretary George Walden in whose flat I spent the next few days before flying out of China. I drank two glasses of *Château Neuf du Pape* with dinner. It was very pleasant to resume contact with civilised living but the immediate impact on me of different food and alcohol was not great. I had never in my long confinement yearned for any particular item of food or drink. I had yearned only for freedom. And if there was one thing I enjoyed above all else it was to be able to talk again. One headline that I saw on a press cutting when I reached England reporting my first evening free had it very succinctly. 'Grey chats on and on and on . . .' That's exactly what I did. That night and on the succeeding nights in Peking I had to stop myself short several times during dinner realising that everybody else had finished their soup, fish, main course or sweet long ago and were politely waiting for me to reach the halfway stage with mine.

Late the first night I sat down and wrote out from memory the Chinese characters from the poster the Red Guards stuck on my back. I eagerly and unashamedly sought – and received – praise from Chinese speakers in the Mission for my Chinese handwriting. I suppose nobody would have been unkind enough to tell me at that time it was terrible! By three o'clock in the morning George Walden and I had long since been left alone and I decided to try my first beer. In fact I had two or three as we continued talking.

But I discovered that showering these new 'poisons' into my alcohol-free system after twenty-six months coupled with the heady effect of freedom was to have a disturbing effect. I went to bed at three thirty a.m. but could only sleep three hours. My body was singing with the effect of the wine and beer although I was not intoxicated. My metabolism so long static and used to its routine intakes was knocked sideways and continued to be for many days. In the succeeding days I went back to drinking warm water and then gradually crept up on my metabolism with the introduction of things like the odd medium sherry, one at a time. Next day my appetite for food disappeared completely. The excitement of release was reaching down to all corners of the system.

On that first night away from the unceasing watch of the Public Security Bureau guards – who as well as imprisoning me had also formed a secure barrier between me and all else outside – I suddenly felt vulnerable. Although I realised I was being ridiculous I couldn't prevent myself dragging a chest of drawers in front of the bedroom door in George Walden's flat before getting into bed. On that first night of freedom I also said a prayer of thanks for the release for which I had prayed so long.

The next day, George Walden, who was to become my constant companion for the next few days, drove me back to my house. During the drive I noticed for the first time my apprehension about moving quickly in a car in traffic after so long in a stationary state. The fear of even a slight accident in Peking which might lead to the foreign occupants of the car being surrounded and hemmed in by crowds only compounded my unease and I was constantly on the point of beseeching the driver to take more care – even though he was, on my account, already driving with exaggerated caution.

At the house I deliberately broke up the pattern of the twelve-foot square room. I moved out my few possessions, took the bedding upstairs and so 'destroyed' it as a living area in the form I had known it for nearly two years, although I left the bed there. I took away my diaries and left again quickly for the comfort and security of the flat in which I was staying in the diplomatic compound. The house was not a place I was at ease in any more.

That evening I met all the staff and their families at the British Mission. A film of the first walk on the moon – an event I'd heard but not seen – was put on specially for me. There too I met again the only foreign correspondent known personally to me who had remained in Peking since my house arrest began. All others had been replaced. But my good friend Milo Saranovic, the Yugoslav correspondent of Tanjug news agency was still there. He was the only non-Briton present at the film show and greeted me with an enormous bear hug. I was glad to embrace the only remaining friend who had shared the tension-fraught days of the summer of 1967. Everyone at the British Mission had been replaced during my confinement so all were new friends. Milo left for home only a day or two later after completing a long assignment in Peking.

At the Mission itself before I left for home I began to discover what it was like on the other side of the journalistic fence. What it was like to be the target of large numbers of reporters instead of being one of them, to be the story instead of the storyteller.

Fleet Street men ringing from Paris, Moscow, Tokyo, claimed they had messages for me from my mother, my girl friend and even from other Reuter correspondents who were unable to get through. All these claims usually proved exaggerated, if not false. I began to smile at the efforts of my fellow journalists to get me to the telephone since I had decided firmly not to talk about my confinement until well clear of China. I was not out of the wood yet. I spoke briefly with Reuter correspondent Lee Casey in Tokyo and asked him what had happened to the golf clubs I left with him in Hong Kong. I was surprised later to find this enquiry went round the world in newspaper headlines as my first words to the Great Outside after the long spell in solitary. I was beginning to rediscover at first hand the intense interest of reporters in the tiniest detail of the personal life of someone in the news. Diplomats in the Mission were busy on the telephone all day giving reporters details of what I had for breakfast, lunch and supper and other ragged bits of information about my first hours and days in freedom. I listened to records of Peter Cook and Dudley Moore and laughed uproariously at them after such a long humourless spell; George Walden played me soothing music by Handel and Telemann on his stereo equipment; I walked in the nearby park of the Altar of the Sun; and these facts were duly recorded in print by newspapers hungry for 'human interest'. It was a salutary experience to discover how persistent *other* journalists can be.

The idea of two years confined totally alone had evoked great sympathy in many people I met in the succeeding weeks and I was often overwhelmed by the kindness offered me. All the British people in Peking were very kind. Wives offered to lend me their husbands' sweaters and warm clothes, there were numerous offers of meals and entertainment, countless small acts of generosity. I had a look at the burned-out hulk of the former British Mission and couldn't suppress a shudder at the stark horror of the period the gutted building recalled. I learned for the first time the details of that night and I learned something too of the political background to my own confinement. There had even been bizarre negotiations in small Chinese restaurants in Hong Kong between British officials and Chinese Communists over whether I should be allowed to have a Bible and Communist prisoners in Hong Kong should be allowed the red booklet of Mao's quotations in their cells.

But politics apart, the thing that made the greatest impact on me in my first five days of freedom in Peking was the mini-skirt. In Peking English and other European girls had worn sober, almost knee-length skirts in the summer of 1967. By the time my release came around the fashion had intensified. Neat all-in-one stocking tights had replaced the somewhat embarrassing stocking tops-and-suspenders arrangement and skirt lengths had shot up to an all-time high. From seeing no girls at all for over two years to suddenly being confronted with beautiful Mission secretaries revealing stunning expanses of their shapely selves just across the coffee table in the evenings was a traumatic experience. Severely shaken by the phenomenon I took a bachelor diplomat aside and asked for guidance. Where on earth did one look nowadays in polite society when sitting at knee level, I pleaded. 'Well,' came the diplomatic answer, 'Don't think you are the only one facing this problem. I suppose you, umm . . . just, well . . . sort of . . . look.'

Five days after I was released, with routine exit visa formalities completed, I left Peking for Shanghai, Dacca, Karachi, Rome – and London.

John Denson took me to Peking airport in his official chauffeur-driven car with the Union Jack fluttering on the wing. A convoy of British cars followed behind. All the British turned out to see me off. There I had my first face to face meeting with the few Western correspondents then in Peking. I tried to be friendly but firmly declined to talk about my experiences in China and personal matters. One correspondent eventually turned in a piece which practically complained of my aggressiveness, nervousness and irascibility and seemed to suggest I was unreasonable in not wanting to talk about personal plans for marriage and my future career – five days after leaving solitary confinement and at the moment when I was about to leave the country which had held me hostage! I was beginning to learn how journalists can sometimes strain the patience and goodwill of their subject.

I received a very warm send-off from the British community and boarded the plane for Shanghai accompanied by George Walden who was to go with me as far as Pakistan. In the Chinese plane the two drably dressed Chinese air hostesses danced and sang Mao's quotations in the aisle between the seats on the flight to Shanghai. Their bright eyes, rosy cheeks and neat pigtails that bounced around as they danced expressed their charming natural vivacity and I joined in the applause. But unlike the other passengers I was applauding the girls for themselves – not the quotations!

In the airport shop in Shanghai I bought some Chinese silk embroidered blouses and embroidered pillow covers as gifts and some gramophone records for myself, including the 'The East is Red', before boarding the Pakistan Airlines Boeing for Dacca. And as we flew across the border between China and Burma on the afternoon of October 9th George ordered a half bottle of champagne and I took one small sip by way of celebration as China finally fell away behind me.

I had chosen to return to London via Shanghai, Pakistan and points west myself since the prospect of going out through the colony of Hong Kong, the way I had come in, left me ill-at-ease. It would have necessitated too, another overnight stop in that Canton hotel, another night exposed to the China which filled me with greater apprehension now, before crossing the border into the colony. And the colony was the place which had exploded into riots and brought about my imprisonment in my own house. Having felt vulnerable the first free night in the guarded diplomatic compound in Peking, I was sure I would not sleep one minute in the colony of four million Chinese.

There was another route out of China via Shanghai, Cambodia and ultimately Paris on the Air France flight – the only Western airline to fly into China. But this once-a-week flight was due to leave at a time when I was becoming unable to sleep or eat properly with the excitement of freedom and feeling unable yet to face the large numbers of newsmen who had been gathering for several days in Hong Kong, and other points in Asia to cover the story of my exit from China. So I had delayed my departure two days to gather myself. During this time the newspaper and television men assigned to cover the story watched and listened, checked flights and rumours assiduously, and prepared to dash to several departure points from China at a moment's notice.

Because movement still upset me after two almost motionless years I flew all the way from Peking to Dacca, the first stop in Pakistan, with my window blind drawn, trying to convince my shaky metabolism I was sitting still in a tube-shaped drawing-room.

We landed at Dacca and again immediately I felt the pressure of press attention. A note was sent on board to me. 'Stay aboard during Dacca stopover. Airline representative will process you for immigration and customs. Terminal full of pressmen – Campbell.'

The note was from Reuters deputy general manager, Doon Campbell, who had come out to escort me home. I pulled up the window blind and stared out at the darkened airport. The unreal feeling of being the sole target of other journalists, of being the object on which all their attention and energy was fixed came to me again. I peered around trying to see the terminal-full, but saw nothing. Then Doon Campbell came aboard with Reuters chief correspondent in Beirut, Ian MacDowall, whom I had known from my time in Germany, and I had the pleasure of meeting my first friends from home.

There was much to talk about, not least how the press corps had been moving itself rapidly around Asia to link up with me. Several had booked themselves on to the flight from Dacca to Karachi and were soon aboard. They trooped in carrying typewriters, news cameras and sound equipment and took seats in the first class cabin around me. As I talked in low whispers with Doon Campbell about things at home, plans for the rest of the trip and so on, I could feel them peering intently at me from the seats all around as if I was a man with two heads.

Soon after the plane took off their natural concern to be polite and considerate was overcome by the vision of the quarry before them that they had been anxiously awaiting and chasing for many days. They were suddenly all around my seat, all talking at once. Tension flashed. 'We want to talk to him,' they shouted. 'Leave him alone,' shouted my escorts.

The voice of Anthony Lawrence, normally quiet and dispassionate on B.B.C. Radio Newsreel, was raised in a shout. I think he was declaring how far he'd come and how long he'd spent doing it. I think I added to the din by shouting I didn't want to be harassed. Semi-pandemonium persisted in the first class cabin for a bit. Such electric explosions of tension are not uncommon among large gatherings of pressmen who go long distances for long hours at strange times of day and night competing hard to get as good a story as the next man and better if possible. But eventually things calmed down and I agreed to talk to one of them briefly about how I felt and he would then distribute the information to others. This is known as a 'pool' system. Ian Brodie of the *Daily Express* squatted in front of my seat taking shorthand notes and soon the first class cabin resounded to the rattle of typewriters as they prepared their stories for touchdown at Karachi where they would dash to cable offices. I had been on planes full of working pressmen before and again felt the strangeness of being the idle object of attention while others worked flat out to meet their deadlines. After the initial clash my fellow journalists were quietly considerate. Some came along quietly to shake hands and wish me well.

Then another storm broke at Karachi. A large crowd of reporters and cameramen had gathered there. Those escorting me tried to arrange an easy passage from the aircraft and I went out by the rear gangway after other passengers had used one at the front door. Halfway down the steps the crowd of newsmen at the foot of the other gangway spotted me and rushed over. A car had been brought near to the plane steps but the newsmen, rather like a pack of hounds in full cry closed round me, flash and arc lights blazing, cameras whirring.

The crowd jostled around me as I edged towards the car. Some were shouting. Then a brawny arm was thrust across the doorway of the car. It belonged to a tall, heavily-built Pakistani who was deliberately barring my entry to the car to keep me longer in his camera lens. The press of the crowd around me, the blinding lights in my eyes and the arm held barring my way suddenly reminded me very forcibly of the occasion outside the Indian embassy in Peking when the screaming Red Guards tried to close round me. It was an unpleasant moment. Then I managed to squeeze under the outstretched arm into the back seat. Cameras and lights were thrust at the open windows. But gradually Doon Campbell, George Walden and Reuters correspondent in Karachi, Nick Moore, made their way into the car and we drove away from the mêlée.

Next morning one Karachi newspaper carried a headline that said 'Reuters and U.K. Mission Weave Hollywood Drama Round Freed Reporter'. I had flown in, the newspaper said, 'in an aura of drama associated with Hollywood's sex symbols'. This amused me no end and almost made the unpleasantness of the previous night worthwhile. One Fleet Street reporter endeared himself to me by writing that I had come down the steps of the plane towards the jostling crowd looking not only bewildered but also faintly amused.

In Karachi I stayed for two days in the house of the British Deputy High Commissioner, Tony Stout, resting and trying to recover appetite and sleep again before the final lap to London. There I met a literary agent who had come out from London to meet me. I was discovering that the subject of a world-wide news story often attracts a volume of enquiries and commercial offers from newspapers, magazines, television and publishers that he himself is unable to handle.

The press corps was briefed daily in their hotel about my activities and showed consideration in not besieging the house where I stayed. I still declined to talk about my twenty-six months in solitary or my experiences with the Red Guards, since I continued to feel an edge of tension about the air journey to come. I was not yet back in London. Throughout the long spell in confinement I had longed to be back in the safety of England and I was to remain keyed up until I got there. But as a journalist I often put myself in the position of those pursuing the story and went out of my way to try to be helpful otherwise. It was a strangely ambivalent position I found myself in.

As I left Karachi during the night the airport was comparatively quiet although there were a few pressmen around. At the bottom of the plane steps a tall, brawny Pakistani photographer waited. Immediately I recognised him. 'I want to apologise and shake your hand,' he said with a wide grin. The hand he held out was the one that had aggressively barred my entry to the car on arrival in Karachi. I prepared to make some mildly cutting remark. But I didn't get a chance. 'That picture I took of you went all round the world,' he said, beaming eagerly. I shook his hand and grinned despite myself. The 'picture' of which he was so proud I discovered later, having been taken in a moment of scuffle in a dark airport by flash light and then having been distorted round the globe by radio transmission, appeared in newspapers at home giving me the appearance of an anguished drug addict who had just stepped on an exploding land mine – or something.

Some Fleet Street men went on the same plane with me to London. It was a long tiring flight and, still in a state of tension, I was not entirely convinced the affair would end well until we reached the ground in London. Even the Channel seemed a wide strip of water as the end neared. The feeling of vulnerability that persisted was not allayed by being many thousands of feet above the earth in that metal-plated flying container that was the BOAC Boeing. I had been invited by the captain of the aircraft to the flight deck to look out at the panoramic view from the nose cockpit as we seemed to hover motionless over the jagged, snow-covered Alps. Mont Blanc jutted up like a frost-covered mole hill. It was a breathtaking sight. But the transition from two solid years in a twelve-foot square room to a spot in the heavens thousands of feet above the Alps – I could see only too clearly there was nothing under my feet – was too much for my earth-bound metabolism. I went and sat down again quickly. And I was flattered that the man in charge of such a vessel with its thousands of dials and mechanical and electrical complexities and crew should ask for an autograph from the likes of me. There had been a number of autograph requests from fellow passengers on both planes home.

It was a final moment of tension as we swooped in to Heathrow airport, London. I closed my eyes and probably said another prayer as we came down. Then the wheels touched the runway smoothly and held. The brakes came on, the speed of the airliner slowed to a survivable rate and then it was taxiing. I allowed my-self to relax but in case reporters were watching, tried not to show the absolute and final relief I felt that at last the ordeal was over and what had so often seemed the impossible had happened – I was safely home.

I moved through the next few hours in a kind of trance. Reuters general manager, Gerald Long, came on board the air-craft to welcome me and shake my hand. An old friend from my first newspaper, Frank Gordon, was among the crowd of reporters and cameramen at the bottom of the steps. I was filmed constantly in the airport. In and out of cars. A large, strangely quiet crowd outside the airport entrance with only the odd shout. 'Take a good holiday now.' 'Get some colour back in your face.' Microphones being stuck out in front of me. Percy Cradock, the former chargé d'affaires in Peking who had returned home, among those welcoming me.

In a separate building a press conference was arranged for a few brief minutes to ease the pressure of publicity on me. I agreed to speak for a few minutes only. I was almost blinded by the television and news camera lights. Questions came at me out of a dark void. Going in and out I recognised the odd friend among the reporters. I have little recollection of what I said. Then a seemingly enormous crowd of cameramen around the car as I went out again to drive into London.

Anybody flying from Pakistan to London would be tired by the tension of the flight in normal circumstances, without anything else, but now I slumped into the back of the car taking me into London practically exhausted. I vaguely recognised Knightsbridge as we drove through and I gathered press cars were following me still. At the Charing Cross Hotel in the centre of London I went up to a room where my mother, sister June and girl friend Shirley waited. I was still consciously tensing myself against extreme emotional reactions and perhaps for several hours didn't really begin to relax. But I was home, it was over.

CHAPTER THIRTY-SEVEN

Getting An Explanation

Mr Michael Stewart, Britain's Foreign and Commonwealth Secretary, pushed a red box of du Maurier cigarettes towards me across the white blotter on his desk and said how glad he was that at last I was sitting there beside him. It was the late afternoon of November 6th, 1969 and I had been home from Peking just over three weeks. The meeting took place in Mr Stewart's office in Whitehall at his invitation. Mr Stewart was the man who all along had the power to order the release of imprisoned Communist newsmen in Hong Kong and so free me from my solitary confinement. Some British newspapers had campaigned editorially for this, criticising Mr Stewart for not ordering the release of the Chinese earlier. Many of my fellow journalists too had expressed strong feelings, both privately and publicly, about this failure to act sooner. As I have already shown, my own feelings as I sat alone in Peking month after month were often bitterly resentful.

I had waited in the corridor outside briefly while an usher had checked whether the Minister was ready to see me. A private secretary who had come from an adjoining office said to me confidentially as we waited, 'He's had a hard day, you know'. I suppressed a smile in the dim corridor wondering whether the secretary was half-expecting me to go in waving my arms and remonstrating wildly with his tiring chief.

I was announced and shown into a very large room lit by a number of table lamps. The high walls of the room held long narrow mirrors and possibly some paintings but it was not easy to see in the gloom beyond the glow from the lamps. Mr Stewart stood waiting for me behind his desk, a shortish man in a grey suit and waistcoat with grey hair and slightly pouched cheeks. He offered his hand, I said 'How do you do' and after the formal handshake, I sat down in the chair offered, close against the side of the rather small desk. Mr Stewart spoke with a slight north-country accent and chose his words when speaking formally with great deliberation, clearly considering carefully what he was committing himself to before uttering them. Mr Stewart offered me a cigarette from his red box of filter-tipped du Maurier and after I declined, lit one himself.

I waited politely for the Minister to begin, curious to know how he would approach the topic. He said how glad he was to see me there at last, then launched immediately into saying how he had felt unable to release the Hong Kong news workers before he did. It had been 'a difficult decision', he said.

He had had to balance the facts and had thought of me sitting there in Peking alone for a long time. But there had been riots in Hong Kong and they felt that to release the convicted news workers would have jeopardised the security of the colony.

'I don't expect you to agree with the decision I made but I wanted to explain it to you,' said Mr Stewart.

He then discussed the question of retaliatory measures that could have been taken against Chinese in London, but said it had been felt that this would have been playing their game and that ultimately the Chinese would always go one better – or worse – and so this kind of action had been eschewed.

Mr Stewart then added that early in the year an offer had been made to send the imprisoned news workers back to China, deport them from Hong Kong, but Peking had refused this.

I listened with great interest to Mr Stewart's explanation and told him that as he had expected, as the innocent prisoner who had suffered the solitary confinement, I did not agree with it. Had there been no possibility of releasing the news workers, say nine months earlier at the beginning of 1969? Mr Stewart repeated that this was not thought possible for reasons of Hong Kong's security.

I asked if the British Government had believed that the thirteen news workers were themselves likely to instigate fresh rioting and were they believed to be dangerous subversive elements in themselves?

They were all 'skilful propagandists' he replied, and it was felt they would possibly have caused new riots if released.

I asked what had led to the release of Wong Chak two years early and the Minister said it was thought at that time it could be

L*

done 'without risk to the situation'. I said that the British Government had not publicly admitted that Wong's release was connected with me and the Minister replied 'Ah well, that was a bit of face'.

I said that while sitting in ignorance in Peking I had wondered whether Britain's broad policy of trying to draw China into the world community of nations had in any way been responsible for Whitehall's reluctance to submit to this kind of blackmail since it would not have encouraged China to behave with a sense of responsibility. To this Mr Stewart said no, he would not have hesitated for these reasons. The decision made was purely because of Hong Kong. He said this was Britain's long term view towards China and he thought perhaps 'internal pressures in China might eventually influence the leadership as they have done already in the Soviet Union'.

I told Mr Stewart that I was very glad to have had the opportunity to come to see him and to ask him questions and he replied that he hoped he had answered them all. But I still wondered how the press treatment of my case had been received in Whitehall.

'I've learned since getting home,' I said, 'of the considerable amount of – sometimes emotional – reporting of my confinement and its effect on myself, family and friends. Did this in any way affect your final decision?'

Mr Stewart thought for a moment before replying cryptically: 'I am responsive to argument.'

I persisted. Had the publicity accorded to my plight in any way influenced the Government's thinking, had it had any effect?

The reply was perhaps a classic politician's evasion. 'Had we ever forgotten it,' he said after a pause, 'the publicity would have reminded us.'

Mr Stewart then asked how I was physically and I told him I was well and briefly described some of the difficulties and strains of my home-coming and the difficulty I still found in meeting with people. He enquired after my mother's health and I said she was resting after the nervous excitement of it all. He asked too how I was spending my leisure and I explained how above all I loved walking in the park in the autumn sunshine.

Quite suddenly Mr Stewart leaned forward and in almost

avuncular tone said, 'You know, I must say I admire the way you can discuss this all so calmly.' Then he asked in which park I took my walks, where was I staying?

I said I was staying in Camberwell and walked in Ruskin Park. Oh well, he too was a 'South Londoner' living in Lewisham and the conversation continued on these lines for a while. Mr Stewart had another cigarette and again offered me one.

I returned to the Minister's starting point that it could hardly be expected that I would agree with the decision not to try to bring about my release earlier but added that there now seemed no point to me in coming along uttering recriminations. I was free now and very happy indeed to be so.

'But,' I added, 'sitting alone in that room in Peking I very often felt very resentful towards yourself and Harold Wilson and in fact everybody who seemed to be doing nothing.'

'I bet you did,' said Mr Stewart quickly, in a manner that suggested he couldn't have agreed more. It was as if the Foreign and Commonwealth Secretary was at last relieved that I had said what he might well have been expecting in a less friendly fashion.

We seemed to have exhausted the topic and I rose to go. Mr Stewart shook hands again and accompanied me across the room to the door and opened it for me to depart. The conversation had lasted some forty minutes.

Outside in Whitehall it was raining and it took me a long time to get a taxi. Once back where I was staying I jotted down what we had said.

After arriving at the Downing Street entrance to the Foreign Office I had been taken up to the office of Mr James Murray, head of the Far Eastern Department. There I was shown three piles of folders on a table – files containing every paper connected with my twenty-six months' confinement. About 1,000 sheets of paper a year had gone into them I was told. I noticed that, perhaps appropriately enough for a government department, the files were bound together with red tapes. The mood of the meeting was friendly and relaxed. The files were referred to light-heartedly as 'The Grey Papers' and it was pointed out that it would be thirty years before they were made public in the government's open archives. At this point I renewed acquaintance with many of the diplomats I had last seen in Peking in the summer of 1967. Then I was shown to Mr Stewart's office.

The British Sunday newspaper *The People* was a leading campaigner for my release, repeatedly urging the Government to release the Chinese prisoners in Hong Kong to secure my freedom. Their campaign caused a flood of letters to be sent to the Foreign Office from people in Britain and in reply a printed letter was sent out in May 1969 explaining the reasons why nothing like that was being done. One of those many people who tried to help sent me a copy of the Foreign Office letter which sets out succinctly the official attitude – and perhaps the dilemma of those faced with the attempted blackmail of hostage-taking. The letter said that there had been no clear guarantee that I would be released if the eleven then-imprisoned news workers were let out and went on to add: 'Even if such a guarantee had been given I am sure that you will appreciate that there are also serious objections to arranging an exchange of this kind. Her Majesty's Government also have responsibilities and a duty to the people of Hong Kong and other British subjects throughout the world and it is for this reason, and not for any fear of "losing face" or allowing the Chinese to claim a "victory" that we have resisted Chinese pressure for the release of these prisoners. The well-being of Hong Kong and the welfare of its people are dependent on continued confidence that the British Government will maintain law and order there so that people can go about their legitimate business unmolested and without fear. If it appeared that by holding British subjects as hostages the Chinese could influence British actions and policy in Hong Kong, this confidence could well be undermined. Furthermore, the release of convicted prisoners to secure the release of an innocent British subject could imperil the position of British subjects visiting China. The Chinese authorities might be encouraged to believe that whenever they wanted to bring pressure to bear on the British Government all they need do would be to detain an innocent British subject. As you can see, the problem raises issues beyond our immediate concern for Mr Grey which involve the welfare of Hong Kong and safety of other Britons abroad. This does not mean, however, that we shall cease to do all we can for Mr Grey.'

*   *   *

The end of the strange affair came on Tuesday, November 11th when at an investiture at Buckingham Palace, Her Majesty the Queen said to me: 'I am very glad to see you here today. This is just a small token for what you have been through.'

I replied: 'It is wonderful to be back home. I am very happy to be here.'

CHAPTER THIRTY-EIGHT

Getting Readjusted

One of the problems of readjustment to normal life after twenty-six months as a hostage in Peking is to be driving up the Strand in a taxi when suddenly the taxi driver, by delayed action, realises that the face of his fare is one he has seen plastered over newspapers and television screens for many months and turns round to stick his hand through the glass partition to shake his fare's hand, apparently oblivious to all other traffic zooming around him. Even if all movement in vehicles after two stationary years does not unsettle you, a friendly taxi man driving blind looking at you in the back is an unnerving experience. If the movement does upset you, it is doubly unnerving.

But the difficulty of writing a chapter with a title like 'Getting Readjusted' is to know exactly when you have got readjusted. Writing this almost four months after the day I was released I have still not yet driven a car, visited a theatre or cinema or read a complete book, or had much desire to do any of these things. I have been preoccupied writing this book. Television I have watched only sporadically. At first the noise and distraction of the bright flickering images on the screen was intolerable to me and for several weeks I could not bear to watch it much at all, apart from the odd news programme.

After twenty-six months confined closely and alone the most enjoyable thing to do is to walk freely, preferably in a park or the countryside among grass and trees and fresh air. The sun is to be preferred too but if it rains it makes little difference. To walk freely in a direction of your own choice for as long or as short as you like, thinking of nothing but the sheer joy of it is perhaps the best thing of all.

Being cut off from normal life and alone for more than two years makes you draw away and see reality with new eyes, as if from a distance. The most frightening question that ever occurred to me in the long reflection and musing of my solitude was 'What is the universe in?' There were times when it was possible to see life not only as the apparently pointless movement of infinitesimal specks of life on the face of a lump of spinning heaven-knows-what plunging through the emptiness of space. There were times when it seemed certain that it was only a peculiar dimension of something else. The very strangeness of life was sensed very strongly after many months quite alone and it was frightening to feel suddenly and surely that the universe must be in something else but that it was impossible to grasp what.

The vague and elusive appreciation of this strangeness perhaps gave me a peculiarly intense awareness of the natural goodness of life on my return to London in the incredibly long, warm sunlit autumn of 1969. But now only four months later I already feel I have lost the bright intensity and clarity with which I saw the colours and textures of life; the greenness of the grass, the fiery tints of the tattered leaves that stayed on the trees long beyond their normal span, the quick, darting, riveting movement of birds on a tree in the garden. Most of the experience is beyond words. But it was as if I was a detached and superior observer of the rows of heaped bricks that were streets, and the scurrying people in them who were so obsessed with the scramble and restrictions of the daily round that they had forgotten how to draw off and look at the good things above and around them.

The artificial entertainments in cinemas, theatres and television sets held not the slightest attraction. Movement in a car or train was a necessary evil but to propel a vehicle personally was an unwanted complication in the beautiful simplicity.

At first not only did I not want to read a book but I could not concentrate long enough to read more than a couple of paragraphs of a news item in the newspapers – unless it was about myself. It was two or three weeks before I could scan the rest of the news with some enthusiasm and then it was still only the headlines and first paragraph. In Peking I had been greatly interested in all news and current affairs programmes when I finally was allowed my radio. But suddenly being projected back into active life, being part of the world again, robbed me of that interest and I became obsessively concerned with only my own activity and interests.

And although when alone I had often told myself I was idealising life at home in freedom and I should be prepared to be disappointed, I was not ready for the disenchantment that sometimes turned to disgust after an initial euphoria. The public obsession with the physical body and sexual indulgence in the 'Permissive Society' which had developed during my two blank years seemed particularly degenerate to one who had lived an austere life of iron-clad discipline, alone and remote. The all-pervading obsessive presentation of female nakedness on magazine and book covers, in newspapers, films and everywhere one looked, added a sordid, decadent patina to the man-constructed areas of life in Britain and perhaps only emphasised the natural beauty of countryside and park that gave me the greatest delight.

The impact of mini-skirt I have already described but the other very noticeable phenomenon was the longness of the hair of many men and boys. It was some time before I was able to prevent myself from becoming unreasonably contemptuous at the sight of a male with hair down to his shoulders in soft waves and curls.

Meeting new people became a strain, mainly because they tended over and over again to want to ask the same questions. How was it, how did you manage? What did you do all the time, how does it feel to be back? Although well-meaning and kindly in what were perfectly natural reactions, it was like constantly having to go back to the beginning again in the attempt to get readjusted. Eventually I found I really only wanted the frequent company of people who could keep pace with my return to normality and help me on, who had heard it all in the early days when I talked so much and so long that each day around mid-afternoon I began to go hoarse and lose my voice. It had been largely unused for two years.

It was nice to get a new set of clothes and cast off the ones that had an aura of the confined house in Peking. But clothes did not seem important. Nor did food. There had been nothing I had yearned for, but suddenly I found something which unconsciously I had missed. And I gobbled them up obsessively at every meal – peas. There had been no peas in Peking and on eating them for the first time I was struck by the deliciousness of their taste. I ate prodigious amounts of peas at many meals after that.

One of the most pleasing sights to me on my release was the paraphernalia behind a bar counter – and I am not including the lady serving the drinks for once. A few evenings after my release I slipped into a pub for the first time. It was just off Fleet Street and I was heavily disguised in dark glasses despite the evening hour – they probably made me more conspicuous but I was very self-conscious about being pursued by working pressmen, and here I was in their backyard! As I sipped my drink I raised my dark glasses briefly to my forehead to let my eyes feast on the play of light on the mellow amber of the uptipped whisky bottles, their shiny silver measuring devices, the glassware and silver tankards, the contrasting deep magentas of the wines and the crystal clarity of the vodkas and gins, the stained wood of the shelves, the shiny pumps, the cut of ham. I felt a flood of pure pleasure that combined in it a feeling of sentimental refreshment at the sight and an aesthetic appreciation, never before so intensely felt, of the trappings of a softly-lit, well-appointed, civilised drinking place.

Because I was alone for twenty-six months I was obsessed with myself. On coming home I was the object of so much attention both from news media and people moved to acts of kindness that it would have been impossible not to go on being self-obsessed. It was then difficult not to become irritable if I felt anyone was being inconsiderate.

There was a strong feeling in me that I had been pushed around for two years by Red Guards and Public Security Bureau guards and I was not going to put up with the slightest pushing around now I was home in my own free country again. It was perhaps an important point in readjustment when, in getting to the counter in a pub one night after being home a week or two, a slightly-drunk man at the counter was consistently rude to me asking who I thought I was and who was I pushing. He didn't know and didn't care and it was possibly the first time anybody had been routinely rude to me. Almost immediately I realised it was a good thing, it brought me nearer earth, nearer to being normal and not special any longer.

Alone in Peking I spoke few words and wrote one letter a month. I therefore used my few words with great precision giving every one definite and exact meaning. From such remoteness, such clearly-defined exactness of word and restricted carefulness of deed, I returned to the seething ant-hill of normal life in which everybody used thousands of words each day hurriedly and imprecisely. They 'promised' to telephone the next day at noon and didn't call till four and I felt nobody meant it when they said promise. They said they would look into it today then were too busy and couldn't manage it and I felt nobody bothered to keep their word. Why did they say it if there was a chance they couldn't do it? My mind, narrowed by solitary confinement, would not for a long time make allowances for the crowded complexities of ordinary life.

But gradually I began to compromise those sharp, rigid ideals of solitary, began to lose the intensity and clarity of the early days of freedom. And this is probably an essential part of readjustment if one is to return from the stark black and white of imagination cut off from the world to the grey mix of reality. I could probably 'promise' something and forget with plausible excuses as well as the next man now.

If left alone at home even for a short time in the early days of freedom I was very nervous. I have already told how I felt vulnerable the first night in freedom and dragged a chest of drawers in front of my bedroom door. This feeling continued. Left alone in a house I started at every sound and found no difficulty in imagining Chinese swarming over the garden wall to get me. Their all-powerful presence had been with me for so long that even in London I still felt illogically vulnerable to this power.

I was impatient with inexact conversation too. If the person to whom I was listening did not appear to be saying anything vital or compelling I turned away as a reflex action. The inconsequential irritated me enormously.

Being intensely busy many days at first, talking and arranging with people who were presenting my story in newspapers and through television, was sometimes tiring since it involved reliving and recalling the unpleasantness. But probably the activity was good therapy. And this book is a kind of therapy in itself, a kind of final cleansing of the experience. To write it has necessitated reliving the experience more closely than any of the news media demanded. Writing this chapter was all part of its title. Until the book was finished I couldn't really begin to stop the obsession with the experience.

On my arrival in London at the Charing Cross Hotel to meet family and friends I immediately, on impulse, said the room I had been given was too small. It was about twelve feet square like the one in Peking I said. I wanted another, different one.

A Reuter man in the room overheard this and added it as an interesting snippet to the end of his story of my arrival home. Newspapers and radio and television stations seized on this, put it in their headlines and soon everyone knew I had arrived home and been given a twelve-foot square room about which I had immediately protested. In fact I later paced out the room and it was much larger than twelve feet square. I think in my keyed up state, perhaps the ceiling was lower than rooms I had been used to and I felt unreasonably oppressed by it. Later in the day, in the corridor, I ran into the hotel manager who though kind and courteous could not conceal his hurt feelings at my brusque rejection of his room. Laughing at myself I promised sometime, somehow to put right the wrong impression that his hotel contained an oppressive, hostage-sized room. Until now I haven't put it right, so this is another factor 'getting readjusted' here.

The fact that I hadn't done any physical work or anything involving great exertion left me sweating quickly and profusely over things like packing a suitcase or swinging a golf club. The fact that I had missed things like glossy magazines and glossy long playing record covers led me impulsively to buy many magazines at bookstalls almost daily because of the novelty of opportunity. I scarcely looked at them once I got them home. I bought batches of L.P's too without giving much thought to whether I wanted them, simply because of the luxury and attraction of their shiny coloured covers.

The idealistic notions I had built up away from the world were brought back to a clearer focus of reality by my being back in it and depression sometimes followed. People back home were not all white and saint-like as they had seemed compared with the oppressors of my confinement. The return to the hard cut and thrust, survival-of-the-fittest Western world where almost every activity and emotion seems to get linked to a commercial value or cost-to-be-calculated sometimes brought on a feeling of disgust. These feelings of elation and depression – in solitary it had hardly seemed conceivable anybody could be depressed in freedom – tended to alternate in decreasing cycles, so that I came down to earth with a series of bumps springing up again each time rather like a man who has jumped from a building into a fireman's escape apparatus. The first bump is hard then up you go again to the former elation, another bump then not quite so far up, then another bump and perhaps a series of smaller ones, then you are firmly on the ground. But being of an optimistic turn of mind and naturally gregarious, through all these phases of readjustment it was never far from my mind how glad I was to be once more an intrinsic part of whatever the world was and not still set apart from it.

It was a very moving experience to find that many people in different parts of the world had *cared* about my solitary confinement. Often two words would recur to me in that room in Peking 'Nothing matters!' If you tripped down the steps into the yard and broke your neck and died or took your own life, the whole thing would be of no consequence, I thought. And was sometimes close to convincing myself. But somehow it always seemed better to keep hanging on in the hope that perhaps, for reasons which nobody has ever been able to pin down, something about life really did matter.

The flood of hundreds of letters I received in the first few weeks in freedom telling me how people in many countries had done what they could to help by prayer and by writing to their parliamentary representatives, to Chinese embassies and the Peking Government, to newspapers and to my Peking house were a moving expression of the goodness in human nature, which is sometimes lost sight of in a cynical world.

I found the weight of letters so moving that over a period of weeks I opened only a small number each day. There were letters like the one from Canada that said: 'Ever since I had read about your being confined to a small room and not allowed any visitors I started praying for you every day...In case you think because I pray that I am a religious fanatic you may put that thought out of your mind as I am an executive secretary for an oil business.'

There was one from a Chinese living in Nottingham: 'I feel it is a great honour to write to congratulate you on your reunion with your mother and friends in this country. I am a Chinese although I am a British subject and I hope you will not bear any personal grudge against the Chinese people in this country...best wishes for your future.'

There was a batch of letters sent just before my release, from every girl in one class at a London convent school which had been saying prayers for me each day. They said things like: 'Ever since our teacher told us that you were being kept in custody by the Chinese our class has prayed for you each morning . . . you may think that nobody cares or remembers you but they do, they really do. You probably say to yourself "Oh it's all very well to say all this trying to give me courage and everything" . . . I hope you are not too bored . . .'

There was one from Gloucestershire which said: '. . . you became a member of an enormous family all trying to help you.'

At Christmas many people who had sent cards to Peking the previous year sent them again knowing this time I would get them. There were cards without addresses like the one saying simply 'Anthony Grey Welcome home and a merry Christmas. Ten Jam Factory Night workers. God Bless.'

Perhaps another letter from Canada summed it up when the writer said 'I kept a magazine with your photograph beside my bed with my other books . . . *you could have been any one of us,* but you made it.'

Those praying were not without their sense of humour either. A man wrote from Torquay: 'At that time I asked the Lord earnestly if it could please Him to translate you physically by His almighty power back to your home in Norwich (what a sock in the eye that would have been for the Chinese!) but it was not to be . . .'

Part of getting readjusted is learning that in 1969 – during which time I and quite a number of other British people were imprisoned unjustly in China – trade between Britain and China broke all records. Britain exported more than £50 million worth of goods to China nearly doubling the previous year's figure. And China sold a record £37 million worth of goods to Britain. While the governments harangued each other merchants in Peking and London went quietly about their business. This is a fact of the world to which one has to readjust. It is a world in which, by the way, trade sanctions are applied on moral grounds against Rhodesia.

Perhaps everybody who reaches celebrity status, even though it is for a short time and accidentally, needs deflating some time. And a friend of a friend tweaked the tail of the outburst of publicity around me with an ironic comment that perhaps can justifiably be included as part of a description of getting readjusted.

He listened with interest to a story connected with my home-coming. It was this: after reading in the newspapers that on the first free day in Peking I had listened to records of Peter Cook and Dudley Moore and music by Handel, Peter Cook and Dudley Moore themselves had invited me to meet them and possibly see a performance. 'Hmm,' said my friend's droll friend, 'and what did Handel say?'

Conclusion

Even after I was back in England Peking's Communist authorities got in their last capricious parting shot at me.

My books were left behind when I flew out from China, to be air-freighted home later. When the box of books arrived at Peking airport the customs officials confiscated several of them, saying that they were 'unfriendly to the Chinese People's Republic and presented facts in a twisted way'.

They were the same books that I had taken into China two years earlier and they had then excited no comment. Among those confiscated was a famous book on China *The Other Side of the River* by Edgar Snow, the American journalist who has a unique relationship with Mao and the other Chinese leaders from having met them in their austere days under blockade in the civil war. The book was very fair to China. If this story needed another bizarre incident as an epitaph, then surely this is it.

I went to China with the intention of reporting fairly and objectively in accordance with the principles of the news agency I represented. That I was there at all was the result of an agreement years before between the British and Chinese Governments to allow each other's journalists to operate in their countries. In that sense my presence there could not be entirely dissociated from politics. But since Reuters was, and is, entirely independent of the British Government, if there was any complaint about my presence or activities there – which there never was – the course for the Chinese should have been to order me out of the country. Perhaps in a backhanded way it is to their credit that they never did accuse me of anything – apart from the vague Red Guard assertions that I was reactionary and imperialist. If you are to indulge in the ruthless business of hostage-taking I suppose it is more honest not to pretend the hostage is guilty of something else. Jail sentences and espionage charges have surrounded hostages in other Communist countries.

This book was born as part of my effort to endure solitude. The promise to myself to write it helped me go on and that was the basis on which I began it. I finish it with the intention of putting the experience behind me. I never dared to think in too much detail about writing the book while still confined since it seemed too much like taking for granted an act of providence that hadn't yet occurred. At no time did I ever know when and if I would be freed.

The experience leaves me with no fierce enmity towards Chinese people in general. Those ordinary Chinese folk I was able to observe closely are as mundanely interested in the ordinary things of life as their counterparts in other countries. They have attractive qualities and the few Chinese I knew I found likeable. The political system is something they cannot do much about, even if they wanted to – and I'm not sure they do. Despite the fact that the régime sometimes does iniquitous things in the eyes of the rest of the world, it has probably provided a better life for the majority of the vast population than any régime that has preceded it. The fact that enormous, over-populated China is governed at all has always seemed something of a miracle to me.

I don't suppose for a moment my solitary confinement was the worst kind of confinement a man can suffer. It was, however, flagrantly unjust. I don't think Peking cared desperately about the news workers in Hong Kong in themselves. I was simply caught up in a battle of face between two intransigent governments. Reflecting on the situation in my Peking room I sometimes thought with bitterness that I was being allowed to suffer for the sake of the business interests in Hong Kong, since this was basically what 'the security of the colony' was all about; that the capitalist West was living up to its Communist image of putting profits before people. And there is probably an underlying truth in this.

Soon after I was released six other Britons were released from mysterious detention in China. An ageing freelance journalist, Norman Barrymaine, sixty-nine, emerged from nineteen months of solitary confinement in a Shanghai prison with amazing jauntiness after being held in a cell twelve feet by eight feet in conditions which seemed much worse than my own. Another journalist, Eric Gordon, aged thirty-eight, a Marxist who was sympathetic to Peking's brand of Communism, and his wife and thirteen-year-old son were freed after being held for nearly two years in the Hsin Chiao hotel where I myself stayed during my first weeks in Peking. Then a forty-six-year-old Scot, Merchant Navy Captain Peter Will, was released after seventeen months in a small prison in the north-east Chinese port of Taku.

Eric Gordon, who had been working for a Chinese publishing house, was accused of insulting Chairman Mao and trying to smuggle information out of China. The 'information' was notes he had made for a book on the Cultural Revolution which he had hidden in framed portraits of Mao in his room. He was interrogated and eventually signed, on his own admission, a 'confession' of a kind before being released. (This Chinese obsession with his notes made me wonder anew at the survival of my diaries.)

Barrymaine was accused of espionage after being taken off a Polish ship in Shanghai and also signed confessions because, he said, in Chinese eyes 'any newspaperman who goes to China spies'. But he denied vehemently that he was a spy. Will was also accused of 'insulting Chairman Mao'.

Gordon and Barrymaine and Will, unlike myself, were all accused of something although not brought for trial. Precise terms were laid down for my release but not for theirs. The timing of their release, however, seemed to suggest that their confinement was seen by the Chinese as lending weight to the direct 'hostage' pressure being put on the British Government through my confinement.

Some people felt the British Government acted wrongly in not trying to bring about my release sooner. I have already described in the course of the book my resentment at the time at the lack of action. But I don't feel, now that it is past, there is much point in going on record with a blanket recrimination. Those who have to make decisions to help or not to help a suffering hostage face a dilemma if the stakes are high, as presumably they were thought to be over Hong Kong's security in my case; and as they were probably thought to be in the case of the London lecturer, Gerald Brooke, imprisoned in the Soviet Union on espionage charges. He was exchanged for Soviet spies Peter and Helen Kroger shortly before my release in 1969. The decision-makers face the prospect of setting a precedent, of encouraging the hostage-taker to do it again.

Oddly enough I'd had an insight into the shady trading in international hostages during my first assignment with Reuters in Berlin. A man who had made the initial approach to Britain through non-diplomatic channels to swop Gerald Brooke for the Krogers in late 1967, some six months after Brooke's trial, gave me an inkling of the attempted deal and I wrote the first story about the exchange attempt from Berlin. This made large front page headlines in all British newspapers the next day. So as I sat in my room in Peking in the summer of 1969 I was delighted to hear the news that Brooke was released. It led me to hope something might be done for me. There was later much criticism of the British Government for doing a deal since Brooke was shown to have acted foolishly in becoming a courier for a subversive organisation. But emotionally I shall always support any similar action on humanitarian grounds having known the awfulness of long confinement. The policy of the British Government in my case, and in that of Brooke too, seemed to be to wait long enough to hope to dissuade the other side from doing it again, but nevertheless ultimately to pay a price for the sake of the individual concerned. An example of British compromise perhaps.

It has been said that Western countries which pride themselves on their humanitarian principles can only lose in this kind of cynical trading in hostages with Communist states. But it is perhaps a losing of which they can be proud. The British Government certainly held out long enough over Brooke and myself – although they were vastly different cases – to make it clear they were no pushover. There was no quick capitulation and presumably there would not be in any future case. Perhaps the international opprobrium showered on the hostage-takers in the course of the long stalemates that have ensued will make them less eager to go in for that kind of blackmail again.

As a footnote to the drawbacks of unsought notoriety mentioned earlier, I feel obliged to add that not everybody thought I was innocent. There was at least one doubter, Christopher, the nine-year-old son of some friends with whom I went to dinner after getting home. His parents told him that somebody whose face he'd seen frequently on television was coming to dinner. Christopher was fascinated. It was Anthony Grey. Ah yes, he remembered. He'd seen that face lots of times. But the cautious

parents thought they'd better check further to avoid possible embarrassment later when the guest arrived.

'You do know exactly who he is, don't you, Christopher?'

'Yes of course I do.'

'Who is he?'

'Umm . . . well he's one of the Great Train Robbers, isn't he?'